PICTURES *left to right*
Street and church
furniture with a
difference:
the red-painted signpost
at Bloxworth, the
boat-prow pulpit in the
parish church at
St Leonard's, and the
mitre-topped lamp-post
at Bishop's Waltham.
The stories behind them
are not always obvious,
but anyone can see
through 'Fred the
Ploughman', Stibbard's
village sign.

TIMPSON'S OTHER ENGLAND
Designed and produced by Parke Sutton Publishing Limited, Norwich
for Jarrold Publishing, Norwich

Text copyright © 1993 John Timpson
This edition copyright © 1993 Jarrold Publishing

ISBN 0-7117-0645-X

Timpson's Other England

a look at the unusual and the definitely odd

JOHN TIMPSON

JARROLD

PICTURES *left to right*
One of eight Parisian elephants in Wickham Church; Horsham's modern version of an ancient device, the 'Sun God' sundial; and England's oldest concrete bridge, at Homersfield. Christleton's sewage lift looks like a dovecote, but there is no mistaking the forge at Claverdon.

Contents

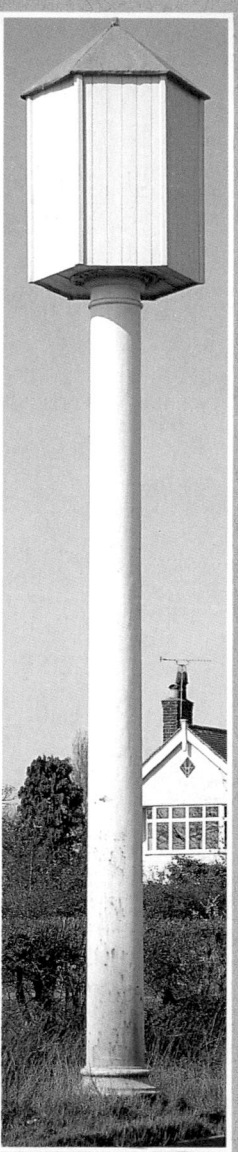

Contributors

AUTHOR
John Timpson OBE

RESEARCHER
Paula Granados

DESIGNER
Gillian Matthews

EDITOR
Anne Priestley

PHOTOGRAPHERS
John Brooks,
Neil Jinkerson,
Andrew Perkins

ILLUSTRATOR
Libby Turner

Introduction

In the Introduction to *Timpson's England* I described it as 'a look beyond the obvious, at the unusual, the unlikely and the undeniably odd'. Well, *Timpson's Other England*, follows the same formula but along different routes and into new fields, as well as filling some of the gaps in areas which I covered before.

I did emphasise in that introduction that *Timpson's England* was far from comprehensive, just a very personal selection, and that has been confirmed, several times over, in the correspondence I have received since. 'Why didn't you mention so-and so?' 'How could you have missed out such-and-such?' 'What about this-and-that?'

I am most grateful to everyone who took the trouble to write, and I felt the best way of expressing my gratitude – and indeed my contrition at having left out so much – was to make a new excursion into the fascinating world of the unusual, the unlikely and the odd.

I ventured, for instance, into tunnels, which hardly got a mention before. We mostly see tunnels through the window of a train or a car, and very boring they are

A shark on a roof, a bed-bug on a weathervane, and a cannon-ball in a church tower.

too, but have you ever noticed the entrances? They can look more like the portals of a stately home than just a hole in the ground. And those hill figures we take so much for granted – we all probably know the ancient White Horse of Uffington, but what about the white horse dug out by schoolboys early in the last century, and why should a giant kiwi land on a Wiltshire hillside?

I was tempted to call one section 'Fascinating things you can see without even getting out of your car', because so many familiar roadside objects have odd tales to tell: pillarboxes, signposts, memorials, even stones. Have you come across one of those coffin-stones where pall-bearers rested their load along the Corpse Trails in the remote Yorkshire Dales? Or the Blowing Stone in an Oxfordshire village which King Alfred is said to have used as a trumpet to summon his men?

Then there are buildings that moved, buildings in disguise, buildings strangely decorated; how would you like to have an eighteen-foot shark diving into *your* roof? And do you know why a Hampshire church has a bed-bug for a weather-vane, or how a Sussex church got a cannon ball embedded in its tower?

Doubtless you know the answers to at least some of these questions, particularly if you live in Headington or Hastings, Kingsclere or Kingston Lisle, Swaledale or Salisbury Plain. But England is marvellously rich in the curious, the quirky, and the slightly bizarre, and in the same way

that I have so often found something unexpected round the next corner and the one after that, I hope that you too will find something unexpected, on the next page and the page after that.

And if in the end you are moved to enquire, 'Why didn't you mention so-and-so?' or 'What about this-and-that?' – well, do check first that it was not in *Timpson's England* or *Timpson's Towns*, then by all means fire away.

Finally, my thanks to all who have played a part in creating this book. There are the photographers who have found their way to so many obscure and improbable locations to provide the pictures, the illustrator who has conjured up quirky moments from the past, the researcher who has delved through more works of reference than it is possible to acknowledge individually (though I have mentioned several in the text), and the production team which has blended it all together. Not least, there are the librarians and archivists, the squires and parsons, the parish clerks and local historians, and the men and women in the village street, who provided so much of the background, the history and the folklore which I have incorporated in it. They are, in fact, the other ingredient in *Timpson's Other England.*

... and the Blowing Stone – did King Alfred use it as a trumpet?

JOHN TIMPSON

A giant kiwi on a Wiltshire hillside ...

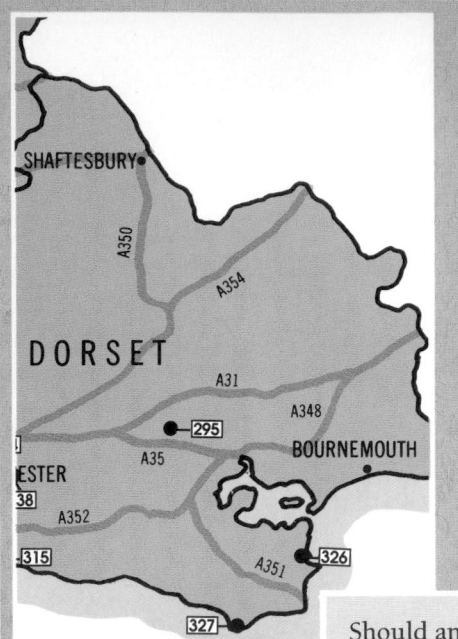

The chapel on St Aldhelm's Head, Dorset, was probably originally intended to be a lighthouse.

Should any readers wish to visit items mentioned in the book, pages 205 to 221 contain maps showing where they can be found. Each map is accompanied by an index giving a short description of each item, and where it is located.

A comprehensive subject index is included at the back of the book.

The central pillar still has a hole where young women dropped in a pin and wished for a husband.

Lock-ups, knees-
ups, run-ups:
the green scene

Lock-ups, knees-ups, run-ups: the green scene

No more 'May Day' emergency calls: this is Wellow's rot-proof, fireproof, steel maypole.

Village greens are traditionally the place for merry-making and malefactors. An archetypal green would have a maypole at one end, a lock-up with stocks and a whipping-post at the other, and in more recent times, a cricket pitch in the middle.

Maypoles have been carefully preserved in some villages, sometimes as a tourist attraction, and at **Ickwell Green** in Bedfordshire, for example, the annual maypole dancing and crowning of the May Queen attracts vast numbers of sightseers. Even in villages which have grown in population and traffic to such an extent that they are in danger of losing their rural atmosphere, they still cling to their maypoles to remind them of their more bucolic past.

Wellow, for instance, which lies on the busy A616 road near Ollerton in Nottinghamshire, with a colliery not far away, still cherishes its village green and the conservation area around it. Dominating the whole village is a gaily striped maypole, sixty feet high and the tallest permanent maypole in England, complete with a cockerel perched on top. The pole, however, is not as traditional as it looks. Give it a tap and you will find it is made of steel. In fact it only dates back to 1976, the Queen's silver jubilee year, when it was erected to replace a wooden one which was rotting away.

Actually, Wellow only joined the maypole scene in the last century, and its successive maypoles seemed to have fairly brief careers before either falling down, being cut down by vandals or, on one spectacular Guy Fawkes Night, accidentally burning down. I gather there was some scepticism when it was proposed to erect yet another one, which turned to astonishment when it was decided to make it of steel. But the reason was very practical: steel doesn't rot, it doesn't burn, and it is very difficult to knock down. Said one parish councillor: 'None of the character of the maypole has been lost by changing to steel.' Said another: 'The pole unites the village and to many it has almost become a shrine.'

So the young folk of Wellow dance around their steel maypole on May Day, but the purists are still not convinced. One travel writer commented rather sourly: 'An important part of the old May Day tradition was the cutting and carrying of the birch saplings from the wood (in Wellow's case, Sherwood Forest), but even pagan ceremonies are now subject to industrial interference.' And he added, even more bitterly: 'Why not, I ask myself, a plastic replica of the village stocks?'

His caustic suggestion has nearly come true at **Woodcote**, in the Surrey suburbs, a 'village' created in recent years largely for the benefit of commuters. The stocks and whipping-post on the green are not made of plastic, but they have certainly been imported as instant relics; they lack only a couple of dummy serfs to complete the illusion. That travel writer was suitably appalled, even without the plastic. 'Everyone who has any concern with Woodcote ought to be thoroughly ashamed,' he fumed. The stocks and whipping-post 'were attempting to give the village an antiquity which is entirely bogus, and they ought to be removed by public demand as a tasteless phoney.' He had yet to see, I imagine, the concrete cows at Milton Keynes . . .

I am sure he would have been much happier with another set of stocks which stand, and have stood for centuries, on the green at **Berkswell** in the West Midlands. This is a genuinely ancient village, with a twelfth-century church, a couple of Tudor mansions, a four-hundred-year-old pub where you can see a cannon captured in the Crimea, and a communal well by the churchyard gate – which gave the village its name. There is a whipping-post too, but it is the stocks which delight me – they have five leg-holes.

The story goes that there was once a perverse old character in the village with only one leg, who was constantly getting into trouble along with a couple of cronies, so the stocks were custom-made to fit the three of them. There is of course a less romantic explanation, that originally there were the standard six holes, but the wood around one of them rotted away and was removed. I know which story I prefer.

Another story about these stocks cannot be refuted, because it happened within living memory. A drunk was put in for claiming he could preach a better sermon than the rector; he was foolish enough to tell the rector so. The villagers, who no doubt had experienced the rector's sermons themselves, asked permission to give the man a drink of tea. They brought a large teapot and poured it into his mouth. The malefactor seemed singularly thirsty, and

Berkswell's five-holer stocks – for a one-legged malefactor and his mates?

Two confusing curiosities on village greens – not an upmarket garden shed and a castle keep, but the wooden lock-up at Barley (right) and Thomas Wright's observatory at Westerton (above).

got through the whole potful. When he was eventually released from the stocks he was more drunk than when he was put in them – the teapot had been full of beer . . .

Stocks, whipping-posts and lock-ups seem rather quaint, even charming these days, but their histories were generally grim, and jolly japes with beer-filled teapots were pretty rare. Lock-ups were dark,

cramped, unventilated and insanitary. At **Baslow** in Derbyshire, for instance, the lock-up was tiny enough to be incorporated in the old bridge over the River Wye. It does have a couple of small oval windows, but it seems little larger than a dog-kennel.

The location of Baslow's lock-up is something of a rarity. Generally they are in a prominent place on the village green, occasionally combined with a pound for keeping lost animals, like the one at **Coveney** in Cambridgeshire, which was built comparatively recently in 1850. They are also usually made of brick or stone, but **Barley** in Hertfordshire has a wooden one, in remarkably good condition and looking like an upmarket garden shed. It is thought to have been built in the seventeenth century, and it was last used for its original purpose in 1890, when a suspected housebreaker was held in it until the police arrived. There was a rather ignominious period when it was indeed a kind of garden shed – the local roadman stored his tools in it – but happily the Parish Council decided to smarten it up again, helped by various grants, and 'The Cage', as they call it locally, now looks as it did when the first miscreant was incarcerated, more than three hundred years ago.

The lock-up at **Lavenham** in Suffolk has been restored even more recently by the National Trust in 1992. Lavenham is famous for its quaint old timbered houses, the subject of countless picture postcards and calendars, but the parish lock-up in the garden of the Guildhall is as gloomy and depressing as any other. It was built in 1833 when the Guildhall was a workhouse and almshouse for eighty paupers, and although the dark little room only measures five feet by seven, up to eight prisoners occupied it. If it was all too much for them, the mortuary was conveniently situated next door.

Not all village lock-ups have fared so well. The one at **Lingfield** in Surrey had a nasty experience with an oak tree. The tree was struck by lightning and some of it fell on the lock-up – an act of God, it was said, to punish the prisoner inside, who had been locked up for using foul language. The language he used when the lightning struck is not recorded, but he emerged unhurt.

The stumpy circular tower on the green at **Westerton** in County Durham looks grim enough to be either a very large lock-up or a very small castle keep, but it is neither. Nor is it a folly, though it has been

called as much by the locals. It is actually the work of a distinguished mathematician and astronomer, Thomas Wright, a well-known and respected figure at Durham University. He was a Westerton man, and he built the tower as his personal observatory in 1750 – in the days before anyone worried too much about private individuals building stone towers for their own use on village greens.

He gave it imitation arrow slits and a forbidding front door, so it was not unreasonable for the locals to call it 'Westerton Folly' – particularly as this was the only way they could make up for the loss of part of their green. But the university authorities thought otherwise, and erected a suitable plaque on the tower in 1950, its two-hundredth anniversary.

Most buildings erected on village greens have a more general benefit for the community, ranging from all those lock-ups to modern cricket pavilions. At **Papworth St Agnes** in Cambridgeshire, for instance, there is a communal bakehouse which was built

Another village green puzzler. Is it a training centre for chimney-sweeps or a pets' crematorium?
No, just the communal bakehouse at Papworth St Agnes.

in the mid-nineteenth century for everyone's use in the village. Again it is a rather forbidding building with its barred windows, but the tall chimney makes it look a little more homely. The chimney was once much higher, probably to ensure that any sparks were kept well clear of the nearby thatched cottages. Inside, the bread was baked in a massive communal cast-iron oven.

The village green at **Harrold** in Bedfordshire has a standard circular lock-up with a conical roof, and a not-so-standard octagonal market house or cross. These structures are generally found in larger places, but Harrold acquired one in the early eighteenth century as a focal point for

More reminders of the past on our village greens. The Cholera Pump at Earls Colne (far right) in thanksgiving for avoiding the epidemic, the market house at Harrold (below), focal point for the local lace-makers in the eighteenth century and, on the same green, a circular lock-up (right), specially designed for miscreants with pointed heads.

A village sign featuring an unusual local character. Stibbard's 'Fred the Ploughman' made entirely of old farm equipment.

the local lace-makers. Before the Industrial Revolution, lace-making was a thriving cottage industry, and the market house was used to distribute work to the villagers, and to act as a collection point when the work was done. The practice died out when lace factories were built at Bedford and the locals went to work there, but the market house, with its eight pillars, lofty tiled roof and handsome cupola, lived on.

Pumps are a more common feature of the traditional village green, and **Earls Colne** in Essex, has a particularly handsome one, handsome enough to be mistaken for a commemorative cross if it were not for the long handle on the side. It is called, rather disconcertingly, the 'Cholera Pump', but it was not the water from it that spread the disease. On the contrary, it was erected in 1853 by a local benefactress, Mary Gee, 'in thankful commemoration for the *absence* of cholera'. This was one village which the epidemic missed.

A more recent arrival on the village green scene is the village sign, which has become a favourite form of communal commemoration, whether it is a golden jubilee, a royal visit, or just a nice thought by the local Women's Institute. It usually takes the form of a carved representation of events and people connected with the village's history, and in some counties there is hardly a village green without one. In *Timpson's England,* for instance, there was a whole chapter about the carvings of Harry Carter, whose village signs can be found all over Norfolk, but there is one obscure Norfolk village which took quite a different approach to its sign.

'Fred the Ploughman' at **Stibbard** was created with great ingenuity and skilful welding by a local sculptress, Ros Newman,

The Biddenden maids born with a shared shoulder and hip . . .

using old bits and pieces of farm equipment to create Fred's life-size, if skeletal, figure. If you study it closely you can pick out two pitchforks, four horseshoes, some chain-link, a tail docker, a pair of pincers, a branding iron, and that very Norfolk tool, a – sugar-beet hook. Fred wears a battered tin hat to protect his hollow head, as he walks behind a real plough on his pedestal beside the village green.

Fred is purely symbolic, but in Kent the **Biddenden** Maids really existed, and they have the distinction of being featured in two kinds of village tradition. They have a sign erected in their memory on the village green, and they inaugurated a bread charity which still operates every Easter Monday. The Maids were reputedly Siamese twins, born sometime in the sixteenth century with a shared shoulder and hip. This made it slightly easier for the sign-carver, who could make one combined figure instead of two separate ones. Eliza and Mary Chulkhurst lived like this for thirty-four years, and left twenty acres of land to provide bread and cheese for the poor of the village.

Many villages have bread charities. **Harrietsham**, for instance, ten miles from Biddenden, uses the interest on a £500 legacy from Sir Charles Booth in 1795 to provide bread for the poor, so long as they attend Divine Service. Many churches have bread cupboards for the same purpose. But Biddenden must have the only bread charity founded by Siamese twins, and they are featured not only on the village sign but on the biscuits which are distributed on Easter Monday.

While there is no shortage of lock-ups, stocks, maypoles, pumps and signs on village greens, it is rare to find one with a grave. Rarer still, the grave of a horse. **Latimer**, a tiny village in the Chess valley in Buckinghamshire, has a minuscule village green, with just enough room for a war memorial, a covered pump with a surround of red tiles said to come from a nearby Roman village – and a horse's grave. To be more accurate, only the heart of a horse is buried there, along with its ceremonial trappings, but it is marked by a handsome cairn which is almost a replica of the war memorial next to it, recording the men who died in the Boer War – the same war in which the horse was involved.

Two distinguished soldiers feature in the life and death of the horse, but there are conflicting versions as to how. One of them was a Frenchman, General de Villebois Marevil, the other was Lord Chesham of Latimer House. We know they both fought at the Battle of Boshof in the South African war, on 6 April 1900, but after that the stories begin to diverge. The most popular version, and certainly the most romantic, is that the two men were fighting alongside each other, when the French general was killed in the act of saving Lord Chesham's life. His horse was wounded also, and Lord Chesham brought it back with him to Latimer, named it Villebois in honour of its former master, and when it died in 1911 had its heart buried on the village green.

However, there are one or two odd aspects of this story. Lord Chesham was a brigadier-general in command of a Yeomanry Brigade, and it seems unusual for two generals to be fighting shoulder to shoulder in the front line. The horse was said to be unnamed until Lord Chesham christened it Villebois, but does a general ride into battle on an anonymous horse? And while there seems to be agreement that it died in 1911, official records show that Lord Chesham was killed in 1907, while out hunting with the Pytchley. The records do not identify the horse he was riding, but it would be a cruel irony if it was Villebois which threw him, after helping to save his life. The point is, though, how did Lord Chesham organise Villebois's funeral four years later?

To confuse the issue still further, a rather different account of the battle-ground incident appeared in a 1974 issue of

A memorial on Latimer's village green to a horse with a strange history. Its heart and trappings are buried underneath.

A typical English village scene at Old Buckenham – but they are playing on Australian turf.

Buckinghamshire and Chiltern Life. This stated that General de Villebois was in fact a Boer, fighting on the opposite side, and Lord Chesham killed him in the battle and commandeered his horse. However, I suspect the real facts are that the two men were friends and when the general was killed, in whatever circumstances, Lord Chesham looked after his horse for old times' sake. Its heart certainly finished up in the right place, under the cairn on Latimer Green.

Perhaps the most English feature of an English village green is the cricket pitch. It can be slightly variable in bounce and slope, and the outfield can be hazardous for unwary visiting teams because of hidden gullies, beds of nettles, and the unexpected tree, but there can be other eccentricities too. The pitch at **Bramshaw**, for instance, straddles the county boundary, so you can hit a six in Hampshire and be run out in Wiltshire.

There are no such complications, however, on one village cricket ground in Norfolk. Although Norfolk is only one of the Minor Counties, having exported its Edriches and its Parfitts to Middlesex and beyond, it can claim to have imported, quite literally, a first-class international wicket. The turf at **Old Buckenham** was brought all the way from Australia by Lionel Robinson of Old Buckenham Hall, who was the leading figure in the village until his death in 1922. A notable county player, McLaren, lived in a cottage nearby, and between them they tempted some distinguished cricketers to play on Old Buckenham's Australian turf. Jack Hobbs, for example, is supposed to have said that it was his favourite ground, and visiting Australian players must have felt particularly at home. It is not often that a cricketer can play on his native turf in an English village, twelve thousand miles from home . . .

If you seek a memorial, then look – very hard – around you

If you seek a memorial, then look – very hard – around you

Wayland Smithy, near Compton Beauchamp, was the scene of overnight miracles in the tenth century. Horses were mysteriously shod overnight – or was it just an Anglo-Saxon 'sting'?

If you seek Sir Christopher Wren's memorial, so the inscription in St Paul's Cathedral advises, you have only to look around you. But memorials are not always quite so easy to spot, because they are not in a churchyard or a church, let alone the church itself. They can be tucked away in very unlikely corners, and commemorate the most unlikely people and events. Usually the individuals concerned are buried elsewhere, in consecrated ground, but there are exceptions, mostly because they have committed some unpleasant crime.

For instance, when suicide was considered in that category it was the custom to dig the grave at a crossroads. Highwaymen and footpads often finished up the same way, being buried either at the scene of their crime or beneath their gallows. At **Boxmoor** in Hertfordshire, for example, near a pub called, rather bizarrely in the circumstances, the Friend at Hand, there is the grave of Robert Snooks, a singularly unsuccessful highwayman – but then, whoever heard of a successful one called Snooks? He was caught after his first attempt, when he held up a post-boy and stole the mail-bags, and was hanged on this spot. In the best tradition of highwaymen, even unsuccessful ones, he joked on his way to the gallows. When he saw the crowd hurrying ahead of him he called out: 'Don't worry; there'll be no fun till I get there!'

A lump of puddingstone marks the grave, near a clump of chestnut trees, together with a headstone bearing his name and the date, 11 March 1802. Legend has it that if, at midnight, you walk round the grave twelve times, you will see him hanging from a nearby tree. You stand a better chance, I suspect, if you have had a few jars at the Friend at Hand first.

However, not every person buried in unconsecrated ground was a highwayman or a suicide. In very early times, of course, there was no consecrated ground to be buried in, hence the megalithic tombs or barrows, dotted around the more remote corners of England which were inhabited three or four thousand years ago. We rarely know the identity of the occupants, but the barrow near **Compton Beauchamp** in Oxfordshire does have a name attached to it, albeit an unlikely one. The tomb dates from about 3700 BC, but its name, Wayland the Smith, was only added in the tenth century AD. Wayland was not a local lad; in Norse legend he was the blacksmith of the gods, with the knack of making armour which rendered the wearer invisible.

His connection with Compton Beauchamp is obscure to say the least, but a story attached to his 'smithy' may explain why the barrow was thus named. The locals maintained that if a horse and a coin were left there overnight, the horse would be shod by the next morning and the coin would be gone. This sounds to me like an Anglo-Saxon 'sting' rather than a Norse legend, and I suspect that many gullible travellers who followed this dubious procedure found next morning that, not only had the coin vanished, but the horse had gone too . . .

A much sadder story is attached to a lonely grave in one of England's most isolated corners, **Sunderland Point** in Lancashire. This little community is

Sambo's Grave (below),
a reminder of the days
when slave ships sailed
from the remote shores
of Sunderland Point
(left).

Memorials you are not
intended to miss: John
Knill's ostentatious
monument (far left) to
himself at St Ives.

connected to the mainland peninsula (itself remote enough) by a causeway which can be covered at high tide. Many of the buildings date from the seventeenth and eighteenth centuries, when it was the seaport for Lancaster, and the place is pervaded by a sense of remoteness and timelessness. The grave, marked by a tombstone in the middle of a field, is itself a period piece, because it is called Sambo's Grave, a name now spurned as racist.

Slave ships sailed from Sunderland Point to pick up their cargoes from Africa and take them to the West Indies and the American colonies, but Sambo was one of the luckier ones. A ship's captain took a fancy to him and made him his personal servant, on shore as well as on ship. That was good news for Sambo; the bad news

was that in 1736 the captain left him behind while he went off on another trip, and the bewildered youngster thought his master had deserted him, so it is said, and died of a broken heart. More probably he caught a chill in the unaccustomed English climate and died of pneumonia.

The locals objected to a heathen being buried in consecrated ground, so he was laid to rest in 'Sambo's Field', as it came to be called. Many years later, in 1796, a clergyman who came to Sunderland Point on holiday, the Revd James Watson, was so moved by Sambo's story that he wrote an epitaph for his tombstone. It starts:

> *Full sixty years the angry winter's wave,*
> *Has thundering dashed this bleak and*
> * barren shore,*
> *Since Sambo's head laid in this lonely*
> * grave,*
> *Lies still, and ne'er will hear their turmoil*
> * more . . .*

At the other end of the social scale, and getting full marks for ostentation, is the memorial to John Knill, an eighteenth-century Mayor of St Ives, Bencher of Gray's Inn, and for good measure, successful smuggler. He had the monument erected in honour of himself on top of Worras Hill, overlooking **St Ives** harbour in Cornwall, and even a writer who is usually very tolerant of such things has described it as obtrusive. It is a lofty stone pyramid like a church steeple, visible for many miles, and its only merit is that it gives an excuse for a civic knees-up every five years. For reasons which I hope were merely eccentric, Mr Knill left a bequest to pay for ten young girls, dressed in white, to dance around his monument every fifth year to the music of a fiddle, whilst singing the hundredth Psalm.

It all sounds like a marvellous exercise in tastelessness; in Eurovision Song Contest jargon I reckon it scores *Knill points*. But in recent years the local council have made the best of it and turned it into quite a party. If you want to book for the next one, I calculate it is due on 25 July 1996.

An even loftier memorial stands in the garden of **Pentlow** Rectory in Essex. It was not erected by the couple it commemorates, but their devoted son. The inscription reads:

> *Erected to the memory of his honoured parents, the Rev. John Bull MA and Margaret his wife, on a spot they loved so well, by Edward Bull MA 1859.*

It is a tower seventy feet high, visible from beyond the Suffolk border, and I imagine that Mr Bull's parents appreciated his grand gesture rather more than the neighbours.

Sir Tatton Sykes also had a prominent memorial, but it was placed in a more convenient position, on a hill outside the village of **Sledmere** on Humberside, where the Sykes family have been squires for centuries. Sir Tatton was the most famous of them, a notable sportsman who founded the Sledmere Stud. The church is full of Sykes memorials, but it is a monument in the village designed by a Sykes in honour of others which is the most striking.

The Waggoners' Memorial commemorates the Yorkshire Waggoners, a corps of drivers raised by Sir Mark Sykes from the farms on the Yorkshire Wolds in 1912. They saw gallant service in the First World War, and many of them were killed. Their colonel, Sir Mark, died himself in 1919, but the memorial was built to his design after his death. The panels show scenes illustrating the Waggoners first as civilians working on the farms, then being called up, taken by ship to France and sent to the front line. Today I suppose it would be called a storyboard.

In more modern times the war memorial with, perhaps, the most unusual story attached to it is the Sherman tank which was salvaged from the sea and installed at **Torcross** in South Devon, in memory of more than a thousand American troops who were killed in a D-Day rehearsal disaster on Slapton Sands in 1944. Some died on the beach because they were landed before the naval bombardment was over, and many more were drowned when German E-boats got through the defences and sank a convoy of landing craft.

Forty years later a local hotelier, Ken Small, bought the tank as a sunken wreck

The 'storyboard' memorial at Sledmere to the Yorkshire Waggoners who died in the First World War, designed by their colonel, Sir Mark Sykes.

The Torcross Tank, a memorial not only to a thousand American servicemen but to one man's single-minded determination.

from the American government for fifty dollars, salvaged and restored it, and installed it on a council car-park in Torcross. His enterprise earned him the personal thanks of the American President, but memorial tank restorers, like prophets, are not always popular in their own country, and Mr Small had several differences of opinion with the council and other residents. Mr Small has admitted that he has been 'obsessive' over his tank, and in 1992 he threatened to move it to a more appreciative holiday resort, but that row was resolved, and the tank remained in place. It is a memorial to one man's single-minded determination, as well as all those American servicemen.

Another example of enterprise and determination in a different field is commemorated at **Colliers End**, near Ware in Hertfordshire. It is indeed in a field, a stone marking the spot where an Italian balloonist, Vincent Lunardi, 'the first Aerial Traveller in Britain', landed his balloon on 15 September 1784. The inscription goes on to say that he 'traversed the Regions of the Air' for two hours and fifteen minutes, but this is not strictly accurate. After taking off from the City of London, Lunardi did make an earlier landing, in a cornfield at South Mimms, but he was only down long enough to disembark his cat, which was suffering from the cold.

It was forty minutes later that he came down at Colliers End, though not without difficulty. It was the first balloon the villagers had seen, and they were so alarmed by it they called it the Devil's Horse, and refused to go near it. Then a young servant girl, encouraged by the shouted promise of five guineas from the still airborne Lunardi, agreed to catch the rope which he threw down to her, and hung on to it until some farmworkers, shamed into action, lent a hand. It is not reported whether she shared the five guineas, but I rather hope not. Lunardi returned to London, where he received a more enthusiastic welcome.

A reminder that 'the first Aerial Traveller in Britain' landed his balloon in this field at Colliers End – but not without difficulty.

This was the highest concrete structure of its kind in England when Judge Peterson built it in 1845. He took quite a chance, putting it in a village called Sway, but happily it didn't, and it stands there still.

He made a number of flights after that, and was last seen in England in 1787 testing a device he invented for saving life at sea, described as 'a sort of barrel-shaped lifejacket with paddles'. It did actually float, but somehow it never caught on. Soon afterwards he returned to Italy, leaving behind him many admirers, a rather well-off servant girl, and a stone with a balloon engraved on it, in the middle of a Hertfordshire field.

Not all aeronauts fared so successfully, of course. A monument beside the River Avon near **Yelvertoft**, in Northamptonshire, marks the place where a gliding machine crashed in 1899 and its pilot, one Percy Pilcher, was killed. Percy had already designed a petrol motor to power a larger glider, four years ahead of the Wright brothers; if he had not crashed, he might have achieved the fame that went to the Wrights. He did at least have his name recorded on a memorial, which is more than another pioneering traveller achieved, who died in the same year. He is remembered only by a sombre little plaque on Grove Hill, **Harrow**, in Middlesex.

'Take Heed,' it warns. 'The first recorded motor accident in Great Britain involving the death of the driver occurred on Grove Hill on 25 February 1899.' Well, at least the poor chap earned a place in motoring history, albeit an anonymous one.

A pioneer in a very different way left a very different memorial in his garden at **Sway** in Hampshire. Andrew Peterson returned to England in 1845, after many years as a High Court judge in India, with a curious passion for concrete. The story goes that he was visited by the ghost of Christopher Wren, who told him he must inaugurate a great new age of building, the Age of Concrete – though why an architect like Wren should be so keen on such an unattractive building material is hard to understand. Another story is that the judge was converted to the Hindu religion, and wanted to build something very high, so his body could be placed on top.

Whatever the motive, up went the tower, constructed entirely without the use of scaffolding. The central staircase was erected first, then they built outwards from that. This was not the first time a no-scaffolding system had been used to erect a tall thin building; John Matson built the lighthouse

Emblems of one man's ingenuity and another man's gratitude. The Marquess of Rockingham built the 'Needle's Eye' at Wentworth Woodhouse (left) to prove he could drive his coach through one; Castrano Celestra built the Romulus and Remus monument at West Horrington (far left) to thank the locals for their kindness while he was an Italian prisoner-of-war.

on **Flamborough Head**, Humberside in this way forty years before. However, that was just 214 feet high, whereas Judge Peterson only stopped when his tower reached 220 feet, the tallest concrete structure of its kind in the country.

It was also probably the most useless. Judge Peterson did display a powerful light on top of it to celebrate his achievement, but had to remove it when the Admiralty warned him it was confusing ships in the Solent. His neighbours, understandably, christened it Peterson's Folly, but I prefer to think of it as Peterson's Memorial – not quite as grand as Christopher Wren's, but just about as high.

In the eighteenth century a great many squires left follies as memorials, but one or two of them did have some sort of purpose, albeit a bizarre one. The second Marquess of Rockingham, for instance, bespattered his estate at **Wentworth Woodhouse** in

South Yorkshire with odd structures, of which the Needle's Eye was apparently the most pointless – except of course for its shape, a pointed pyramid with an arch through it, and a large urn on top. It did have an object, however; to win a bet.

The Marquess was a great gambling man, who once wagered £500 on a race between turkeys and geese, and when someone bet him that he could not drive a carriage through the eye of a needle, he was unable to resist the challenge. So he built the Needle, with an 'eye' wide enough to take his carriage. It still stands as a monument to his ingenuity – but I hope he had the grace not to take the money.

An equally useless-looking monument stands near the A39 road at **West Horrington** in Somerset, but it is in fact a memorial of thanksgiving. It stands twelve feet high and consists of four decorated columns supporting a statue of the twins

Romulus and Remus, being suckled by the she-wolf which, according to legend, reared them. The twins were later responsible for building Rome, and Romulus went on to kill his brother and organise the rape of the Sabine women, a full and active life which seems to have little connection with the peaceful Somerset countryside.

The monument was, in fact, built by an Italian – not a Roman legionary stationed in this outpost of empire, but a prisoner captured during the Second World War. Castrano Celestra was a stonemason before joining the Italian army, and was called in by a local farmer to repair a wall which had been damaged in a German air raid. When he finished the wall Castrano asked permission to build something extra, to express his gratitude for the kind treatment he had received from the locals. Romulus and Remus were the result. It would be difficult to devise a less appropriate subject as a thank-offering to an English rural community, but it is the thought that counts, and I hope the locals were nice about it.

A rather more practical memorial was left by the Revd Thomas Remington, Vicar of **Grange-over-Sands** in Cumbria some 160 years ago. In 1834, on the summit of Hampsfell, he built a little shelter for the use of travellers who found themselves marooned on the fell overnight. He put a poem on the wall, setting out the delights the little hospice had to offer, not least the view from the roof. 'A flight of steps requireth care,' he wrote, 'The roof will show a prospect rare.'

The poem ended with a gentle plea to visitors:

A lengthened chain holds guard around,
To keep the cattle from the ground;
Kind reader freely take your pleasure,
But do no mischief to my treasure.

He reinforced this appeal with a rather more forceful, warning to vandals:

All persons visiting this 'hospice' by
permission of the owner, are requested to
respect private property, and not by acts
of wanton mischief and destruction show
that they possess more muscle than brain.

But he added fatalistically:

I have no hope that this request will be
attended to, for as Solomon says, 'Though
thou shouldest bray a fool in a mortar
among wheat with a pestle yet will not his
foolishness depart from him.'

Sure enough, some graffiti was added to the walls, but in equally elegant style. Also

The Revd Thomas Remington's refuge on the summit of Hampsfell, notable for its splendid views and elegant graffiti.

It has to be said that he made rather a mess of it. His plan was to put the town to the torch, but the torch, made of canvas dipped in brimstone, refused to light. In addition, a large number of his men disappeared into a pub on the quayside as soon as they landed, and lost interest in the proceedings altogether. John Paul Jones had to limit his activities to spiking the cannon round the harbour, though he did manage to set fire to one boat before he left – helped, perhaps, by the fact that it was loaded with coal.

Officially the authorities were outraged by all this, but the locals seemed to find it rather entertaining, and the portrait was painted in his memory, alongside one of the cannon he spiked. The picture is actually quite flattering, depicting him with a superior, rather supercilious expression, as if he had achieved a famous victory instead of a rather ludicrous debacle.

Finally, a memorial connected with a much earlier chapter in the colonisation of America, which you might expect to find in

written in verse, it dealt first with the vicar's poem and its reference to the view from the roof:

> The 'flight of steps requireth care'
> Then why not have a handrail there;
> That feeble old and timid fair
> May mount and view the prospect there.

The final verse, however, offered reassurance to the rector over his fears about vandals doing mischief to his treasure:

> No good man would think it pleasure
> To climb the fell to spoil your treasure.
> Your offer made in kindly spirit
> I hope you'll find our conduct merit.

The good vicar was so taken with this response that he had the verses printed and hung on the wall opposite his own, under the title *The Answer*. And indeed the answer must have been an effective one; the little shelter has survived without any serious damage ever since.

Further up the Cumbrian coast, at **Whitehaven**, there is a different memorial in the form of an old cannon, and close by it on the cliff wall is a weather-beaten portrait of the man it commemorates, John Paul Jones. Whitehaven had the distinction of being the only port in England which came under attack during the American War of Independence, and it was John Paul Jones, an American colonist who was born in Scotland and trained as a seaman at Whitehaven, who led the raid in 1778.

John Paul Jones (left), who brought the American War of Independence to Britain by leading a raid on Whitehaven. It wasn't too successful, but he did manage to spike the odd cannon (above left). Beyond the cannon is the Candlestick Chimney, which ventilated a coalmine. Some say it got its name after being set on fire by lightning, but I prefer the story that when the mine-owner, Lord Lonsdale, was asked to suggest a design for it he pointed at a candlestick on the dining table and said 'Build it like that . . .'

The memorial marking the place where the Pilgrim Fathers first set sail from England in search of religious freedom – not in the *Mayflower* from Plymouth, but thirteen years earlier from near Boston in Lincolnshire. The captain gave them away and they were all arrested.

Plymouth, but it actually stands beside an obscure creek in **Fishtoft**, Lincolnshire. The inscription says simply:

*Near this place
in September 1607 those later
known as the Pilgrim Fathers
set sail on their first attempt
to find religious freedom
across the seas.*

Yes, the *first* attempt, thirteen years before the date which is always associated with the Pilgrim Fathers, the sailing of the *Mayflower* in 1620. Many of those who eventually sailed on her were, in fact, from Lincolnshire and the neighbouring counties. They were known as Separatists, a more extreme branch of the Puritan movement, and their determination to worship separately from the Church of England made them very unpopular with the authorities. One of their centres in Lincolnshire was the village of Scrooby, where William Brewster set up a Separatist church in his manor house. Richard Clyfton, a former Church of England Rector of nearby Babworth, took the services.

The pressure on the Separatists increased so much that in September 1607 the entire Scrooby congregation sold all their belongings, made their way to Boston, sixty miles away, and hired a ship to take them to Holland. They boarded it at Scotia Creek, about three miles down-river from Boston, and that was as far as they got. The captain

had passed the word to the authorities. 'Bailiffs put them into open boats and there rifled and ransacked them, searching them to their shirts for money – even the women.'

Most of them were just sent back home, but the leaders, including Brewster and Clyfton, were held in Boston Guildhall cells for some time, until they too returned to Scrooby, virtually destitute. Undeterred, six months later they tried again. They raised enough money to contract another ship, this time with a Dutch owner, and arranged a rendezvous at Killingholme Creek, on a remote stretch of coast north of Grimsby. The men of Scrooby walked there, the women and children went by barge. The men arrived first and were already on the ship when the captain saw armed men on the shore and set sail, refusing to wait for the families. The women and children were arrested again, including Mary Brewster with two small children and Ann Clyfton with her nine-year-old son.

The story continues in the same dramatic fashion. I find it astonishing that no television producer has seized upon it for an upmarket Sunday night serial, probably with Ian McShane as William Brewster. The ship with the men on board was caught in a storm and swept off course to Norway before managing to head home to Amsterdam. Meanwhile, nobody knew what to do with the womenfolk, and the authorities were eventually 'glad to get rid of them on any terms'. Sympathisers arranged a passage for them to Holland, where the families were reunited.

The Scrooby Separatists might have lived happily in Holland ever after, but the irrepressible Brewster started printing inflammatory pamphlets to smuggle back to England, and after twelve years they had to move on. He and his followers sailed to Southampton to link up with the *Mayflower*, and in due course they sailed to the New World, where Brewster became one of the notable Founding Fathers, author of the 'Mayflower Compact', the constitution which introduced democratic elections in the colonies.

One might say, then, that if you seek a memorial to that band of Lincolnshire Separatists, you have only to look at America. If the sight of that does not appeal to you, there is always that lonely monument at Scotia Creek.

A pillar to post –
Trollope's most
novel idea

A pillar to post – Trollope's most novel idea

When Anthony Trollope was not writing novels – fifty of them altogether and almost a full-time job in itself – he had a day job in the Surveyors Department of the Post Office, and in 1851, as a change from romantic fiction, he turned his pen to the nineteenth-century equivalent of an internal office memo. It resulted in an even better legacy to the nation, in its way, than the *Barchester Chronicles*. He suggested to his superiors that they could save the public much inconvenience, and incidentally encourage more business, 'by the provision of iron posts for the safe reception of letters, which may be erected at the corner of streets at such situations as may be desirable.'

Thus, within a few months, the British pillar-box was born, and Trollope has gone down in Post Office folklore as the man who invented it. However, I happened to meet his biographer, Victoria Glendinning, and when I tried to show off my knowledge of Trollope and his pillar-box brainwave, she told me the full story.

Alas, far from being an essentially English creation, as we all like to think, the pillar-box actually originated in France. Trollope came across them on a visit to the Continent, and brought the idea back with him. Significantly, it was in the Channel Islands, so closely linked with France, that the first British pillar-boxes were installed in 1852. The idea caught on, and the new boxes soon spread to the mainland. Even then they were not the traditional Post Office red; the earliest ones were sage-green. But the letter-writing public soon spotted them, and their usefulness became immediately apparent.

Up until then, letters had to be taken to central receiving houses, which could involve quite lengthy journeys. One example of these receiving houses is the Craven Arms, a coaching inn at **Southam** in Warwickshire, where a receptacle for letters was uncovered during renovations in 1925. A notice beside it says a number of coins were found inside it dating back to 1689, though why anyone should post their loose change into a letter-box is not clear. Perhaps it was also used for depositing letters brought on the coaches, in which case the coins may have been left there as a tip for the driver by the grateful recipients – and nobody ever told him.

Certainly letters were delivered by the stage-coaches to the inns along their route; at **Hurstbourne Tarrant** in Hampshire, for example, the sixteenth-century George and Dragon still has its original oak mail rack in the bar.

The pillar-box changed the postal collection system, and since its introduction designers have been changing the pillar-box, sometimes with bizarre results. Mr Trollope, I imagine, just visualised some sort of sturdy metal box with a hole near the top to put the letters in, and a door near the bottom to get them out. His basic idea has remained unchanged, but the box has sometimes been six-sided, sometimes eight-sided, sometimes fluted, sometimes just plain round. The apertures have varied from vertical to horizontal, and the decorations have ranged from crowns and balls on top of the box to leaves around the openings and white enamel plates on the doors. Sometimes there was a Royal cipher, sometimes it just said 'Letter Box' or 'Post Office', sometimes there was nothing at all. In one extraordinary case the manufacturers misread the specifications and made a pillar-box eight feet high, with a vast dome on the top; one still survives in the Post Office Museum.

Then came the wall letter-boxes, tucked into Post Office frontages and boundary walls. Some of them were individually designed by the local postmaster, like the early wooden one at **St German's** in Cornwall, which suits all tastes by having both a vertical and a horizontal slot. Finally, as late as 1896, came the lamp-boxes, attached to lamp-posts and telegraph poles and any other upright that was handy. Over the years, in fact, Mr Trollope's boxes went from pillar to post . . .

To the average poster of letters a post-box is just a post-box, but whole books have

Two of the earliest pillars in which to post: the crowned 'Liverpool Special' in Albert Dock Village . . .

aptly-named **World's End** in Hampshire. Up until then, 1859, local Post Office Surveyors ordered their own favourite design for their own area, and when a national design was introduced it did not go down too well in independently-minded places like Liverpool.

The Liverpudlian Postmaster reckoned that the standard box was too small to hold enough letters, the aperture was the wrong size, and the new-fangled wire guard inside the door, which stopped the letters falling into the mud when it was opened, took up too much room. He couldn't do much about the first two objections, but instead of the wire guard he continued to use the original system of hanging a mailbag inside the box to catch the letters. On top of the

. . . and an example of the first national standard design, still in use at World's End.

been written about these humble, but familiar, features of the roadside scene, and just as a philatelist can get excited over a rare Penny Black, so a pillar-box buff (a 'pillartelist', perhaps?) can be enraptured by a genuine Penfold original – six-sided, acanthus leaves and a ball on top, designed by J. W. Penfold in 1866. There would be positive ecstasy over a Liverpool Special – cylindrical, 'Post Office' under the aperture, large solid crown on top, circa 1863.

There are over a hundred Penfolds surviving, which by vintage pillar-box standards makes them fairly common, but only one Liverpool Special remains in use, on a pavement in **Albert Dock Village**, Liverpool. You may spot another one outside **Liverpool** Head Post Office, but beware, it is only there for decoration. The Special was a local variation on what the Post Office hoped would be the first national standard pillar-box, the type which can still be found in remote corners like the

Unlikely places to find a letter-box: at Rochdale (above) the box is in the bottom of a lamp-post, and on Cranmore Station (right) it is in the back of a telephone kiosk. Neither idea caught on.

box he added what is officially described as a crown, but it looks to me suspiciously like a red rose . . .

There is an even more distinctive variation on the standard design in Toad Lane, **Rochdale** in Greater Manchester, near the shop where the Co-operative movement was born. The pillar-box must be an example of co-operative action itself, because the Post Office agreed that the local lighting authority could install a lamp-post on top of it. So far as I know this is the only 'lampillarbox' in the country, but at **Cranmore** railway station, headquarters of the East Somerset Railway, there is another, more complex concoction which might be called a 'letterphone-stampbox'. To Post Office aficionados it is known simply as the K4. There are about ten still surviving, but this is the only one which actually functions.

It came about as the result of a Post Office experiment by its engineering department which left them with faces as red as the K4 itself. The standard pillar-box with its various modifications had been around for nearly sixty years before it was decided to introduce a standard telephone box too. The first type, the K1, never caught on, but the K2, designed by Sir Giles Gilbert Scott in 1924, proved a winner, and it remained basically unchanged for half a century along with its grey equivalent for rural areas, the K3. However, the engineering department were reluctant to leave well alone, and decided it could be improved. In the late 1920s they produced the ill-fated K4.

It was one of those ideas which look jolly good on paper, and sound great in the boardroom, but do not quite work in practice. Let's create a post office in miniature, said the engineering department. We'll take Scott's kiosk, add a chunk on the back of it which will hold a letter-box and two stamp machines, stick a lamp above them, add the royal cipher, and there we are, three Post Office services in one.

There they were, in fact, with what became known as the Vermilion Giant, the Post Office equivalent of a white elephant. It was so big that local authorities complained it blocked the pavement and caused a traffic hazard. The stamp machines were so noisy that anyone making a phone call inside the kiosk could hardly hear themselves speak, let alone the voice at the other end. And the stamp machines themselves were so open to the elements that when it rained, all the stamps got wet and stuck together.

They made just fifty K4s, then the Post Office cut its losses and returned to Scott's original design. Of those that have survived, only the K4 at Cranmore has been restored to anything like its former glory. After long disuse on a Bristol pavement it was rescued by the chairman of the East Somerset Railway, the wildlife artist David Shepherd, whose devotion to elephants and rhinos in his paintings is reflected in his affection for this survivor of an endangered species.

It was restored by a K4 enthusiast, a retired general manager of British Telecom, Andrew Hurley, who adapted one or two of its functions to local use. When you lift the receiver and put a coin in the box, you just hear a recorded message from David Shepherd, extolling the delights of his railway – and thanking you for your dona-tion. But the letter-box is still emptied by the postman, or at any rate it was while I was there for the unveiling ceremony in the summer of 1992. In my view it is quite the most imposing pillar-box still in business.

The oldest functioning pillar-box in England is much less conspicuous. You have to find your way to a lonely cottage at **Barnes Cross**, near Sherborne in Dorset. On the grass outside is an obviously well-cherished veteran of some 140 summers and winters, an eight-sided pillar-box with a vertical slot for letters.

In the early days it was thought that a slot which went up and down instead of side-ways made it more difficult for a thief to reach inside and steal the letters. After a few

years, however, it was realised that not many thieves had flat forearms three feet long. They also found that vertical slots let in the rain, and anyway it was impossible for cartoonists to draw them as mouths and make them smile on Post Office advertise-ments. But the Barnes Cross pillar-box and one or two other rare examples, like the

England's oldest functioning pillar-box, at Barnes Cross, dating from the 1850s and still boasting its original 'VR'.

box at **Eton** in Berkshire, still look down their vertical noses at the world and remain resolutely glum.

In *Timpson's England* there was a picture opposite the title-page of a pillar-box with spikes on top. I had a theory that the spikes were put there to prevent very tall pedestrians from playing leap-frog, but this explanation was never actually published, perhaps wisely. I have now discovered their real purpose.

These days the box stands in the middle of the pavement in Priors Road, **Cambridge**, which prompted my leap-frog theory, with all those undergraduates around, but the experts say that originally it must have been located beside a high garden wall, and the householder insisted on the spikes so that burglars could not use it as a stepping-stone to climb over the wall. I think the leap-frog idea is rather more entertaining, but I expect they are right.

It is also, incidentally, an 'anonymous' pillar-box, with no royal cipher, just the maker's name, Andrew Handyside of Derby. These anonymous boxes went into production in 1879, and surprisingly it was eight years before anyone noticed that something

Pillar-boxes with anti-crime devices: the one at Cambridge has spikes so it cannot be used for climbing over walls . . .

. . . and the much earlier one at Eton still has the vertical slit which was supposed to foil letter-thieves with long flat forearms.

was missing. There was a gentle murmur of 'Whoops!' and Andrew Handyside had to concede pride of place to the more illustrious 'VR'. I imagine that, as usual, Queen Victoria was not terribly amused, and maybe it was she who suggested adding those spikes, on which to impale the presumptuous Mr Handyside.

Yes, on thinking about it, I like that theory best of all.

Distances and directions, left, right – and centre?

Distances and directions, left, right – and centre?

When the Romans vacated their fort at Vindolanda they left behind one of their milestones which is now the only one remaining in England in its original position.

The longest mile, they say, is the last mile home, but for the Roman soldiers marching up the length of England to the northernmost defence line, the longest miles were the last ones to the Wall. To give them a little encouragement, the Roman road engineers planted milestones along the route, and one of them still stands on the final stretch, near the remains of the Roman fort of Vindolanda, or **Chesterholm**, just north of Bardon Mill in Northumberland – the only Roman milestone in England which is still in its original position. You can hardly miss it, because it stands six feet high.

The Romans, of course, not only invented the milestone, they invented the mile, based on a thousand paces. I once commented that the average Roman soldier must have either very long legs or quite a spring in his step, because in a thousand paces he covered 1,620 yards. Kindly historians have pointed out to me that a Roman 'pace' was actually the distance covered by one foot from where it left the ground to where it landed again, while the other foot landed somewhere in between. I would call that two paces, but then I am not a Roman.

Anyway, it does reduce Roman legs to more normal proportions, even if their milestones were rather large.

Since then the milestone industry has never looked back, though it may have problems if we ever switch to metrestones. In its heyday it was even providing milestones where no miles were involved; at **Fordingbridge** in Hampshire, for example, there is one which gives the useful information: 'Fordingbridge, 0'. It also seems a little superfluous for a stonemason in Northumbria to have spelt out in full, 'Cambo, Half a Mile', when Cambo was only just up the road anyway.

Not content with this, some milestone-makers have added elegant patterns and crests but, more poignant, is the milestone in the churchyard alongside the Old Dover Road on **Shooter's Hill**, the route taken by many First World War Tommies as they marched out of London to the coast. It gives the routine information on one side, 'London 12 miles', – or rather, it used to, until vandals removed it – but on the other it says:

130 miles to YPRES. In defending the salient our casualties were 90,000 killed, 70,500 missing, 410,000 wounded.

Not so much a milestone, more a war memorial, and a very telling one at that.

(Right) You can work out the location of this milestone for yourself . . .

The stone signpost at Wroxton not only provided helping hands but told you the time as well.

130 MILES TO YPRES. IN DEFENDING THE SALIENT OUR CASUALTIES WERE:- 90,000 KILLED, 70,500 MISSING, 410,000 WOUNDED.

HYDE PARK CORNER 120
BLANDFORD 16
BRIDPORT 15

At Shooter's Hill, a reminder in milestone form of the First World War . . .

. . . and in Dorchester, a reminder of the coaching days when travel information was provided at coach-top level for the drivers.

Milestones were handy for the Roman foot-soldier and even for the charioteer, but when the stagecoach was invented the driver was perched ten feet or so above the ground, and he almost needed a telescope to read them. Maybe that was when sign-posts came into their own. Certainly we still have one or two surviving which were obviously designed for the convenience of high-riding coachmen. In *Timpson's England* I quoted the lofty post by the Evesham road at **Chipping Campden** in Gloucestershire, and the same idea was taken up in **Dorchester**, Dorset, where you have to peer up to coachtop level to spot the information carved into a wall: 'Hyde Park Corner 120'.

However, not every seventeenth-century signpost catered for coachmen. A stone signpost at **Wroxton** in Oxfordshire is

An early example of helpful guidance for travellers: the pillar at Dunston used to have lanterns on top to help travellers at night.

was how to spot them at night, let alone read what they said. One or two places therefore offered alternative forms of guidance. In *Timpson's England* I mentioned the lantern on the church tower at **Weldon-in-the-Woods** in Northamptonshire, paid for by a stranger who had got lost in the woods. Sir Francis Dashwood had the same thought in mind in 1751 when he erected a pillar with lanterns on top, like an inland lighthouse, at **Dunston** in Lincolnshire. Sir Francis, of Hellfire Club fame, was not renowned for philanthropy, and I suspect the pillar was largely for his own benefit, after he had inherited some property at Dunston from his wife. It was a long coach-ride from his main home at West Wycombe in Buckinghamshire, and no doubt he often arrived after dark.

Some time after his death, in 1810, the lanterns were removed and a statue of King George III was put on the pillar instead. Presumably patriotism had taken precedence over public-spiritedness, or maybe the locals preferred strangers not to find them anyway. Then in the Second World War George III became a danger to low-flying aircraft, and the pillar became just another pillar.

The modern equivalent of Dashwood's elevated lantern is the lamp-post, which is often a fairly humdrum affair, built to a standard pattern and singularly lacking in character and charm. Sometimes, however, the lamps are attached to existing buildings rather than put on a post, and at **Deeping St James** in Lincolnshire the old lock-up was given a new lease of life in this way.

This was no ordinary village lock-up. It started life in the fifteenth century as a market cross, a central point for street traders, and originally it was solid. In 1819 it was converted by a local man called Tailby Johnson, who hollowed it out and created a gloomy little room about four feet square, containing three stone seats with chains across them, to which the prisoners were manacled. Tailby omitted to provide any ventilation, except for the bars in the door, and it must have been a very unsavoury little cell. Sympathetic villagers tried to supply drinks to the occupants by poking a long-spouted teapot through the bars, but as the recipients could hardly move and the pourers could hardly see, most of it probably went on the floor.

indeed nearly ten feet high, but all a coachman would see is the sundial on top. That was handy if he had forgotten his watch, but it didn't help if he was lost. The actual directions are much lower down on the plinth, where stone hands have been carved to indicate the routes to London, Stratford, Banbury and Chipping Norton. The post was given to the village in 1686 by a Mr Francis White, and the story goes that his spelling did not quite measure up to his generosity, one side said 'Chiping Norton'. In 1974 the village preservation society had the post restored by a local mason, who not only freshened up the stonework but gave the battered fingers on the hands a nice manicure, adding a ring or two for good measure. If you are in too much of a hurry to study all the details, the highway authority has thoughtfully erected a modern signpost a few yards away.

The snag with signposts in the days before street lighting and bright headlights

The lock-up was also the village's main source of water, as it had a pump on one wall, and its two tiers of stone seats still provide a resting place for weary shoppers. When street lighting was introduced it achieved yet another use, as one of England's most unlikely lamp-posts.

Even the routine ones are sometimes given a little extra ornamentation to provide local colour as well as local light. At **Bungay** in Suffolk, a lamp-post in the centre of the town is surmounted by the Black Dog of Bungay, a replica of the legendary hound which once terrorised the neighbourhood. While lamp-posts naturally attract dogs, I like to think this is the only one in England which has a dog on top of it, instead of at the foot . . .

In contrast, a Victorian lamp-post in St George's Square, **Bishop's Waltham**, Hampshire is surmounted by a bishop's mitre, a reminder that the town was once the seat of the Bishops of Winchester; the remains of the bishop's palace and its moat are still there. The last bishop to live there was besieged by the Roundheads and had to escape in a dung-cart, which would have provided a more dramatic decoration for the lamp-post, but the Victorians discreetly plumped for a mitre instead. It was originally on top of the Market House clock but the Market House fell into disuse and was demolished in 1841, and the lamp-post now stands on the site. No doubt those who regretted the passing of the old building rejoiced when the mitre survived. 'The lamp has got its hat on, let's sing hip-hip-hooray . . .'

In the days of the episcopal dung-cart, the alternative to a lantern for guiding travellers at night was a bell. There were the church bells, of course, and if they happened to be ringing for a late-night service they could be a great help to wandering strangers. But this could backfire on the ringers too, as the good monks of **Blanchland Abbey** in Northumberland discovered. The abbey was due to be dissolved by Henry VIII, but his Commissioners got lost in the mist and went off across the fells in the wrong direction. The monks were so delighted that they rang the bells in thanksgiving – and guided the King's Commissioners straight back to the monastery.

That was a rather exceptional case. On the whole it was bona fide travellers who benefited from the ringing of church bells on foggy nights. They were particularly fortunate if they got lost in the vicinity of a village with a curfew bell – so long as it happened to be curfew time. Sir Robert Fry struck lucky in this way when he got lost on Moreton Common on his way home from London to **Moreton-in-Marsh**, in Gloucestershire. The sound of the bell in the Curfew Tower led him straight home, and he was so grateful that he left an endowment of ten shillings a year to pay the bellringer, and another pound a year for winding the clock. The bell is dated 1633, and it was rung regularly at eight o'clock every evening until 1860.

The last man to ring it was William Webb, who also doubled as parish constable. This was quite convenient as the lock-up was on the ground floor of the bell tower, so he could combine his duties of winding the clock, ringing the bell and guarding offenders, all under one roof. He retired at the age of seventy-six, after breaking a leg in a struggle with a drunk he was trying to put in the cell, and the curfew bell stopped functioning too.

Street lamps with a difference: this lamp at Bishop's Waltham (above) is no doubt proud of its episcopal connections, but the one at Deeping St James (left) may not enjoy being stuck on the old lock-up.

Lanterns and bells for guiding travellers became superfluous in due course, and signposts became more sophisticated in the information they provided. The old West Riding of Yorkshire, for example, added a circle on top of its signposts bearing the local grid reference and the name of the county. When parts of Yorkshire were transferred into Lancashire this created a problem, and the solution proved to be drastic. As a correspondent wrote heatedly to *The Countryman* magazine:

'Hardly was the ink dry on the Act of Parliament than the hacksaw gang from County Hall, Preston, removed the upper part of the circle from those signposts bearing the erstwhile county's name. Although I live in Lancashire by choice, I have never forgiven Lancashire County Council for this deed!'

There is one of these semi-capitated signposts at **Bolton-by-Bowland**.

Understandably, most modern signposts are painted white for clarity, and the newest ones are even fluorescent white for easier reading by headlight, but a signpost near **Bloxworth** on the road from Wimborne to Bere Regis in Dorset has always been painted red. It would be tempting to conjure up a legend about some bloody crime committed at this crossroads, or perhaps recall highwaymen's bodies dangling from the post, but its history is rather less gruesome, though indeed rather sad.

The road was on the route from Dorchester Prison to Portsmouth, where prisoners were taken after being sentenced to transportation. They stopped overnight in a barn down the side lane to Bloxworth, and as the guards were assumed to be illiterate, the signpost was painted red to show them where to turn off. It might have been simpler, perhaps, and less disconcerting for other travellers, just to put a red arrow pointing down the lane, but the prison service preferred to do it the quirky way. Equally quirkily, and much to its credit, the highway authority still paints the post red. Incidentally, the barn is still there too, easily recognisable with its prison-like windows.

A much more imaginative, and considerably more cheerful, form of signpost has been created for travellers on the Grand Union Canal at **Wolverton** by the Inland Waterways Association and Milton Keynes Council. Wolverton is not the most attractive corner of the new 'City', as Milton Keynes likes to be called; it was created mainly to build carriages and engines for the railway, and the unprepossessing carriage works are now flanked by a gravel works, which is no great improvement. To

The directions on the signpost are clear enough, but can you guess why it is red?

Part of a 350-foot 'signpost' beside the canal at Wolverton . .

round it all off, a long blank wall next to the canal was permanently covered with the more basic varieties of graffiti.

In 1986 the two authorities decided to cheer up this depressing vista, and a local artist called Bill Billings was commissioned to design a massive mural, more than 350 feet long and 8 feet high. He was helped by over a hundred playgroup members and community service workers, and it took them four months to complete. The result is not only the biggest mural in Milton Keynes, but also, since it incorporates the distances along the canal to Birmingham, Brentford and the places in between, it must be in the running for the biggest signpost in England. The paint is touched up each year, and happily the graffiti writers have taken their talents elsewhere.

There is another kind of signpost which can be found at various points along a line running north and south of Greenwich. They take various forms, ranging from the monument in the middle of **Peacehaven** in Sussex to the round stone with a line bisecting it in a field outside **Frampton** in Lincolnshire, but they all carry the same message. They stand on longitude zero, and divide the world in two – the western hemisphere on one side, the eastern hemisphere on the other.

Another kind of measurement post indicates the height above sea level. These four-foot concrete cones were sprinkled all over the English countryside about sixty years

ago by Ordnance Survey, as a guide to map makers and surveyors in plotting precise locations. One of them stands in a field near my cottage, a source of some irritation to the farmer, since he has to plough around it, drill around it, spray around it, and combine his crops around it. It records a height of twenty-three metres, which amounts to quite a hill in Norfolk – some of the Ordnance Survey 'trig-points' in East Anglia are actually below sea level.

With the new satellite technology, however, about five thousand of these blocks of concrete became redundant, and Ordnance Survey have hit on a jolly scheme called 'Adopt-a-Trig-Pillar'. They must be the ultimate in gifts for the person who has

. . . and one of the trig-pillars which Ordnance Survey offered for 'adoption'. So far as I know, this one on the Peddars Way at Castle Acre is still an orphan.

Lillington's 'Midland Oak' plaque, reputed to mark the centre of England . . .

. . . but High Cross has a claim to the title too. And don't forget Minsworth . . .

everything, though they are a mixed blessing for whoever adopts them, because they have to be protected from vandals, belligerent animals and the weather. They cannot actually be delivered, and a special access agreement has to be arranged with the landowner if they are on private property. However, they can be suitably inscribed and, no doubt, gift-wrapped for the presentation ceremony.

Some of the more spectacular sites, like the trig-pillar on top of Snowdon, were snapped up straight away, but I cannot visualise a queue for the one in my neighbour's field. It will be interesting to see what future generations make of these chunks of concrete, with the brass fitting for a theodolite on top, a pipe down the centre, and something like 'To Libby with love from Robin' inscribed on the side. They may well regard them as civilisation's equivalent of all those Devil's Stones which have been handed down to us from the past.

Greenwich Meridian signs and Ordnance Survey trig-pillars are sited with great scientific accuracy, but it is not so easy to pinpoint another geographical feature which rates an identifying mark, the precise centre of England. **Meriden** in the West Midlands is the popular choice, if only because its name sounds vaguely cartographical. Medieval map-makers certainly thought so, and put a cross in the middle of the village to prove it, but there are at least three other claimants.

In Warwickshire **Lillington** planted an oak tree on what it says is England's central point, while **Copston Magna** traces its claim back to a sixteenth-century Warwickshire poet called Michael Drayton. Just outside Copston Magna is **High Cross**, where two former Roman roads, Watling Street and the Fosse Way, intersect. This is the crossroads which Drayton referred to when he wrote:

> Here, Muse, divert thy course to
>   Dunsmore, by the Cross
> Where those two mighty ways, the
>   Watling and the Foss,
> Our centre seems to cut . . .

A hundred years later another writer called Celia Fiennes referred to 'High Cross, which is esteemed the middle of England', and when a monument was erected there in 1712 that seemed to clinch it. Actually the monument was donated by local landowners 'to serve as a perpetual remembrance of peace at last restored by Queen Anne', and High Cross just seemed a handy place to put it. The monument was short-lived anyway – it was struck by lightning in 1791, and the remains were last spotted in somebody's garden. It all seems very inconclusive.

My own money goes on the fourth claimant, which entered the ring fairly recently with the sort of scientific proof that I can understand. Apparently a master at King Edward's Grammar School in Birmingham had the bright idea of getting the boys to cut out forty cardboard maps of England, then balance them on a large pin to find their centre of gravity. It turned out to be in a suburb of Birmingham called **Minsworth** – and that is good enough for me. So Meriden, Lillington, Copston Magna – eat your centres out: Minsworth is the place to be. But let's not all rush there at once – we may tip over . . .

Dig that rock, man – for fires, flavouring, funerals . . .

Dig that rock, man – for fires, flavouring, funerals . . .

Grimes Graves (above) with its mysterious craters baffled the experts for centuries, until a Victorian archeologist discovered they were ancient flint-mines. The main shaft (right) is the only one open to the public.

People have been digging very large holes in the English countryside, for various reasons, since long before it was England. Sometimes it was to extract stones for weapons, sometimes to carve out a home or create a line of defence, sometimes just to bury the dead. In more recent centuries the main object has been to find fuel, starting with the peat-cutters, then the coal-miners now the oil prospectors. They have left us a heritage of curious caverns, strange and sinister stones – and a few major problems.

The earliest diggers were after flints. The flint-knappers converted them into axe-heads, to chop down trees, to hunt for food and to protect themselves from the local wildlife – and of course, human nature being what it is, to thump one another. The main centre of the flint-knapping industry, the Sheffield of the Stone Age, was a place known as **Grimes Graves**, on the Norfolk–Suffolk border near Brandon. The name confuses visitors; they are inclined to ask who Mr Grime was and why he needed so many graves. So far as I know, there was no Mr Grime. My own assumption was that some early traveller thought these pits in the heart of the forest looked pretty grim, and the description, slightly adjusted, stuck. However, the experts say that 'Grim' is another name for the Anglo-Saxon god Woden, and they thought this weird moonscape of craters looked so fantastic that only a god could have created it, so they named it after him.

'Graves' seems more logical, since the craters do look a bit like burial places, but again the experts have a different answer: to the Anglo-Saxons, 'graves' just meant holes or hollows. Succeeding generations were understandably perplexed by all this, and nobody knew what the craters really were until an enterprising Victorian archaeologist – who should have been a Mr Grime, to add to the confusion, but was actually a Canon Greenwell from Durham – dug down into one of the 'graves' and found a forty-foot pit shaft, clogged up with rubble.

The men who first excavated it, four thousand years ago, just had picks made from the antlers of the local red deer. They dug galleries at the foot of the shafts to extract the flints, and in their tea breaks they drew patterns in the chalk with their antler picks. Both the drawings and the antlers are still there, and one or two of the antlers still have fingerprints in the chalky paste on the handles.

No great harm came from digging the flint-mines at Grimes Graves, except for the people who got thumped with the flints, but some excavations have caused a considerable upheaval – or more accurately, downheaval. The medieval peat-diggers, in another part of East Anglia, left massive holes which filled up with water from the nearby rivers and eventually linked up to form the series of waterways now known as the Norfolk Broads. These days it is the gravel-diggers who make the holes, and the end result is not always so attractive, but in our new 'green' environment there is much more effort to restore old gravel workings, and places like **Pensthorpe** Waterfowl Park and Nature Reserve, near Fakenham, are the result.

In earlier centuries, though, nobody bothered too much about the effects of digging holes, or where they dug them. The result was subsidence, which was generally associated with coal-mining areas, but it happened in other excavated areas too. Occasionally the effect is rather bizarre; the whole nation chuckled at the sight of a doubledecker bus stuck nose-first in a hole which suddenly appeared in a Norwich main road, over some old chalk workings. But it can also be most disconcerting, singularly uncomfortable, and sometimes downright dangerous.

Droitwich Spa, in Hereford and Worcester, is a notable example of what can happen to a town where there has been indiscriminate tunnelling for centuries. What attracted the tunnellers to Droitwich was the salt. The prehistoric salt-makers started chipping away on the surface first; the Romans dug rather deeper into the site they called Salinas, the place of salt, and the Anglo-Saxons of the seventh and eighth centuries sank their brine wells in what was by now Saltwic, named after the local tribe, the Hwicce. By the time the *Domesday Book* was compiled, there were at least 250 salt-houses and five brine pits in Wich, the next adaptation of the name.

Over the years the more sophisticated extraction plants created more and more salt, and the salt created more and more money for Droitwich, as it finally became. The town took as its motto *Sal Sapit Omnia*, Salt Flavours All, such was the wealth it created. But it also created bigger and bigger holes as the deposits were removed,

and in the High Street you can see the result. Some of the old buildings tilt at very strange angles, to such an extent that a pub called the Waggon and Horses was renamed the Crooked House.

Upstairs the beds had to be tied to the walls to stop them sliding across the room, and down in the smoke-room a table apparently sloped at an angle of thirty degrees, yet a billiard ball placed in the centre would unexpectedly roll upwards. This might have helped the locals to win a few bets with strangers, who stationed themselves at the wrong end of the table to catch the ball, but in the long term they must have found it too unsettling to drink in such lopsided surroundings. Business, like the billiard ball, fell off, the Crooked House became a butcher's shop, and was considerably altered, inside and out.

The most obvious building these days to have been affected by subsidence is the Bullock Cafe, an Elizabethan building with odd-shaped walls and beams which slope far more than the builders intended. The owners made gallant efforts to keep the business going, but things got so tricky that the place had to be shored up, and the last I heard, it was closed with its future in doubt.

The damage resulting from the excavations at Droitwich, however, was paltry

Some of the 'crooked houses' of Droitwich Spa, caused by centuries of underground tunnelling for salt. For the occupants the term 'salt cellar' has nothing to do with cruets . . .

compared with the effect that was felt at **Hallsands** in Devon on a dramatic night in January 1917, when the sea rushed in and the whole village had to be abandoned. It was not just an act of God – man was responsible too and, in particular, the men who dug out half a million tons of shingle and gravel on the shore and undermined the village's natural sea defences.

The dredging took place at the turn of the century to provide material for extending Devonport dockyard, and as a result the beach level at Hallsands dropped by some fifteen feet. The high water mark had been 150 feet away from the cliff; after the excavations the sea came right up to it. There were a number of less serious floods over the years, and each time it happened the sea-wall was strengthened, but when the final disaster came it was not the wall but part of the cliff which gave way. At the subsequent enquiry, according to the local paper, 'the expert evidence was convincing that the romantic hamlet was rendered vulnerable by the removal of pebbles for the dockyard extension scheme at Devonport'.

Hallsands was virtually obliterated by the floods. Nearly every building was in ruins and, in due course, new homes were built for the villagers further from the sea. Only one resident stayed on, thirty-two-year-old Miss Elizabeth Prettejohn, and she was still living on her own in the ruined village until she was well into her seventies. She acted as unofficial guardian and guide, gathered driftwood on the beach to augment her meagre income, and resisted all the efforts of the local authorities to move her to an old people's home. Miss Prettejohn died in 1964, leaving Hallsands to the seagulls, the summer sightseers – and the sea.

Miraculously, no lives were lost when that disaster occurred – only the village died. But in a far greater tragedy in Staffordshire which also involved excavations, seventy people were killed, and this time man was entirely to blame.

There have been gypsum mines in the Hanbury area of Staffordshire since the twelfth century, and before the Second World War the RAF requisitioned some of the underground galleries at **Fauld** as a

The ruined village of Hallsands, destroyed when the sea broke down defences which had been weakened by excessive dredging for sand and shingle.

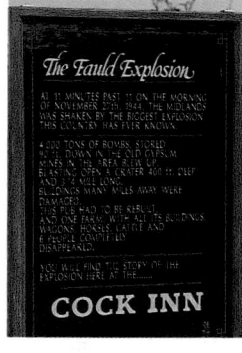

A reminder of the Fauld explosion at the local pub (estimates of the crater size vary) and (above) the crater itself today. The Royston cavern (top left) is a hole with a happier history – though theories about its origin can vary too.

storage dump for bombs and ammunition – nearly 15,000 tons of assorted high explosives. On 27 November 1944, for reasons which have never been established, but probably because of careless handling, there was a massive underground explosion, the biggest detonation of the Second World War apart from the atomic bomb. It was heard as far away as Leicester and Birmingham, and the tremor was registered in Rome and Geneva, where they thought it was an earth tremor.

Only about four thousand tons of explosives went up; if the entire stock had been involved, a vast area of Staffordshire would have been blown to bits. As it was, three million cubic yards of earth and rock were thrown up and deposited over an area of a square mile. The actual crater was 800 feet long, 300 feet wide and 120 feet deep. Around it was a sea of mud, like a First World War battlefield, and as recently as the 1970s a local farmer ploughed up a forty-foot oak tree which had been buried upside down.

Fortunately the area was mostly farmland and sparsely populated, apart from the village of Hanbury, about a mile away, which was extensively damaged. Unfortunately there was a fully staffed plaster factory at the entrance to the mine, and in the mine itself many civilians and RAF personnel were working. The search for bodies took days; eighteen were never recovered.

Today the massive crater is overgrown with scrub and bushes, and fences have been erected round it by the Ministry of Defence with warnings of unexploded bombs. Another notice erected by the Countryside Commission 'welcomes us rather too gleefully', as one visitor put it, to 'the scene of the biggest explosion ever to happen in the United Kingdom'. A white granite memorial stands there, a gift from the Italian Air Force; six Italian prisoners-of-war died in the explosion.

It is not a big step from man-made craters to man-made caves, but it is a big step back in time from the Hanbury crater to the **Royston** cavern in Hertfordshire. Underneath a busy street in the centre of the town is a bell-shaped cavern carved out of the chalk, lit only by a hole in the middle of the roof, which is covered by a grating. The site is very close to the Midland Bank, but prospective raiders will find that the grating opens onto the pavement outside the bank, not the vaults inside . . .

Originally the hole was blocked by a millstone about two feet below pavement level. Workmen came across it accidentally in 1742, when they were trying to drive a post

Roche Rocks, scene of Jan Tregeagle's unpleasant experience with the 'hounds of hell'.

into the ground. Under the stone they found a narrow shaft, and an intrepid lad with a candle was lowered into it. He found a chamber, half-filled with rubble, and the walls covered with drawings. The rubble has long since been cleared, and a less precarious mode of entry has been created down a flight of steps, so the drawings can be seen to full advantage – and the experts have been arguing about them ever since.

The range of drawings is quite remarkable, from St Laurence with his gridiron and St Catharine with her spiked wheel, to Richard the Lionheart and Henry II. There are assorted horses, spirals and naked ladies in between. The range of theories about their origin is nearly as varied, from a hermit's cell to an oratory for the Knights Templar. Personally I would go for a connection with Lady Roisia, the Norman lady who is supposed to have given her name to Royse's Town, and might have retired into this cell after the death of her second husband. It must have been very boring down there, so she probably whiled away the time by doodling on the walls – partly for her own amusement, but partly, I like to think, in order to baffle the experts centuries later.

Hermits' cells have always been a fascinating subject for conjecture. A surprising number of medieval mystics liked to spend their days sitting in caverns thinking great thoughts – like, what sort of a drawing can we confuse them with next? Some of them lived in greater luxury than others. The hermitage at **Warkworth Castle** in Northumberland, for instance, is quite an elaborate affair. The living quarters are cut into the cliff overlooking the river, together with a tiny chapel with vaulted roof cut into the rock, and another lump of rock carved into an altar. It could only be reached by boat, so privacy was ensured, and in the fourteenth century it must have been a cosy hide-away for an upmarket hermit, who was no doubt an associate of the Percys in the castle just up the river.

The Hermit's Cell on **Roche Rocks** in Cornwall is the opposite extreme; one could hardly find a more exposed and inhospitable site. This too was created in the fourteenth century, not by carving into the rock-face but by cutting chunks out of it and using it to build on top of the great granite mass that comprises Roche Rocks. It all looks rather gloomy and depressing, and the stories attached to it are gloomy and depressing too.

The earliest one features a man struck down by leprosy, who moved into it to avoid spreading the disease among his family. His daughter, however, continued to bring him food and drink, and achieved sainthood as St Gundred. Rather more fanciful, and considerably more depressing, is the legend of Jan Tregeagle, an unscrupulous seventeenth-century magistrate who used his office to commit all manner of frauds and malpractices, and died a rich man. After his death, however, one of the men he had swindled was brought to court, and created an unusual precedent by calling the dead man as a witness for the defence.

Not even Perry Mason could have achieved this, but in the seventeenth century nobody thought twice about it when Tregeagle's ghost duly appeared in the witness box, and admitted it was all his fault. Taking this in their stride, the jury found the defendant not guilty, and added a plea for mitigation on behalf of the ghostly Tregeagle, for behaving so sportingly.

The local clergy debated how they could save his soul, and decided to give him a task that would last for ever, so that the Devil would never find work for his idle hands. They issued him with a cracked limpet-shell and told him to empty Dozmary Pool, a lake on Bodmin Moor which was reputed to be bottomless. To make sure he kept at it, they arranged for a pack of headless hounds to guard him.

After a while, though, Tregeagle's spirit got rather fed up with all this pointless baling, and decided to make a run for it. With the hounds in hot pursuit he climbed the Roche Rocks, reached the hermit's chapel and took a dive through a window, hoping to gain sanctuary within. Unlike most spirits his body was still pretty solid, and he only got his head inside the window. 'His body remained outside, exposed to the fury of the storm and the snarling fangs of the hounds of hell.'

This does not quite tally with the hounds being headless, unless the heads came along independently, but it was undoubtedly a very unpleasant situation for a spirit, with or without any fangs at the rear, and it is said the screams could be heard for miles around. A priest came to his rescue and extracted him from the window – but only to send him back to his endless task at Dozmary Pool. In *Timpson's England* I noted that, according to quite a different legend, Dozmary could have been the pool where Bedivere hurled King Arthur's sword

Excalibur; maybe one day Jan Tregeagle will find it, and all that baling will have been worthwhile. Meanwhile the Roche Rocks with their hermit's cell continue to glower down on the Cornish countryside, waiting for the next legend to come along.

Ancient rocks and boulders do seem to attract weird tales, particularly if they are in churchyards. The Devil, it seems, was in the habit of hurling stones at churches, but happily he always seemed to miss. In *Timpson's England* I mentioned the **Rudston** monolith on Humberside, the tallest standing stone in England, which he threw just wide of the church, and there are more of his 'arrows' – three standing stones almost in a line – on the moors near **Ripon** in North Yorkshire, which were aimed at an early Christian settlement at Aldborough and went even wider. He was not only a rotten shot, but clumsy to boot; the Agglestone, a seventeen-foot boulder near **Studland** in Dorset, was destined to be dropped on Salisbury Cathedral, but it slipped out of his grasp on the way.

However, legends about churchyard stones don't always involve the Devil. A massive split boulder by the church porch at **St Levan**, on the south Cornish coast, is supposed to mark the spot where Levan

A dog can negotiate the gap in the boulder, but happily it is too narrow for a laden pack-horse – otherwise the world might end! So says the legend of St Levan's Stone.

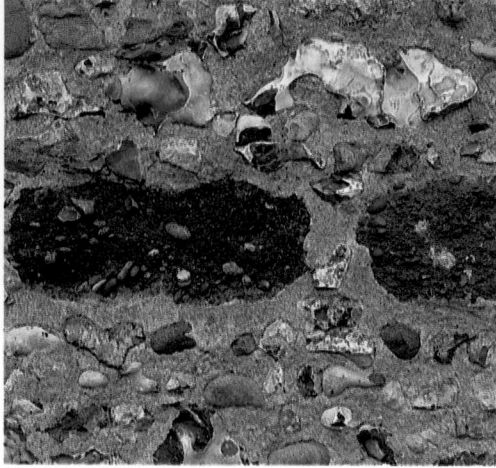

Puddingstone was used in building Great Munden Church (above) because of its solidity and strength, but it is also reputed to have the power to reproduce itself . . . On the other hand the Long Stone at Minchinhampton (far right) was supposed to cure rickets.

relaxed between fishing trips. It might be called the Domesday Rock rather than the St Levan Stone, because an odd little verse is attributed to him:

When with panniers astride,
A pack-horse one can ride
Through St Levan's Stone,
The world will be done.

Happily the gap is only between fourteen and twenty inches wide, far too small for a pack-horse, even without panniers. Happier still, the stone is granite, which lacks the curious ability possessed by another kind of rock, called puddingstone, to grow larger. Puddingstone is an ancient conglomerate of pebbles from prehistoric seas, crushed together in what has been described as a sixty-million-year-old mud pie – but incredibly hard.

As well as growing larger, reproducing itself, marking the 'ley lines' along which pagan monuments were sited, and being able to ward off evil spirits – just a few of puddingstone's legendary powers – it is also excellent building material. In Hertfordshire, which has large deposits of the rock, medieval masons used it extensively for building churches; apart from its solidity, its ability to ward off spirits made it particularly popular. **Great Munden** Church is one of those which has several pieces of puddingstone in its walls.

It also makes a very attractive ornament when split open and polished, and curio shops around **St Alban's** Abbey do quite a brisk trade in it. There is one enormous chunk of it – not for sale – quite near the museum, which is supposed to have lain in

the nearby river until some merry-makers from the local pub hauled it out for a bet.

Puddingstone has so many useful qualities for mystics, masons and memento-hunters that enthusiasts say, when supplies eventually get low, it will become as valuable as gold. There is supposed to be a vein of ten thousand tons of it under the Gade Valley, near Hemel Hempstead, which could be bad news for the Gade Valley, if it is ever invaded by puddingstone prospectors. Meanwhile geologists remain suitably sceptical about its legendary powers; they would like to have proof of this particular pudding without any eating . . .

For a wide assortment of legends, healing properties, traditional customs and cautionary tales, you can't beat a stone with a hole in it. In *Timpson's England* I mentioned the Bargain Stone at **Wolverhampton**, where a buyer and seller shook hands through the hole to seal their bargain, and the massive **Blidworth** Boulder, which is supposed to be a sacred relic of the Druids (if you are short of a legend, there's always the Druids). **Minchinhampton** in Gloucestershire offers something quite different, the Long

The Blowing Stone at Kingston Lisle (left) which King Alfred is said to have blown through to summon his men to battle. The Bradling Stone at Norton-in-Hales (far left) has felt a good blow or two as well – it was used as a punishment block for anyone who worked after noon on Shrove Tuesday.

Stone near the entrance to Gatcombe Lodge. It stands over seven feet high and is said to be the same length below ground. It could be the remains of a long barrow – there are many Stone Age relics in the area – but in medieval times it was supposed to have the power of curing rickets. The child had to be passed through the hole in it, ostensibly to absorb the stone's strength.

The Blowing Stone at **Kingston Lisle** in Oxfordshire has several holes in it, but if you pick the right one and blow through it, you can produce a note which is graphically described in *Tom Brown's Schooldays* as 'a gruesome sound between a moan and a roar, sounding over the valley, up the hillside and into the woods – a ghost-like, awful voice'. Others reckon it sounds like the bellowing of a calf, though it must be a very lusty calf; the eerie noise is said to have startled worshippers in Faringdon Church, six miles away. In coarser vein it has been likened to the sound of a monumental raspberry, 'a sound guaranteed to

exclude the blower from polite society for at least a month'.

Inevitably the Blowing Stone has attracted the legend-writers. According to some it was used by ancient Celtic tribes to call in the nomadic families on the Downs if danger threatened. Others say it was King Alfred's hunting-horn, which he blew to summon his men for battle. Cynics, however, regard it as nothing more than an oddity which was used by the landlord of the nearby village inn to entertain his customers. It is generally agreed, though, that it was brought down from White Horse Hill during the last century, probably by the village blacksmith; a nearby cottage was once a smithy. So I like to think that, if you can blow the right note on the Blowing Stone, the White Horse will get up off the hillside and come down to the smithy to be shod ...

The Bradling Stone on the green at **Norton-in-Hales** in Shropshire is hole-less, but it has known a good blow or two, because there was a tradition that any man found working after noon on Shrove Tuesday would be 'bradled', or bumped on the Bradling Stone. It was a rather drastic way of enforcing the observance of a religious holiday, but it was probably more effective than its present-day equivalent, the Sunday Trading Act.

A flat stone near **Ivelet Bridge** in Swaledale, North Yorkshire, had a much more macabre purpose. It was one of the coffin-stones on the route which funeral parties took from the head of the dale to the church at Grinton. The journey along the Corpse Way could take a couple of days, and the wickerwork coffins were placed on these stones while the bearers took a breather. Sceptics argue that this coffin-stone got its name because it is roughly the shape of a coffin, and the funeral parties never came near it, but there is no doubt that coffin-stones existed, and if one of them happened to be the ideal shape for the job, then so much the better.

Finally a very modern stone, though it looks as if it ought to be much older. It is a tall, flattened stone head, which sticks up from the ground like one of those prehistoric Standing Stones, surrounded by a circle of smaller stone blocks. The layout suggests some ancient Druid rite, and maybe in centuries to come the Druids will get the credit for this set of stones as well. They do indeed have a connection with the rays of the sun, but they were only put there two or three years ago to decorate a 'fragrance garden' behind the council offices at **Horsham** in West Sussex.

They form, in fact, an outsize sundial, the work of sculptor John Skelton. He carved the stone head to represent a sun-god, and the small blocks mark the hours. Each block bears a letter, making up a Latin tag which means: 'I count not the hours unless they be happy.' Alas, only a sun-god could be quite as blithe as that . . .

A circle of latter-day 'Standing Stones' with a sun god in the centre? Actually a modern sundial at Horsham.

Oaken hokum,
an old chestnut,
and a yew turn

Oaken hokum, an old chestnut, and a yew turn

The oak tree holds a special place in the affections of the English. The Druids venerated it, the Tudors built their ships with it, assorted monarchs have sheltered in it, held a parliament under it, heard news of their ascension while sitting beneath it, and even ordered the hanging of an abbot from it (that was the Abbot's oak near **Woburn Abbey**, and the monarch, inevitably, was Henry VIII).

There are many more variations in English oak-lore. An oak in **Windsor Great Park** was said to be haunted by Herne the Hunter and his pack of spectral dogs, and when it was blown down in 1863, Queen Victoria thought highly enough of it to have another one planted in its place. The Honour Oak at **Whitchurch** in Devon was used as a repository during the cholera epidemic of 1832; money was left in it by villagers in the affected area in exchange for food. Years earlier, the same oak was the boundary mark for French prisoners-of-war on parole from what is now Dartmoor Prison. They too were on their honour.

The Reformation Oak on **Mousehold Heath**, just outside Norwich, also served two purposes. It was the rallying point for the followers of Robert Kett during his Peasants' Revolt, and when the revolt was put down, it became the gallows for nine of its ringleaders. And then there is the oak in **Godington Park**, near Ashford in Kent, which achieved two mentions in the history books, some eight hundred years apart. It was originally called King Stephen's Oak, presumably because he rode past it or sat beneath it, but in 1939 it earned a much more dramatic title. On September 3rd, at the moment when Neville Chamberlain was announcing on the radio that Britain was at war with Germany, the tree crashed to the ground, and from then on it has been known as the Domesday Oak.

Years later there was some interesting speculation as to how it had happened. A correspondent in *Country Life* put forward an ingenious theory: 'Is it conceivable that the intense and widespread mental agitation could at that moment have set up some kind of telepathic disturbance, sufficient to cause disintegration of tenuously cohering material such as a very old tree?'

Even I find it difficult to believe that a very large old oak could be felled by telepathy, but there is no doubt that it collapsed on that day, and the mass of tangled wood still lies where it fell.

All through English history, then, the oak has played its part, and the longer it lives and the larger it gets, telepathy permitting, the more we cherish it. So it is a bold man who claims that any particular oak is the largest or the oldest in England, and I am relieved that when I wrote about the **Marton** Oak in Cheshire in *Timpson's England* I only suggested it might have been the biggest, before its trunk split into four, leaving enough room for a Wendy house inside. Other claims have poured in, some from people who say the Marton Oak is now the Marton Oaks, and hardly qualifies as one tree.

The sight of that Wendy house, however, may have inspired other claimants to judge their oaks by a different yardstick. They quote, not just the size of the girth, but how many people can get inside it, standing up, sitting down and even having a meal in it. Thus one of the major contestants, which indeed is named the Major Oak, not only boasts a circumference of thirty-eight feet, but also a holding capacity of seven people seated for breakfast, or fifteen standing up, albeit jammed together in the intimate style of rush-hour travellers on the London Underground.

It is situated near **Edwinstowe** in Sherwood Forest, the village where Robin Hood is supposed to have married Maid Marian, and you may marvel that with such connections it was not called the Robin Hood Oak, but actually he already had an oak named after him, a couple of miles away. It was known as Robin Hood's Larder, and it is said he hung his deer there until the Merry Men came home for supper. We don't know its precise deer capacity, because a hundred years ago some school-girls lit a fire inside it to boil their kettle, and burnt most of it down. The remnants were then blown down in a gale in 1966. All that remains of Robin Hood's Larder is a sliver of wood, suitably inscribed, which the Duke of Portland presented to the Mayor of Toronto, presumably a Robin Hood fan.

There is another oak with a thirty-eight foot girth at **Fredville Park**, near Nonington in Kent, but this is a 'maiden', which means, among other things, that its trunk is still intact, so its holding capacity is nil, except for the odd squirrel. The record in terms of both girth and capacity is supposed to be held by the **Bowthorpe** Oak, near **Witham-on-the-Hill** in Lincolnshire. When it was measured in 1973 it was just over thirty-nine feet round, but more dramatically it is claimed that thirty-nine people once stood in it, and on another occasion sixteen people sat down to tea.

I have to say that I have been inside the Bowthorpe Oak myself, and those thirty-nine people must have been either acrobats, or midgets, or they knew each other very well indeed. It would hardly surprise me,

therefore, if supporters of the **Cowthorpe** Oak near Wetherby in North Yorkshire will contest the title, because they claim it will hold up to seventy.

Personally I would bet on the tree which W.H. Davies referred to in 'The Old Oak Tree':

I sit beneath your leaves, old oak,
You mighty one of all the trees;
Within whose hollow trunk a man
Could stable his big horse with ease.

What a challenge for the good folk of Bowthorpe and Cowthorpe: have you tried sharing your tree with a horse?

After all this oaken hokum you might think that the oak is the only English tree to reach any size or achieve any historical significance. This is not so, of course, and in *Timpson's England* I quoted some yew trees, for instance, which are a lot bigger and older than any oak. There is also the **Tortworth** Chestnut in Avon, which was known as the Great Chestnut back in King Stephen's time, and King John is said to have admired it while out hunting. No one

All that is left of the Domesday Oak in Godington Park; it crashed to the ground at the moment when Neville Chamberlain announced that Britain was at war with Germany.

The Rebels' Tree at Clifton was used as a gallows for captured Highlanders after the last battle on English soil. Some of the gravestones from the battle still survive in the churchyard.

scene of the last battle fought on English soil. The Young Pretender's forces clashed with the English here as they were retreating to Scotland. The dead were buried in Clifton churchyard, but some of the captured Highlanders were hanged on the Rebels' Tree, and it is still a place of pilgrimage for the Scots. The tree stands in a farmyard, and I gather that one Hogmanay dawn, the farmer was disconcerted at milking time to hear the sound of bagpipes in the yard; it was a piper playing a lament.

If the English run short of single trees with tales to tell, they are inclined to plant combinations of them to create new ones. Thus, in Warwickshire the **Packwood House** yews were planted to represent the Sermon on the Mount. The timbered house on the road from Stratford to Birmingham dates back to the sixteenth century, but the Sermon was started a little later, and was not completed for a couple of centuries. John Featherstone inherited the house in 1634 and began to create the Sermon on a mound in the garden. He planted a single yew on the summit to represent Christ, then four more to represent evangelists, and another twelve for the apostles.

is sure of its age or its size, because its roots and branches cover such a wide area, but a plaque was put on it in 1800 which said that, even then, it was six hundred years old. It is actually of foreign extraction, a Spanish chestnut, but it has claimed a place in English history.

Of more sinister significance is the Rebels' Tree at **Clifton** in Cumbria, the

That was as far as he got before he died in 1670, and there seems to have been a hiatus for a couple of centuries, perhaps to allow this group to grow to a more imposing size before adding the other ingredient, the Multitude. During the 1850s the house was rented for a few years by William Whitehouse, and it was during this period that the Multitude were planted round the Mount. The entire ensemble is kept neatly clipped, but the Multitude grows steadily around the King of the Yews.

Another religious theme was taken up in in the 1930s by Edmund Kell Blyth. Mention **Whipsnade** in Bedfordshire and you probably think of animals, but Mr Blyth thought of trees. On a hillside on the Downs he planted his Tree Cathedral, as a living memorial to the friends he lost during the First World War. Around a natural dewpond he planted the nave, transepts and chancel, a Lady Chapel, the cloisters, and four Chapels of the Seasons. The trees were not limited to yews; all kinds of native and foreign varieties have been used. Oaks form an archway at the entrance, limes line the aisle, and the chapels have doorways of cherry trees and

Two groups of trees with a religious theme: the Packwood House yews (above), planted to represent the Sermon on the Mount, and part of the Tree Cathedral at Whipsnade (left), created by Edmund Kell Blyth in memory of friends who died in the First World War.

are made up of cedar, rowan, elm and spruce, with flowering shrubs inside.

After Edmund Kell Blyth's death his son Tom continued the planting, and more trees were donated. Two thousand pines were sent from Berlin, where his father served with the Government of Occupation. The Men of the Trees, a conservation group, presented a red oak, and Tom Blyth himself is now remembered by a blue Atlantic pine in one of the transepts.

These days the Tree Cathedral is owned by the National Trust, and managed by a group of trustees; local volunteers keep it in good shape. It is a cathedral which remains unconsecrated – the churches believe, understandably, that you cannot consecrate Nature – but non-denominational services are held in it, and a grassed area at the end of the aisle has been raised to act as a platform for outdoor plays and concerts. Mainly, however, it continues to fulfil the vision of Edmund Kell Blyth – as a place of rest and contemplation, a safe arbour in fact, to be enjoyed, not under a roof as in other cathedrals, but out there under the sky, among the trees.

Finally, a wood which became a memorial, complete with stone monument in one corner. After the First World War an area of woodland at **Petts Wood** in Kent was put on the market, and the residents of nearby Chislehurst feared that it would be bought by a developer and turned into a housing estate. Petts Wood's best-known resident, apart from the Petts who gave it their name, was William Willett, who had the distinction – a dubious one in some people's view – of leading the campaign for British Summer Time. As one historian wrote, 'he aroused much scorn, and even ridicule', and the idea is not universally popular even today, but we duly got BST, though it was only introduced after the death of Mr Willett in 1915.

When the wood came on the market, the locals thought of an ingenious way of saving it from development and immortalising Mr Willett's memory in one go. It was, after all, while riding in the wood that he was supposed to have thought of British Summer Time in the first place, so there was a good excuse to link the two. A fund was opened which appealed both to William Willett's admirers and to the anti-development campaigners, and enough money was raised to buy the wood and erect a memorial. It took the form of a sundial – set, of course, to British Summer Time.

The sundial was unveiled on 21 May 1927, eleven years to the day after daylight saving was adopted. That corner of Petts Wood became Willett Wood, and these days the National Trust continues to preserve it from the property developers. Under the circumstances, few people mention that William Willett, whose memory it hallows, was actually a property developer himself . . .

The woodland memorial at Petts Wood to William Willett, who led the campaign for 'daylight saving' eighty-odd years ago. The sundial, as you might expect, is set to British Summer Time.

HORAS NON NUMERO NISI ÆSTIVAS

Which way to the minotaur – or the virgins?

Which way to the minotaur – or the virgins?

The handy thing about mazes, from my point of view, is that nobody is quite certain where or when they started, what they were for, or even what names to give them, and some of the theories put forward by the experts are so far-fetched that I am encouraged to have a go myself. For instance, it seems quite likely to me that the writer of 'Amazing Grace' was inspired by the legend of the monstrous Minotaur, symbol of evil, being subdued and imprisoned inside a labyrinth; that labyrinth was of course 'A-maze-in Greece' . . .

More seriously, mazes have been regarded as a symbol of death, as a map of the Underworld, as a path of penance, and more cheerfully, as a venue for a Springtime fertility rite. In Scandinavia, where they are very advanced in such things, mazes were called *Jungfraudanser*, or Virgin Dances; the virgins duly danced in the centre of the maze, and young men had to find the right route to them. The French had a quite different use for mazes, and a different name. A number of cathedrals, such as Chartres, have pavement mazes along which pilgrims had to crawl on their knees as the symbolic route to salvation, and the maze was called *Chemin de Jérusalem*.

Some of the earliest mazes were just in the form of rock carvings, but again there are different theories about how old they

Early mazes in unusual places: a Bronze Age carving (or was it a hoax?) in Rocky Valley (below) and a Norman font in Lewannick Church (above right).

are and why they were put there. For instance, there is one such carving in **Rocky Valley**, near Tintagel in Cornwall. Some experts believe it dates back to the Bronze Age; other experts say it was carved by a local miller, just to confuse the first experts. There are similar carvings in Italy believed to date back to the fifth century BC, others in Spain which could be 900 BC, and one at the entrance to a tomb in Sardinia which might go back a thousand years before that, so really you can take your pick.

The one by the Sardinian tomb obviously had some pagan link with death, and Christianity took over the same theme and adapted it to Christian beliefs. As a result, the maze pops up in a number of our medieval English churches, sometimes in the most unlikely corners. One of the oldest is in **St Mary Redcliffe** Church in Bristol, but you will have quite a job to spot it, because it is tucked away in the roof on a tiny boss. It is much easier to locate the

maze in **Lewannick** Church in Cornwall, where it is incorporated in the Norman font, and in **Bourn** Church in Cambridgeshire, where it is in the floor. There is one in **Ely** Cathedral too, but that is a bit misleading (as I suppose a good maze should be) because it is not medieval, it was only put there in 1870.

The best church for maze-spotters is at **Alkborough** on Humberside, where there is one in the floor of the porch, another in the stained glass of the east window, and a third not far away in the cemetery, set into a brass plate on a tombstone. It marks the grave of the squire, J. Goulton-Constable, a

Alkborough – a mazehunter's paradise! There is a maze in the floor of the porch (above), a maze in a stained-glass window (left) . . .

great labyrinth-lover. Until his death in 1922 he was responsible for maintaining Alkborough's fourth and most prominent maze, known as Julian's Bower.

This is where we get into turf mazes, and the remarkable assortment of names attached to them. Sometimes they are called the City of Troy, or more endearingly, Troy Town – shades of Larry the Lamb and Mr Growser. Sometimes they have names linked with local customs, like Shepherds' Race (because they did) and at **Sneinton** in Nottinghamshire Robin Hood's Race (because every tourist attraction in that area has to be connected with Robin Hood). But Julian's Bower at Alkborough is perhaps the most delightful name, with a delightful story to go with it. Or rather, three.

According to one set of experts – and they are divided on this, as on many other maze matters – it originates from the Julius who was the son of Aeneas, a Trojan prince who escaped the sack of Troy and settled with his family and followers near Rome. They took with them the maze games that were popular in Troy – hence all those Troy Towns – and these eventually spread throughout the rest of Europe, even as far as Alkborough. But I prefer the medieval legend of St Julian the Hospitator, partly because he was the patron saint of innkeepers, and obviously shares my tastes.

. . . a maze on the squire's gravestone . . .

However, Julian accidentally killed his parents, and in atonement he created a hospice by a ford for travellers, which became known as Julian's Bower, on the same principle as Fred's Caff. One of the travellers was a leper, and Julian gave him his own bed to sleep in – whereupon the leper turned into an angel, forgave Julian his sins, and they all lived happily in Julian's Bower ever after.

So what is the connection with mazes? I am not too sure, but it is a fact that some mazes are near fords, and the one at Alkborough, for instance, is close to both the Trent and the Ouse. Maybe it is all to do with travelling life's tortuous path – or something. But it's a nice story, and Julian's Bower at Alkborough is a nice maze. If you don't go much for Julian and his Bower, there is an alternative story. It is said that one of the knights who killed Thomas à Becket was told to go on a pilgrimage to Jerusalem to atone for his crime, but he took the easy way out by adopting the French *Chemin de Jérusalem* approach and made this maze to crawl round instead.

Whatever religious significance the Alkborough maze may have had to start with – and there was a small monastery nearby in medieval times, which might account for its existence – it no longer applied by 1700, when a contemporary chronicler wrote that it was 'nothing but a great labyrinth cut upon the ground with a hill cast up round about for the spectators to sitt round about on to behold the sport'. It was referred to by this time as Gillian's Bower, which suggests that its use had developed along Scandinavian lines. Certainly games were played in it on the eve of May Day, the traditional season for fertility rites, but according to another writer the games must have been highly

. . . and where they all started, the turf maze at Alkborough, known as Julian's Bower.

respectable, even spiritual, because they were played 'under an indefinite persuasion of something unseen and unknown co-operating with them'. It's an ingenious argument, but would it stand up in court?

J. Goulton-Constable must have believed in the religious aspect of those frolics because he not only looked after the maze, he had a copy of it cut into the floor of the church porch in 1887. He would be glad to know that, exactly a hundred years later, Julian's Bower was re-cut, and is still in excellent shape – the original medieval design with eleven rings, measuring about forty-four feet across.

That is a fair size as turf mazes go, but nowhere near the biggest. Until quite recently the title was held by the Town Maze at **Saffron Walden** in Essex, but a larger copy of it has now been created at **Milton Keynes** in Buckinghamshire, complete with an oak tree in the middle. It is claimed to be, not merely the largest in England, but in the world.

The idea of putting something prominent in the heart of a maze may have been borrowed from **Hilton** in Cambridgeshire, where the maze on the village green has a monument to William Sparrow, the man

William Sparrow's maze and monument at Hilton. Both maze and monument have altered over the years – that stone ball on the pillar was once put on a farm gatepost.

who was supposed to have created it in the seventeenth century. Again I have to say 'supposed to', because it is also argued that he was merely re-cutting an earlier maze which had been destroyed by Cromwell's men, along with maypoles and other 'relics of vile heathenism'. In support of that theory there was the discovery in 1945,

Brandsby maze has the dual distinction of being the smallest surviving turf maze in England and also the most northerly. Like most of the others, no one is quite sure of its history.

behind some wall panels in William Sparrow's farmhouse, of two paintings of a woman dressed as a man. She was Mary Frith, a remarkable lady who lived a double life in the style of Margaret Lockwood's 'Wicked Lady', riding forth in men's clothes to hold up travellers on the highway. But she only held up supporters of Cromwell, including on one occasion General Fairfax, one of his top aides. Manifestly the Sparrow family sympathised with her activities, and William might well have cut the maze to celebrate the restoration of King Charles – both happened in 1660.

Whether he did or not, the maze has been re-cut so often since – seven times at the last count – that nobody is quite sure what his looked like. At various times it has been paved with pebbles, it has been reduced from eleven rings to nine – Sparrow's monument may cover the two nearest the centre – and it has had banking on the turns removed. The banking suggests it was used for races, but local legend has it that young men walked the maze to see if they would be lucky in marriage. They had to complete it without stopping, tripping or taking the wrong turning. If they failed, they had the choice of a miserable marriage or being 'possessed by the Devil' – whichever seemed less unpleasant.

Sparrow's monument started off as a square pillar with a stone ball on top, and a sundial on top of that, but at one stage the ball was removed and put on a farm gatepost. When it was replaced the sundial was at the wrong angle, and it is said the wording on the pillar has been altered too, but it says in Latin: 'Thus passed the world's glory. William Sparrow, Gentleman, born 1641, died at the age of 88, formed these circuits in 1660' – and that's good enough for me.

The Hilton maze is fifty-five feet across, a little smaller than the Mizmaze – there's another splendid name – in the grounds of **Breamore House** in Hampshire. One at **Wing** in Leicestershire is a mere forty feet, but the smallest surviving maze in England, and also the most northerly, is in Yorkshire, near the village of **Brandsby**. This is a City of Troy maze, for which the locals have yet another explanation. The walls of Troy were apparently riddled with passages leading nowhere in particular, so if an enemy got inside he never found his way

out again. As Brandsby's City of Troy is only twenty-seven feet by twenty-four, nobody gets lost in it today. There is the usual ambivalence about its history. Some say it existed for centuries closer to the road, but so many horses and carts went across it that in 1900 it was re-cut further away, still retaining its seven-ring design. Others argue that it was originally created about that time by a local farmer, Thomas Dobson of Dalby Hall, who copied the design from a newspaper. Either way, its future is assured; the County Council adopted it in 1934.

The enthusiasm for mazes is by no means dead. Apart from all the hedge mazes we enjoy exploring in places like Hampton Court and Longleat, the maze motif still crops up in memorials. In *Timpson's England* I mentioned the Wells Memorial Chapel at **Compton** in Surrey, an early

Two more recent maze motifs: in the Wells Memorial Chapel at Compton, on the bodies of the angels, and on the next page . . .

example of slightly eccentric do-it-yourself architecture, but I omitted to draw attention to the little classical mazes which rest snugly on the stomachs of the angels on the interior corbels. Mrs Mary Watts, who built the chapel in memory of her husband, also put a maze on the altar, supported by three more angels, with the inscription, 'He shall dwell with them'. I hope he enjoyed mazes too.

Finally, in **Hadstock** churchyard in Essex, there is the grave of the latter-day expert on all matters labyrinthine, Michael Ayrton. He died in 1975, and on his tombstone is a bronze plaque showing the maze he completed in New York State in 1969, based on the original labyrinth occupied by the Minotaur. This remarkable achievement – I nearly wrote 'amazing' – took him two years, during which he used two hundred thousand bricks to build walls ten feet high, enough to contain the mightiest of Minotaurs. The maze leads to two central chambers, and in them are bronzes made by Ayrton of the characters which inspired him. One portrays Daedalus, who designed the first labyrinth with his high-flying son Icarus, and the other is the Minotaur itself.

Michael Ayrton not only created brick mazes and bronze statues, and wrote books about them; he was also a philosopher. In *The Maze Maker* he wrote: 'Each man's life is a labyrinth at the centre of which lies his death, and even after his death it may be that he passes through a final maze before it is all ended for him.'

It's a sobering thought to associate with mazes. I think I prefer the Scandinavian approach . . .

. . . on the tombstone of master maze-maker Michael Ayrton at Hadstock. He spent two years in New York State re-creating the original Minotaur's labyrinth with its two central chambers, and this is the same design.

The age of
shovelry is not
dead

The age of shovelry is not dead

Not exactly in the same class as the ancient White Horse of Uffington, but not a bad effort for a bunch of schoolboys. They carved out this emaciated steed on a hill above Preshute in 1804.

Nobody is quite sure how it all started, this curiously English practice of cutting designs into hillsides – mostly horses, but also the odd giant and, in more recent times, almost anything from a crown to a kiwi. It may have been some Neolithic artist, who got bored with scratching pictures in caves and thought he would go for a larger canvas, or perhaps a Saxon Stubbs with a passion for horses, but too poor to afford a paintbox and easel. In the case of the Cerne Giant in Dorset, with its thirty-foot appendage, it could have been a rich Roman with a crude sense of humour, who wanted to shock the neighbours.

The difficulty of tracing the history of this early art-form is matched only by the difficulty of finding a name for it. One chap who ought to know, Morris Marples, who wrote the definitive book on the subject, is not really a great help. You cannot call it turf-cutting, he says, because that is what the peat-cutters do, for a totally different reason. They are not 'chalk figures' because not all of them are chalk – there is a well-known Red Horse, for instance, and another one marked out by flints. 'Hillside figures' was a term used by Mr Marples' father, who actually created one himself in 1937, the White Horse at **Pewsey** in Wiltshire, but Morris thinks that is still a bit too general.

He quotes two quite appalling words which were devised to pinpoint the art of carving figures on hills – 'bolotomy', which sounds like a rather unpleasant surgical operation and 'caespiticidy', pronounced 'sespit-icidy', which would be more appropriate to the art of digging latrines.

Morris actually has a go at inventing a word for it himself, albeit half-jokingly. He suggests 'leucippotomy', for the cutting of horses, and 'gigantotomy' for giants. I fear they are a bit of a mouthful too, even more so with your tongue in your cheek. My own offering is more basic. These hill figures involve artistry with a shovel, so I settle for 'shovelry'.

In *Timpson's England* I mentioned only one example, the Long Man of **Wilmington** on the South Downs, because there seemed too many White Horses to choose from, and the Long Man did hold the distinction of being the largest representation of a human figure in the world. It was only after consulting Morris Marples and other shovelry buffs that I found some White Horses had unexpected tales to tell, and the twentieth century has also produced some curious examples of this ancient art. The age of shovelry, in fact, is not yet dead . . .

The Horses for a start. There have been seventeen in England altogether, of which all but four are in the south of England, and nine of them in Wiltshire, although two or three have been obliterated. The Wiltshire Horses are young foals compared with the sire of them all, the White Horse of **Uffington**, said to have been carved by King Alfred, though it may date back even earlier. It lies, or rather gallops, in the Vale of the White Horse, an area of the Berkshire Downs which is now, confusingly in Oxfordshire. The history of this particular Horse is obscure, but nearly all those in Wiltshire are just a couple of centuries old or less, and folk like Morris Marples have uncovered most of their secrets.

I was intrigued to discover, for example, that the Horse on **Granham Hill**, just above the village of Preshute, was a very elaborate schoolboy jape, carried out in 1804 by the pupils of a Marlborough school. This was not the college, which didn't exist then, but a humbler establishment run by a Mr Greasley, who apparently approved of instant ancient monuments, and indeed made sure the Horse was scoured and smartened up by the boys each year, on what could have been called Grooming Day. We even know the name of the boy who designed it, a William Canning of Ogbourne St George; he marked out the pattern on the hillside with pegs, and his fellow pupils did the shovelry.

Morris Marples is rather rude about young William's creation. 'It has a somewhat grotesque and angular appearance,' he wrote. 'The head, with its short thick muzzle, pricked ears, and large round eye, scarcely resembles that of a horse at all.' But he adds, more generously: 'It must be admitted it has a particularly perky charm of its own.'

Mr Greasley died in about 1830 and his school died with him, but the Horse lived on, though no longer quite so perky. It was, in fact, getting distinctly tatty when a Captain Read, who had been one of the boys who worked on it, arranged to have it restored. That was in 1873 and, as Morris Marples points out, he must have been in his eighties by then. He obviously cherished a nostalgic affection for this youthful escapade, and he would be gratified to know that it has earned a place in the official reference books.

Appropriately, in view of its youthful creators, when the White Horse of Preshute (or Marlborough, depending on your allegiance) was smartened up again to mark King George V's silver jubilee in 1935, it was the Boy Scouts who did the work. Their efforts only lasted until the war, when the Marlborough (or Preshute) Horse, like all its fellows, was camouflaged to confuse enemy airmen – though with so many White Horses in that part of Wiltshire, leaving them on show might have confused the enemy even more. Perhaps that is what Mr Greasley's lads had in mind in the first place.

If Morris Marples was rather scathing about this Horse, he was even ruder about the one at **Woolbury** in Hampshire: 'a very crude little animal, angular and shapeless,

The Osmington Horse, the only one of its kind with a rider. He is supposed to be George III, a regular visitor to nearby Weymouth, but Thomas Hardy had a different theory.

having only two stumpy legs and defective in detail . . . It is without eye, or nostril, or even ears, and has a strange tapering tail projecting behind.'

Nevertheless the Woolbury Horse has three distinctions. At twenty-seven feet long it is the smallest hill-figure horse in the country, it was created by sticking flints in the ground instead of removing the turf, and it has a romantic story attached to it which I am afraid Mr Marples decries, but it does come from more than one source and is as reliable as many other country tales.

Tradition has it that a traveller was attacked and killed on the road between Stockbridge and Winchester, at what is known as Robbers' Roost. A cross of flints marks the spot there where he died, but his horse was only wounded, and staggered away towards Woolbury before it too expired. The White Horse of Woolbury, they say, dates from that time, and it would be nice to think that on each anniversary of that fateful attack it rises from the turf and returns to the cross at the roadside to seek its master.

Of all the horses that shovelry has produced, only one that I know of has a rider, the **Osmington** Horse in Dorset, and a very dashing fellow he is, with a tall cocked hat, a long pointed nose and chin, a slim body, and carrying a neat little whip. Horse and rider between them are 354 feet

high and 279 feet across, covering nearly an acre of ground, and according to one admirer, 'the carving exudes a kind of cumbersome stateliness'.

So it should, because the figure is said to represent George III, a stately chap if ever there was one. On his regular visits to nearby Weymouth he used to go swimming accompanied by a bathing-machine full of violinists playing 'God Save the King'. He no doubt regarded this as a demonstration of their devotion, but it may have been their lack of faith in his prowess as a swimmer. Anyway the locals were delighted to have his custom, and it is generally thought they commissioned the Osmington Horse (and Rider) in his honour. The actual work is supposed to have been carried out by militiamen from a nearby camp, in a display of soldierly shovelry.

Thomas Hardy, however, had a different theory. In *The Trumpet Major* he suggests the Horse commemorates the victory at Trafalgar, and he described how the trumpet major and his girl-friend, while out for a stroll, saw figures at work on a distant hillside. 'When they reached the hill they found forty navvies at work removing the dark sod, so as to lay bare the chalk beneath. The equestrian figure that their shovels were forming was scarcely intelligible to John and Anne now they were close, and after pacing from the horse's head down his breast to his hoof, back by way of the king's bridle-arm, past the bridge of his nose, and into his cocked hat, Anne said she had had enough of it.'

And so, I am sure, have you. No more horses, then, royal or otherwise, and on to another form of regal shovelry. On the North Downs near **Wye** in Kent is a massive crown, 165 feet wide, and cunningly sited above a chalk pit, so it appears from a distance to be resting on a white cushion. Students from a nearby agricultural college carved it in 1902 to mark the coronation of Edward VII. It involved moving four thousand barrow-loads of soil, presumably a useful exercise for agricultural students, and I hope some of them were still around many years later when the crown was floodlit for the coronation of George VI.

It is still the only shovelry crown in England, but regimental badges were rather more popular. There are a dozen of them

The Fovant Badges, left behind by the British and Commonwealth troops who were stationed in the area during the Second World War.

The Giant Kiwi of Bulford, designed by a New Zealander who had never actually seen a kiwi. Who would have guessed?

on the Downs near **Fovant**, **Sutton Mandeville** and **Compton Chamberlayne**, where thousands of British and Commonwealth troops were stationed during the First World War. They range from the elaborate crest of the London Rifle Brigade to the simple inverted triangle of the YMCA. The latest one was added in 1949, when the Fovant Home Guard Old Comrades Association carved the crest of their own Wiltshire Regiment.

The badges are about 150 feet across, and they include a map of Australia left behind by the Australian Commonwealth Military Forces. For once, however, the Australians have been dwarfed by the New Zealanders, because at **Bulford**, about fifteen miles to the north, New Zealand troops have left behind a truly monstrous kiwi, 420 feet long and covering about one-and-a-half acres. It has a 150-foot beak, and the initials NZ beside it are 65 feet high.

This bulky bird was carved in 1918, when the war had ended and the men were being kept occupied until they could be shipped home. The rather curious shape of the bird, however, was not the result of their eagerness to get it finished and get home, but a design problem on the part of the man detailed to map it out, a Sergeant Major Percy Blenkarne of the New Zealand Education Corps. In spite of being a native New Zealander, the hapless Blenkarne had never seen a kiwi; it was not an experience commonly enjoyed in the Education Corps. He freely admitted he had no idea what a kiwi looked like, and was forthwith told to find out.

This test of initiative led him, not to the nearest library as one might expect, but all the way to the British Natural History Museum. I suspect he rather fancied a free day out in London. He did not actually reach the museum until late evening, and understandably had some difficulty in convincing the caretaker that he was making a genuine enquiry – one can imagine how the caretaker felt, being woken up late at night by a New Zealand soldier looking for a kiwi. Blenkarne talked his way in, found a book with a kiwi in it,

Not just another chalk carving, but a detachable spire. The ingenious Edward Horn had the White Mark cut into the hillside above Watlington so that he could see a 'spire' on the parish church. Well, nearly!

and made a rough copy. Based on that, he pegged out the shape of the bird which still stares down at us from its roost on the Wiltshire hillside.

I am glad to report that Percy Blenkarne got safely home to Auckland and became a successful merchant, while the ornithological oddity he left behind was adopted and maintained by the Kiwi Boot Polish Company, ostensibly as a tribute to the New Zealand forces, but more likely because it provided them with the biggest advertising hoarding in the country. However, in 1967 the company decided to pull out, and since then it has been looked after, with varying degrees of enthusiasm, by local army units.

They have quite a problem. It needs about twenty tons of chalk applied twice a year to keep it spruce, and a major restoration in 1981 occupied 160 officers and men for three days. Perhaps one way to ensure its future preservation is to make its bill spoon-shaped, and turn it into that breed of duck known as a shoveler – a fitting emblem for all followers of the ancient art of shovelry . . .

It would not be the first time that the art has attracted the less than serious exponent. Edward Horn, for example, created an entertaining little leg-pull when he had the White Mark cut near **Watlington** in Oxfordshire. The Victoria County History records it merely as 'an eighteenth-century Folly, 270 feet long and 36 feet wide, and originally intended to represent an obelisk,' but local legend has it that Mr Horn had something rather more subtle in mind than just an obelisk.

He felt that Watlington Church would look better with a spire, and he devised an ingenious way of providing one, without wasting time on building regulations or planning permission. He had the White Mark cut on the hillside beyond the church, in such a position that if he stood at a certain point on the road from Oxford to Watlington, it looked for all the world like a white spire perched on the church tower. Anyone who disliked this effect only had to travel a little further along the road and the White Mark was just a white mark again. I am not sure if the church authorities approved, but to my mind Mr Horn qualifies for the Order of Shovelry, *Coup d'Oeil* Class.

Hadrian's service
station – and a
splash for
Beau Nash

THIS PUMP WAS
ERECTED BY ORDER OF
BEAU NASH OF BATH IN 1754

Hadrian's service station – and a splash for Beau Nash

The Holy Well at Holystone, where St Paulinus is reputed to have baptised three thousand people in a single day in AD 627. But who was counting?

There is nothing like a hole in the ground with water in it for attracting strange tales and legends, and if it is in a churchyard, so much the better. Sometimes it is the water which has mysterious healing qualities. Sometimes it is connected with some holy person who has drunk from it, or lived beside it, or carried out baptisms in it. Sometimes it dates back to the Romans, part of the sophisticated water supply systems which they left behind when they went back home. Sometimes its name has been altered and adjusted over the years until nobody is quite sure what its significance originally was. And sometimes, very rarely, you will get a combination of all these factors, to make it a very complicated waterhole indeed.

One notable example is the well at **Holystone** in Northumberland, which, like so many ancient 'wells', is not actually a well at all; it is more like a miniature swimming-pool, fed by a spring. But that is just the start of the confusion over its name. It is not called Holystone Well, though it does have a 'holy' stone beside it, a modest piece of rock about two foot by three, with no obvious holy connections. Holy Well is the workaday name, but it is also called St Ninian's Well, Lady or Lady's Well, and even Mungo's Well, because it is sometimes confused with another, slightly less holy well, not far away.

Let me deal with that one first, Mungo's Well. St Mungo had a lot of churches and wells and other holy places in Northumberland, but there is no particular reason why this one should be named after him. Some experts point out that 'Mungo's Well' could be a corruption of Muggers' Well, which conjures up dramatic pictures of roving footpads having a quick dip before waylaying the next innocent traveller. In medieval times, however, muggers were just itinerant pedlars who sold mugs, and a group of them may have made camp beside this well; there is another one at **Simonburn** which has the same name, for the same reason.

The Holystone Muggers' Well is just beside an old track which was much used by these early travelling salesmen, on a hillside above the village, and it would have been a convenient spot to pause for a wash-and-brush-up before going down to meet their clients. The water was excellent quality for drinking too, so good in fact that in more recent times it was piped down to a conduit on the village green for general consumption.

The history of the other well goes back much further. The most popular story is that St Paulinus baptised three thousand people in it in AD 627, in the space of a single day. I don't know who was counting, but if the figure is anywhere near right, Paulinus must have been quite a worker, and the whole operation was as well organised as a Billy Graham rally. Alas, it may have been just another mix-up over the name; early chroniclers may have confused the Latin 'Sancta Petra', Holy Stone, with 'Sancta Petri', St Peter, because the Venerable Bede, that most reliable of historians, records that on Easter Day, AD 627, Paulinus carried out a baptism at St Peter's Church in York. The only recipient he names is King Edwin; there is no mention of the other two thousand, nine hundred and ninety-nine.

Nevertheless, when the walls of the Well were rebuilt in 1780, a statue of Paulinus was brought from Alnwick and put on a pedestal in the pool, thus perpetuating the legend. A hundred years later some doubts may have crept in, because Paulinus was moved to a less conspicuous position and replaced by a non-committal cross.

The link with St Ninian is even more tenuous. It is possible he passed this way and consecrated the Well; it is equally possible he did not. Then again, Lady or Lady's Well could have been a dedication to Our Lady, or derived from the ladies of Holystone nunnery, or be totally unconnected with either. One might even suggest that, with two wells close to the village, one was set aside for ladies and the other for gents. Your guess, and the guesses of the historians, are as good as mine.

The statue of St Paulinus at the Holy Well, scene of his great baptism marathon – but he may have been in York at the time.

However, there seems no doubt about a Roman connection. The Roman road from Redesdale to the Devil's Causeway passes close by, and it would have been a welcome watering-hole for the Roman patrols as they marched around this inhospitable countryside, north of Hadrian's Wall. It was probably they who built the first wall around the spring to create a refreshing pool.

Andrew Stobart would have no problem in picturing Roman squaddies enjoying their equivalent of a mug of tea and a fag beside the well, because he has an eye for such things. A Fellow of the Royal Society of Arts, he believes that the Romans had a rather more elaborate roadside watering-place, a chariot-way station, in fact, near his former home at **Great Ouseburn** in Yorkshire. The site is just outside the village, some fifteen Roman miles north of York on Dere Street. It is also the site, he believes, of one of the oldest-established pubs in England, with origins going back to the construction of Dere Street, around AD 71. Here is his reasoning:

'Little Ouseburn has Roman stone in its church and, reportedly, the foundations of a Roman villa under the house beside it. Where the road dips past the turning to the village, there stands the Green Tree, which the landlord tells me has deeds going back many centuries. The evergreen garland was the sign for a wine-shop, and from the green garland to the Green Tree is not very far. Fifteen miles is about right for a stop for breakfast on the way north, and for a clean-up and getting into parade armour on the way south after a successful foray, before entering the Eboracum fortress.

'The present building is not old, but I firmly believe it is one of the oldest

watering-holes in the country.' And on the strength of that, he has tried to persuade the landlord to erect a sign, 'Hadrian drank here' . . .

The Romans did not confine their water-holes to the North Country. They may well have had one at **Bisley**, a village perched high on a hillside in the South Cotswolds, where numerous Roman remains have been found. One of the main features of Bisley is Seven Wells, a semi-circle of springs emptying into a central pool, as they have done for centuries. The pool was restored in memory of Thomas Keble, a long-serving Victorian vicar, and the water now gushes out of elaborate little gabled recesses in the stone wall.

At one time the village was known as Beggarly Bisley, because the local clothing trade died out and the weavers were left destitute. As one historian wrote: 'The decline of Bisley from a populous village to a bleak, poverty-stricken hamlet must have made mockery of those sparkling waters.' Perhaps it was to cheer them all up that Mr Keble introduced the custom of well-dressing on Ascension Day, and I think the

Bisley's Seven Wells, centuries old but restored in memory of a Victorian vicar who made sure they were well-dressed on Ascension Day.

Water is still drunk from Glastonbury's Chalice Well – in glasses.

Romans would have appreciated the irony of this, because it was originally a pagan rite, an offering to the water gods, and no doubt they came across it when they arrived in Britain. If they returned to Bisley on Ascension Day they might think the clock had been turned back twenty centuries – and they would have been disconcerted to find that this pagan offering was introduced by a Christian parson.

They may also have been familiar with another water-hole at **Duntisbourne Abbots**, some ten miles away over the hills. Certainly the semi-circular stone trough in the centre of the village has a Romanesque look about it, with none of Bisley's Victorian trimmings. The water overflows into a brook which runs between raised pavements to form a water lane, the only one left in the Cotswolds. Waggoners drove through it to wash their horses' hooves and clean the wheels after travelling along the muddy country roads – and it would be nice to think the Romans drove their chariots through it as well.

They would certainly have known about the Chalice Well at **Glastonbury** in Somerset, though hardly as a watering-hole

Water from the Duntisbourne Abbots' well (left) formed a 'water lane' in which waggoners washed their wheels and their horses' hooves. The telephone box came later.

Knaresborough's 'petrified forest'. Water from the Dropping Well can in effect turn objects into stone.

or a chariot-wash. It was a very holy place, and anyway there is so much iron content in the water that it can be an off-putting rust-red, giving the well its other name of Blood Spring. The colour of the water may have encouraged the legend that Joseph of Arimathea hid the Holy Grail in the well, the chalice which Jesus used at the Last Supper. It is the blood of Jesus, says the legend, which makes the water red, and in spite of all the geological evidence, the legend lives on, along with the story of the Glastonbury thorn tree which sprang from Joseph's staff. The well is in a garden at the foot of Glastonbury Tor, and in spite of its high iron content it is eminently drinkable.

However, I would not recommend the water from the Dropping Well at **Knaresborough** in North Yorkshire. Knaresborough has other unusual features which I mentioned in *Timpson's England* – the sixteenth-century cave dwelling, the oldest chemist's shop and oldest linen mill in England, the redoubtable Mother

Shipton and her suspect prophecies – but the Dropping Well could be the oddest of the lot, because its water can, in effect, turn objects into stone. It contains a strong lime deposit which acts as a petrifying agent, and there is generally a bizarre assortment of items in the well, being given a coating of limestone and getting, as it were, well stoned . . .

Wells could be decorative as well as utilitarian, sometimes in the most unexpected way. **Stoke Row** in Oxfordshire must have the most unlikely village well-head in England, an ornate oriental canopy with a domed cupola and a cast-iron elephant on top. It was given to the village in 1864 by the Maharajah of Benares, as a gesture of appreciation to a local resident, Edward Reade. When Reade was governor of India's North-West Province, he organised an up-to-date water supply for Benares, and when he told the Maharajah that Stoke Row had water problems too, this was the result – a 368-foot well and the fanciest well-top in rural England.

The fanciest, but far from the biggest. I think that title must go to **Nottington**, near Weymouth in Dorset, where a village spring has been surmounted by a three-

Two unlikely wellheads: the Spa House (left) built over the village spring at Nottington, and the village well at Stoke Row (below) provided by the Maharajah of Benares.

storey octagonal house. The medicinal qualities of the spring are said to have been discovered in the seventeenth century by a shepherd, while he was driving his flock through the village. Some of the sheep drank the water from the spring and walked through the pool, and those which were suffering from sheep-scab were miraculously cured.

The fame of Nottington's water spread beyond the shepherd fraternity, as far up the social ladder as George III, who visited Nottington in 1791, tried the water, and presumably became immune from sheep-scab – there are certainly no reports that he ever caught it. The spring became so famous that the local landowner built this Spa House in 1830 to cope with the rush. It was a philanthropic gesture, he insisted, but it must have made him a bob or two as well. The reason the Spa House is eight-sided, so the story goes, is that he built a room for each of his seven sons and an eighth one for himself. This hardly tallies with the philanthropy theory, but at least he has left us with one of England's more curious water-holes.

The Beau Nash pumps have no pretensions to philanthropy at all. They were installed at regular intervals along the Bath Road for the sole benefit of a Regency buck called Beau Nash and his friends, when they drove from Bath to London for high jinks with the Prince Regent. The pumps were to make the journey more tolerable, not as a source of refreshment but to settle the dust. When he set out on a journey, two

outriders went ahead and turned on the pumps to damp down the road before his carriage passed. There are still a few of these pumps left, including one at **Poyle**, not far from Heathrow Airport, where even the first-class passengers might envy the individual attention that Beau Nash organised for himself on his journeys, more than two centuries ago.

One of the roadside pumps (right) installed by Beau Nash to ensure a dust-free coach-ride from Bath to London.

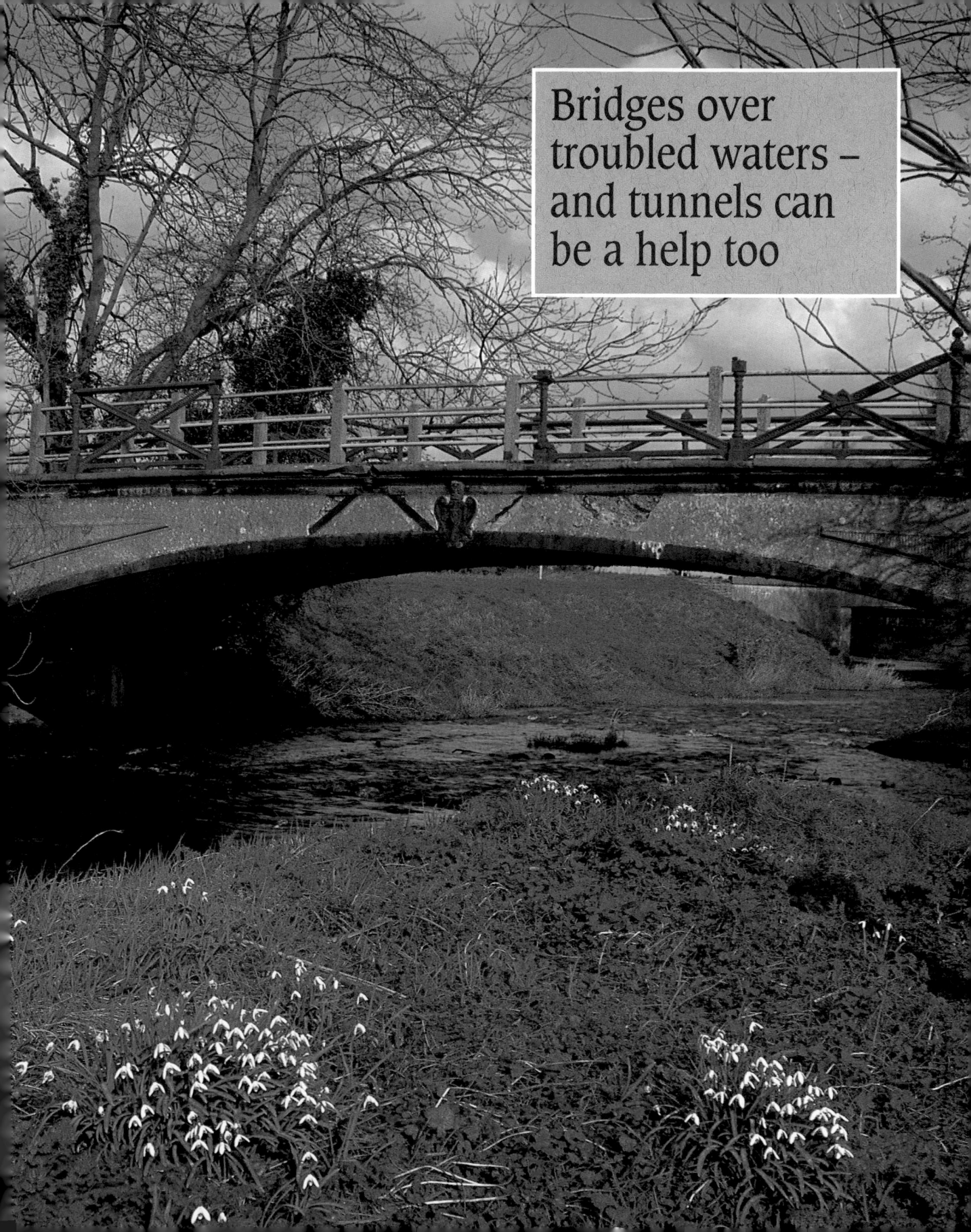

Bridges over troubled waters – and tunnels can be a help too

Bridges over troubled waters – and tunnels can be a help too

The English, on the whole, do not have a lot of time for tunnels. In one or two cases, like the Channel Tunnel, they can actively dislike them, but in general they just find

The plaque at the entrance to Horn Hill Tunnel, extolling the 'zealous exertions' of the man responsible for it, Giles Russell.
He provided Beaminster with a more direct route to the outside world.

them boring. Let's face it, the inside of one tunnel is very much like any other, and the prime object of most people in tunnels is to get out of them.

English tunnels cannot claim any records of note, compared with those in America and Switzerland and Japan. Our longest rail tunnel, for example, is the Northern Line on the London Underground, and I know of no one who is thrilled about the Northern Line. No, tunnels in England are not the stuff which picture postcards and tourist brochures are made of, and I confess that in *Timpson's England* I ignored them, and concentrated on bridges instead.

This was an oversight I must now put right, and indeed I shall give tunnels precedence over bridges. After all, they do have the edge on them in one romantic respect, as any fairground operator can confirm. I doubt that a bridge would have the pulling power of a Tunnel of Love. But apart from that, we do have some very intriguing tunnels tucked away under the English landscape, not just rail or canal tunnels, but at least one fascinating road tunnel – and

this in a country where traditionally the roads wind round natural obstacles rather than go straight under them.

The tunnel I have in mind does not look too spectacular. It is little more than a hundred yards long, and only wide enough for two small stagecoaches to pass, but when it was built it was the longest road tunnel in the British Isles, and for the locals it was as important a link with the outside world as the Channel Tunnel is today.

The little country town of **Beaminster** lies in the heart of steep hills, which gives it one of the most attractive settings in Dorset. Unfortunately one of those hills is on the route to Crewkerne and the north, and it caused considerable problems for the horse-drawn traffic of the early nineteenth century. That was a time for expansion in the rest of England, but Horn Hill was effectively the stopper in Beaminster's bottle. The man who uncorked it is commemorated on the stone plaque above the entrance to **Horn Hill** Tunnel. 'The public,' it says, 'are principally indebted for the erection of this Tunnel to the zealous exertions of Giles Russell, of Beaminster, Gent.'

Mr Russell's zealous exertions started with convincing his fellow townsfolk that the idea was practicable, then persuading them to pay for it. He was not only a Gent but a solicitor, which meant that in addition to being an eloquent advocate he also coped with the legal procedures. Even in 1830 you were not allowed to go around digging road tunnels wherever you fancied, and Mr Russell managed to get the Bill through Parliament which authorised it.

He was still waxing eloquent when the first sod was cut, at a rather jolly little ceremony involving considerable quantities of cider, on Easter Monday, 1830. According to the local paper, 'G. Russell Esq. addressed the party assembled in a neat and most impressive speech, in which he emphatically exemplified the benefits that would accrue to the different towns in the neighbourhood, but more particularly to Beaminster and its environs.' This date, you will doubtless discover, does not tally with the starting date on the stone plaque, August 1831, but the experts say that must denote the laying of the first brick.

On 29 June 1832 – and this time all the dates tally – there was an even jollier celebration to mark the tunnel's completion. A procession formed up which was actually eight times as long as the tunnel itself, headed by two bands, a mail coach carrying the engineers and officials, an open carriage in which rode the triumphant G. Russell Esq., and then assorted dignitaries in carriages or on horseback. Finally came the men who had actually dug the tunnel, walking two by two and carrying their picks and shovels and other tools. A twenty-one-gun salute was fired on the summit of Horn Hill, a balloonist ascended from a nearby field, and fireworks were let off from the church tower – well away, one hopes, from the balloon.

Cider flowed in all the pubs, and at a dinner for the gentry the praises of Mr Russell and his tunnel were sung in a nine-verse ditty which culminated in the chorus:

> *Now will we all in loud acclaim*
> *Our worthy patriot cheer,*
> *United with whose envied name*
> *Horn Tunnel shall appear!*

It was such a jolly party, in fact, that the good folk of Beaminster repeated it the following year, and went on doing so for about half a century, in what was known as the Tunnel Fair, until the celebrators had probably forgotten what they were celebrating. In 1881, at about the time that the Tunnel Fair expired, the gates of the tunnel were taken away, and many years later the turnpike house was demolished, ironically to widen the road. But Horn Hill Tunnel itself remains as it always was, a monument to one man's vision and initiative and a reminder, at a time when there is talk of building new roads by private enterprise, that there are few things new under the sun.

One can hardly argue, however, that the tunnel is picturesque. Its portals are plain brick, plus that slightly confusing plaque, and most of our road tunnels are just as utilitarian. It was the railway engineers who put a little more imagination into their tunnel entrances, sometimes for their own satisfaction, sometimes to placate the local landowner, who probably never wanted the railway in the first place. There is a fair example of the latter at **Shugborough Park** in Staffordshire, where the first Earl of Lichfield ordered that the western portal of the tunnel under his park should be 'properly and sufficiently guarded by a stone wall or battlement to hide the sight of the trains as they pass in and out'.

The park was already littered with eccentric monuments erected by his forebear Thomas Anson in the 1760s, ranging from a copy of the Arch of Hadrian in Athens, with

Shugborough Park was already well-equipped with eccentric monuments like the Triumphal Arch (left) when the railway added its own contribution, a castellated tunnel (below). These days the power gantries rather spoil the effect.

The house with a hole in it: the occupants of the Clayton Tunnel entrance get a splendid view of the trains, but there must be quite a noise under the floorboards.

a bust of his brother Admiral Lord Anson on top, to a bulky obelisk erected in memory of the admiral's cat. Maybe the Earl thought he could go one better, or maybe the railway company took a look around and decided that, amongst that lot, one more peculiar structure would not look out of place. One way or the other, the result is a grandiose arch surmounted by battlements and towers which look more like the entrance to a Norman castle than a hole in the ground. The other end of the 770-yard tunnel comes out immediately below the Admiral's Arch, and, perhaps slightly cowed by this, the railway engineers built a more modest portal, on vaguely Egyptian lines.

Chroniclers of Shugborough Park and its contents seem so overwhelmed by Thomas Anson's monuments that they pay little attention to the tunnel, and the local library could find only one reference to it, an account of an accident in 1875 when a platelayer was killed in it by a passing train. Apparently the engineer who designed the tunnel, although very strong on castellated towers, was rather slack about health and safety, and omitted to put any manholes in the tunnel for workmen to jump into when a train went through. The railway company was instructed to install them forthwith, but that was small consolation for the platelayer.

Shugborough Park is still the family home of the Lichfields, but the current Earl understandably prefers to photograph fashion models rather than entrances to railway tunnels, however grandiose. The property is actually owned by the National Trust, but they are not too bothered about the tunnel either, and it is not mentioned in their handbook. Your only chance of seeing the 'castle' is to find your own way through the beech wood which surrounds it – unless of course you happen to be a train-driver.

There is no such problem with another railway 'castle', the entrance to the **Clayton Tunnel** in West Sussex. When I used to stay with my mother in nearby Hassocks, it was a regular treat for the family to go and see the trains from London to Brighton disappearing into this mock-medieval jumble of towers and battlements built onto the hillside. There is actually an inhabited house tucked between the twin turrets over the entrance, and I often wondered whether to envy the occupants for their splendid view of the trains, or sympathise with them over the constant racket under the floorboards. High on the Downs above Clayton are two much more famous landmarks, the Jack and Jill windmills, but for me that fairy-tale castle with its roaring 'dragons' was a much bigger draw.

There are one or two cases where the intriguing feature of a tunnel is not so much its appearance as its name. For instance, on the main line between Taunton and Tiverton, where it crosses the border from Somerset into Devon, is the **White Ball Tunnel**, completed in 1844. The name is not too odd in itself, and it might be easily explained if there were a white stone ball over the entrance, but there isn't. Instead you will find that in nearby **Sampford Arundel** there is a pub called the Blue Ball, and just across the border in Devon is a hamlet called **Red Ball**.

One begins to picture some eccentric millionaire snooker-player who has renamed everything in sight after a different-coloured ball on the table, and I quite expected to find a Green Ball gardening centre and a gentlemen's club called the Black Ball. The real reason, however, is quite different. The countryside in that area has a variegated clay soil, and the names come from the different-coloured ball clays found in the area. White Ball seems to be the most popular variety; in addition to the White Ball Tunnel there was, until 1930, a pub on the main road called the White Ball Inn, now a private house, and an area right on the county boundary is called **White Ball Gate**. It has one house which actually straddles the border; most of it is in Devon but the front porch is in Somerset. When they beat the bounds in White Ball Gate every four years, a small boy actually climbs over the porch to follow the boundary line. The only alternative, I suppose, was to dig another tunnel . . .

Railways did not, of course, have the monopoly of tunnels. The canal-builders

Sampford Arundel has White Ball Gate (left) and White Ball Tunnel, a Blue Ball Inn (above) and a nearby hamlet called Red Ball – but the name of the game is clay, not snooker.

were at it years before, and some of them were as partial to Norman arches and battlements as the first Earl of Lichfield. There are a couple of castellated creations at each end of **Sapperton Tunnel** in Gloucestershire, on the old Thames and

The elaborate east portal of Sapperton Tunnel . . .

. . . and the more subdued version at the other end.

The Greywell Tunnel is not notable for any battlements, just bats.

Severn Canal. The tunnel was completed in 1789, more than half a century ahead of the one at Shugborough Park, and it runs dead straight under the Cotswolds for two-and-a-quarter miles, the second longest canal tunnel in England. The canal-men propelled their boats through it by lying on their backs and pushing against the roof with their feet.

There was a pub near each entrance where they could gather strength for this upside-down marathon, and if their posture was uncomfortable, at least it cured any hiccups. The pubs are still there, and so are the elaborate portals; the one below

Sapperton, in the Golden Valley, favours a Gothic style, while the other one near Coates goes in for Doric columns and niches. The tunnel itself, however, has been out of action since the canal was abandoned in 1927.

The portals of the **Greywell Tunnel** on the Basingstoke Canal, in Hampshire, hardly come up to Sapperton standards. One end is basically just a hole, the other was restored in the 1970s, but is still a plain brick archway with not a battlement in sight. Greywell, however, shares Sapperton's tradition of attracting upside-down activity, because it is famous, not for its battlements, but for its bats. Ever since part of the tunnel collapsed in 1932, turning it effectively into a very long cave, it has provided a cosy winter refuge for up to two thousand bats of five different varieties. According to the Nature Conservancy Council it is the largest site for hibernating bats in Britain.

In the mid-1980s, though, the local canal restoration society decided that it wanted to reopen the tunnel, and the two groups of conservationists met head-on. The bat-lovers argued that bats and boats didn't mix; the canal-lovers said that they did in other tunnels and they could in the Greywell. In 1985 the canal enthusiasts came up with an ingenious compromise; as the local headline-writer inevitably put it: 'Canal Society Has A Batty Solution'. The idea was to create a form of time-share, in which boats would use the tunnel during the summer, and bats would use it during the hibernating and breeding seasons in the winter and spring.

The Nature Conservancy Council was not convinced. Any sort of disturbance, it said, would scare the bats away for ever. But the Canal Society kept trying – or as that headline-writer had to put it: 'Bats? The Flap Continues'.

From then on, however, the headlines became rather repetitive. In March 1986 the *Basingstoke Gazette* announced what it called a new solution, but the headline sounded strangely familiar: 'Bats Could Be Saved By Time-Share'. In May 1987, up it came again: 'Bats And Boats: "What About A Time-Share?" ' Three years later, in September 1990, the situation seemed no further forward: 'Tunnel Plan: Experts Fear For Bats'.

The Canal Society produced a glossy fifty-two page booklet presenting the case for restoration. Three pages were devoted to bats, and the familiar time-share proposal was put forward again, but with an extra ingredient. If the unblocking of the tunnel took away its cave atmosphere, so beloved of bats, then how about a removable partition which could be floated in during the winter months to cut off one end of the tunnel and re-create the cave environment?

There was the proviso, however, that the partition should be fitted with a door so that a maintenance crew could get through in an emergency, and I am not sure how the breeding bats would fancy producing their offspring in a cave with a back door, which might be opened unexpectedly during their most intimate moments by a boatload of maintenance engineers.

Perhaps the Society had its doubts about this too, because it went on to make a quite different proposal – a separate bat tunnel parallel to the Greywell, lined with brick and built with lime mortar, leaving crevices for the bats. There could even be a water-proof membrane to keep the brick face dry. It sounded like a luxury bat hotel; beside it, the Greywell would seem a mere doss-house. You might think, therefore, that the Nature Conservancy Council would be thrilled to bits – except for the final paragraph. The cost of the tunnel, it said, should be met by the Nature Conservancy Council; the Canal Society 'might provide voluntary labour'.

That was three years ago. The last I heard, Greywell Tunnel was still blocked and the bats were still in it. Or were they? The Canal Society has a fresh line of argument: maybe there are not all that many bats in the Greywell anyway. It claims that numbers have been declining for years. In 1984 an NCC expert counted 450; the last count was less than 200. Society engineers inspect the tunnel each year, and while they used to see three or four bats, for the last three years they have seen none at all.

One perceives what the Society is driving at. But if the Conservancy Council does not accept its argument, what then? 'Well, we've devised this time-share scheme . . .'

Now from tunnels to bridges, and the transition is not too difficult. In fact, further along the Basingstoke Canal there is a combination of both, the **Little Tunnel Bridge**, which in my view has earned its listed building status by its name alone. 'When is a tunnel not a tunnel? When it's a Little Tunnel Bridge . . .' And from there one can move on to canal bridges proper, like the ingenious snaily bridge on the Macclesfield Canal at **Congleton** in Cheshire, which allows the towing horse to

Congleton's curly canal bridge, which allows a towing horse to cross from one towpath to the other without being unhitched. Modern narrowboats are not too bothered.

cross the canal from one towpath to the other without being unhitched. I gather the locals call it 'snaily' because it is curved rather like a snail-shell, but I have heard it called a 'snake bridge' too, so I imagine anything with a wiggle will do.

The Macclesfield Canal was one of the late starters in the canal world. It was only completed in 1831, when railways were already entering the scene. Most canals, and their bridges, were built long before the age of steam, but there is one railway bridge which goes back a hundred years earlier than that snaily bridge at Congleton. Admittedly the rails were made of wood and the wagons which ran on them were hauled by horses, but the **Causey Arch**, near **Tanfield** in County Durham, qualifies as England's oldest surviving railway bridge, completed in 1727.

Local mine-owners paid £12,000 to have it built across the Causey Burn, to carry coal from the nearby Tanfield Colliery. It is eighty feet high, with a span of a hundred feet, quite a major engineering project for the man who built it, 'a common mason', as one chronicler describes him, by the name of Ralph Wood. Mr Wood tried his hand at

a wooden bridge first, but unfortunately it fell down, so he switched to stone instead. However, the memory of his previous failure must have preyed on his mind, because before the stone bridge was completed he leapt to his death from the parapet, perhaps fearing that history would repeat itself. He might be consoled – or perhaps just exasperated – to know that the Causey Arch stands there still, as sturdy as ever, and in due course it was able to take the strain of steam engines running on iron rails, until the line was closed in 1962. Indeed, local railway enthusiasts are planning to reopen the train service across the bridge, which its creator expected to collapse nearly 270 years ago.

Engineers were still building bridges for horse tram-roads a century later, but on a rather grander scale, and the **Treffry Viaduct** which spans the Carmears Valley between St Blazey and Luxulyan in Cornwall was designed to carry an aqueduct as well. Joseph Treffry was a Fowey man with rather grand ideas, not only about bridges but about his own status. He was born Joseph Austen, but acquired a new name with a coat of arms to go with it, and

The Causey Arch, England's oldest surviving railway bridge, built when the rails were made of wood and the waggons were hauled by horses.

The Treffry Viaduct, which carries an aqueduct as well as a tramroad a hundred feet above the Carmears Valley.

he incorporated his instant family crest on the side of the viaduct.

There are ten granite arches nearly a hundred feet high, with a total length of 650 feet. The tram-road linked Treffry's quarry with a canal which ran to Par on the coast – he built the harbour there as well. The water which flowed through the aqueduct under the rails was used to power the water-wheels at a local copper mine. Although the railway has gone, the aque-duct is still used by the china-clay industry, and Treffry's Viaduct would seem to be as permanent a feature of the English land-scape as the Causey Arch.

The same could not be said, alas, for another viaduct which was built thirty years later, and was hailed at the time as a much greater achievement than either of them – though a hundred years afterwards, with the help of hindsight, it was described as 'a gallant monument to an age of reckless

All that remains of the Solway Viaduct, the embankment on the Bowness side.
The bridge was rendered useless by a combination of ice floes, Anglo-Scottish antipathy, and market forces.

enterprise'. The **Solway Viaduct** was built across the neck of the Solway Firth, which is little more than a mile wide at that point, to link the rich ore mines of Cumberland with the iron foundries of Lanarkshire, as well as providing a passenger service twenty miles shorter than the route round the coast. It seemed, as they say, a good idea at the time, and after three years' work the viaduct was duly completed in 1869, an iron structure standing forty feet above the bed of the Firth. The first goods train went across a year later, the first passenger train a year after that, and the directors of the Solway Railway Company sat back to watch the profits pour in.

Unfortunately they had failed to consider three rather vital factors. First, they could not have checked on the reserves of ore in the Cumbrian mines, or how the price would compare with the same product overseas. Very soon the supplies began to dwindle, and the Scottish foundries imported cheaper Spanish ore instead.

Second, nobody had apparently told them about the Saga of the Bowness Bells. Many years before the viaduct was built, a boat-load of marauding Scots managed to extract the bells from Bowness Church, and were back in the boat with them before the unobservant locals realised what was

happening. Much incensed, the Cumbrians gave chase, caught up with the Scots in mid-Firth, and fell upon them so energetically that the bells were tipped overboard and disappeared for ever.

This might have ended the matter, but the Cumbrians decided to have their revenge. A few days later they rowed to the northern shore, and in an operation which must have been even more discreet than the previous one, removed the bells from Middlebie Church without being detected. They brought them back to Bowness and hung them in the church tower.

Perhaps surprisingly, the Scots left it at that – except that each time a new rector arrived in Bowness he got a letter from his counterpart in Middlebie saying in effect, 'Please may we have our bells back'. The traditional answer was always, 'Yes of course – if you give us back ours'. The Scots maintained that when the bells in Bowness Church were rung you could hear them pealing, 'Take me back to bonnie Scotland.'

All this may still have been in people's minds when the viaduct was opened, but certainly there was no rush for tickets. Any Scottish passenger coming to Bowness might have been suspected of bell-hunting, and any Englishman crossing to the Scottish side would probably have been thumped anyway. In either case, the atmosphere on the train would probably have made a football special seem a haven of tranquillity. Passenger traffic was officially described as 'sporadic', and from the railway staff's point of view it was probably just as well.

The third factor the company overlooked was a far more decisive one. The Solway Firth can be very cold in winter, so cold that ice floes can build up in it, and the floes can be very substantial indeed. On the night of 29 January 1881, the ebbing tide brought a mass of ice ten feet thick crashing against the viaduct. Four men had been stationed in the signal-box on the viaduct to watch out for ice, but it was not the sort you can warn off with a red flag, and they had to run for their lives as great gaps were smashed in the superstructure and the cast-iron pillars were buckled and bent.

The pounding continued for the next three days. Each time the tide ebbed and flowed it forced more ice against the viaduct, until long sections of it were reduced to a mass of tangled wreckage. But amazingly this was not the end of it. Parliament granted £30,000 to repair it, and after three years the trains were running again, albeit not very profitably. It came into its own during the First World War, when it carried pig-iron to the shipyards on Clydeside, but that was its final fling, and the company closed it in the early 1920s.

However, intrepid pedestrians still ventured across the rusting girders, and I rather think it would have been an ideal route for a spot of bell-stealing, but nobody bothered. In due course a watchman was posted, like Horatio, to guard the bridge, and even the foot passengers petered out. In 1935 the derelict viaduct was at last demolished, and much of the scrap metal was shipped to Japan to be turned into armaments for their war against China.

All that remain are the embankments at each end of the bridge. The one on the Cumbrian side, made of rough-hewn sandstone, stretched for over four hundred yards across the mudflats from the old Bowness station to the shore, and thirty years ago there were still some of the foundations of the ironwork left. A *Carlisle Journal* reporter wrote: 'Blocks of sandstone have fallen away to expose rusting steel pillars, looking for all the world like columns marking the site of some ancient Greek settlement.' But even then the sandstone was covered in thistles and couch grass, and today it takes a fair amount of imagination to connect this overgrown mound with what at one time was the longest viaduct in Britain.

A number of bridges from a much earlier era, instead of having a signal-box in the middle, had a little chapel, or a lock-up, or some kind of toll-keeper's shelter; I mentioned a few in *Timpson's England*. However, **Wilton Bridge** near Ross-on-Wye in Hereford and Worcester is the only bridge I know which has a sundial standing guard halfway across. There are four faces to the sundial and a stone ball on top, all perched on a lofty plinth which stands high above the parapet of the bridge to survey

The sundial on Wilton Bridge has four faces, a stone ball, and a gloomy message.

the river below. The bridge was built in 1599, but the sundial was added much later, possibly by the Puritans when the bridge had to be restored after a fierce encounter on it during the Civil War. The Puritan connection is strengthened by the verse on the sundial, which as one maga-

'Not more than half the Mortar or Cement is required, as is commonly used, consequently that part of the Work most likely to decay, is much reduced, and if affected by frost, will not be more than half the usual expense to replace the face of the Joints.'

The bridge at Watton-on-Stone was built with Hitch's Patent Bricks – but the bricks ran into a hitch, and the idea never caught on.

zine writer commented in 1907, 'cannot be commended either for its grammar or its poetry'. Judge for yourself:

Esteem thy precious time,
Which pass so swift away;
Prepare then for eternity
And do not make delay.

The nineteenth century produced some interesting ideas in bridge-building materials to supersede ironwork and stone, and one of them was Hitch's Patent Brick. Of course bricks have been used by builders as far back as the Romans, but even a small bridge takes a lot of bricks, a lot of mortar, a lot of time and a lot of money, and there seemed scope for speeding things up. In 1828 Caleb Hitch thought he had got the answer. It was a brick with flanges on it, which would interlock with the ones around it. The main advantage, according to the prospectus he issued to the building trade in 1830, was the saving in cement:

There was more. Hitch's Patent Brick was 'equal in durability to any of the Ancient Walls now found', it had a sound face for stucco work, it was 'very proper for Garden Walling, having no sort of vacuum to admit insects', and it was ideal for aquatic walls, 'being faced so securely, using not half the cement as is now necessary'.

In Mr Hitch's home town of Ware in Hertfordshire a number of buildings were erected using his Patent Brick, but maybe the prospectus was a little too optimistic, particularly the line about 'equal in durability to any of the Ancient Walls now found', because nearly all of them have now disappeared. There is, however, just one example of his Aquatic Walls, the three-arch bridge over the river at nearby **Watton-at-Stone**. You can't spot the flanging, of course, but the bricks are larger than the standard size, a foot long and six inches square – and this in fact was the hitch to Hitch's Patent Brick.

Bricklayers found it was too cumbersome to cope with; it did not fit comfortably into one hand while using the other hand to lay the mortar. It may have been tried out in other Hertfordshire towns – perhaps they took to Hitch in Hitchin? – but it never caught on nationwide. And alas, when some of the patent bricks started to crumble on the parapet of Watton Bridge, they were replaced by the standard variety. Interlocking bricks were forgotten for a century and a half – until along came a certain Mr Lego . . .

However, later in the nineteenth century a much brighter idea cropped up in the bridge-building world, which is still very much in use today. You can find the earliest example of it in East Anglia, for once ahead of its time. Linking Norfolk with Suffolk across the River Waveney at **Homersfield** is the oldest surviving concrete bridge in England. It is very little like the concrete bridges of today – there is the new one which replaced it a hundred yards down-river for comparison – but it did involve the extensive use of concrete and it was quite a daring innovation in its day.

It was built for Lord Waveney of nearby Flixton Hall in 1870, and as a reminder that it was privately owned he closed it on one day a year from sunrise to sunset. A chain was erected across it and his staff charged vehicle drivers tuppence per wheel to cross. Very shrewdly he always chose a day when the river was in flood, so nobody could dodge payment by driving through the water. Pedestrians were allowed to cross for nothing if they were nimble enough to step over the chain.

Flixton Hall has long since gone, and so has Lord Waveney and his title, but the bridge is still used for foot traffic and there is currently a joint plan by local authorities and conservation interests on both sides of the river to restore it. Its appearance was not improved, when I last saw it, by a gas pipe attached to the side, but if that is removed it will be easier to see Lord Waveney's coat of arms, the curious Adair family crest which features four red hands.

Legend has it that the hands have no connection with the familiar Red Hand of Ulster. They are linked with a much more local story, of a pantry boy who was murdered in a bedroom at Flixton Hall. It is said he was thrashed to death, but as he lay

dying he tried to struggle to the door, and his hands made four bloody imprints on the wall. So the Adairs were cursed by having four red hands on their crest, and a white flag bearing those red hands was flown over the Hall. The curse was to last four generations, one hand being removed from the crest as each generation died, but Lord Waveney had no direct heirs and the title became extinct, so the four bloody hands remain on Homersfield Bridge.

I have to say that the story of a bloody hand crops up in other distinguished families. At **Aston** Church in Birmingham a stained glass window depicts the crest of the Holte family, which includes a red hand

England's oldest surviving concrete bridge, linking Norfolk with Suffolk across the Waveney. The four red hands on the shield have a gory story to tell.

minus a finger. Sir Thomas Holte was rumoured to have killed his cook in 1606, either by running him through with a spit or splitting his head with a cleaver. Either method would have made his hands very red indeed. Sir Thomas took a neighbour to court for spreading this story and won the case, but the rumours persisted, and by the nineteenth century everyone was convinced that the red hand in the coat of arms was symbolic of Sir Thomas's crime. The missing finger is explained on the same lines as the Homersfield story – one was removed for each generation, and this was the first to go.

There are similar tales at Wateringbury in Kent and at Stoke d'Abernon in Surrey, but I suspect they are all linked in some way with the armorial Red Hand, which is not confined to Ulster but appears on the coats of arms of English, as well as Irish, baronets. However, if the red hands on Homersfield Bridge do really link it with bloodshed, it would not be the only one. As I mentioned in *Timpson's England*, a great many bridges have tales of accidents, suicides and murders. Even the picture postcard bridge over the River Exe at **Bickleigh** in Devon has a strange associa-tion with a headless horseman who gallops across it on Christmas Eve. Sceptics suggest that the story was devised by local land-lords to increase their sales, but it may be connected with an encounter that took place on the bridge in the sixteenth century between a Courtenay and a Carew, members of two well-known local families. Neither would give way, and in the resul-tant fight the Courtenay threw the Carew to his death in the river below.

However, Bickleigh Bridge has a much happier connection. It is said to be the bridge which inspired an American song-writer while he was on a visit to the West Country. His name was Paul Simon, and the song he wrote was an international smash hit called 'Bridge Over Troubled Water'.

The locals I spoke to had not actually heard they had been immortalised in this way, and it may all hinge on a visit that Paul Simon made when he was still a folk singer and had never even met Mr Garfunkel. Nevertheless, it is just as good a story to latch on to as the one about the headless horseman, and if I were a local hotelier I would probably seize it with both hands . . .

Bickleigh Bridge – the original 'Bridge Over Troubled Water'?

When doves had
luxury flats –
and a deer's home
was his castle

When doves had luxury flats – and a deer's home was his castle

The formidable gateway to the manor house at Hinton-on-the-Green was designed, not for defence, but for doves.

The English are reputed to be inordinately fond of anything with four legs or a beak. As proof of this it is constantly pointed out that, while we have a 'national' society for preventing cruelty to children, we have 'royal' societies for protecting animals and birds – though this may just indicate greater enterprise (pushiness?) on the part of the RSPCA and RSPB to acquire royal patronage, and a becoming modesty on the part of the NSPCC. Our fondness for our four-legged or feathered friends can also be a mixed blessing for the recipients, because we often house and nurture them and generally look after their welfare merely so that, in due course, we can kill them and eat them. However, there is no disputing that over the centuries the English have built some rather splendid accommodation for those creatures whose company – or flavour – they take a fancy to.

Perhaps the earliest example is what the Romans called a columbarium, and we call a dovecote. Its other name is a pigeon-house, which is just as accurate but somehow sounds less attractive. There is hardly any difference between a pigeon and a dove, and over the years the names have become interchangeable; the bird may live in a dovecote, but in a pie it's a pigeon. It is interesting that when people talk about doves, they mean the pretty little creatures that fly around with olive branches, and make soothing noises on window-sills; when they talk about pigeons they mean the ones that eat all the crops, have a silly walk and make a filthy mess. Doves in fact are the good guys and pigeons are the bad ones, but to our forefathers they all amounted to the same thing – a steady source of fresh meat all the year round.

That only applied, though, if your particular forefather was a lord of the manor, an abbot, or otherwise entitled to keep pigeons. If you did not qualify and your neighbour did, that could be very bad news for you, because pigeons worked on the principle of robbing the poor to feed the rich; they lived off the crops of the neighbouring peasants, and if a peasant tried to do something about it, like kill them, he was liable to be strung up himself. It was Good Queen Bess who showed just how good she was by decreeing that a lord of the manor must provide enough crops around his dovecote to discourage his birds from taking other people's. Queen Elizabeth is generally remembered for her triumphs over the Spanish, but to her pigeon-pestered peasantry, this decree was undoubtedly her greatest coo . . .

At one time there were 26,000 dovecotes dotted around the English countryside, but once the farmers got the hang of using root crops for winter fodder, ensuring a year-round supply of fresh meat, the demand for pigeon pie decreased. For a time in the nineteenth century the birds were bred for shooting rather than eating, but the gentry came to prefer bigger game, and dovecotes became redundant. Most of them were left to crumble; it is only recently that Dovecote Trusts have sprung up to restore and preserve them.

In the Middle Ages dovecotes were made circular, because the nesting boxes could then be reached by a ladder which revolved around a central post, called a potence. By 1984 most of the potences had become, as it were, impotent, and there were only four which still worked and were on view to the public – at **Dunster** in Somerset, **Broughton** and **Basingstoke** in Hampshire, and **Alcester** in Warwickshire. The row upon row of nesting boxes, soaring up into the roof, look like a circular block of flats seen through the wrong end of a telescope.

After the Middle Ages, dovecotes began to develop more decorative, if less practical lines, until they no longer looked like traditional dovecotes at all. Sometimes they were built in pairs to act as portals to big estates. At **Hinton-on-the-Green** in Worcestershire, for example, the drive to the manor house passes beneath twin arches connecting two rectangular stone dovecotes. At **Hamstall Ridware** in Staffordshire the two dovecotes are octagonal with domed roofs, and look more like watch-towers outside a prison than the entrance to the family home of the FitzHerberts.

In some cases the dovecotes are built above the entrance rather than on each side of it. There is a timber-framed version over the entrance to the splendid eight-gabled Tudor house at **Dowdeswell** in Gloucestershire. It is only recognisable as a dovecote by the belfry-like entrance on the roof.

This was a very modest structure compared with the massive dovecotes built by some sixteenth-century landowners, as much to impress the neighbours, no doubt, as to increase the comfort of the pigeons. At **Willington** in Bedfordshire lived Sir John Goswick, who was Cardinal Wolsey's Master of Horse (why should a cardinal need so many horses that they rated a Master, one wonders). He built a dovecote large enough to earn him the title of Master of Pigeons as well. It had accommodation for thirteen hundred pairs of birds, and the roof is an elaborate affair with crow-stepped gables – or should that be pigeon-stepped?

Even this was not as large as a stone-built dovecote at **Culham Manor** in Oxfordshire, dated 1685, which has three thousand nesting niches, and in pigeon terms was not so much a block of flats as a vast housing estate.

A more picturesque approach: the timber-framed dovecote-cum-gatehouse at Dowdeswell.

Half a dovecote is better than none: the Rev. Sabine Baring-Gould's semi-circular version at Lewtrenchard.

As the popularity of pigeon pie decreased, so did the size of the birds' living quarters. The Revd Sabine Baring-Gould, Rector and Squire of **Lewtrenchard** in Devon at the end of the last century, designed a dovecote which followed the traditional circular pattern on one side, with a sort of pinnacled dormer window to let the birds in, but the other side was flat to form part of a wall. It was in fact the dovecote equivalent of a semi-detached, without the other semi.

A birdhouse? Tell it to the birds . . . But this Egyptian pyramid at Tong was actually built as an aviary; pigeons in the upper storeys, poultry down below.

This half-size near-folly was primarily intended to balance an ornamental pavilion on the other side of the rector's house, but it really did contain doves.

So did the Egyptian pyramid at **Tong** in Shropshire, one of the more bizarre birdhouses in the English countryside. The man who built it in the early nineteenth century, George Durant, preferred to call it an aviary. Pigeons lived in the four upper storeys, and poultry on the ground floor. He provided the pigeons with flightholes and ledges, but omitted any nesting boxes,

which must have made life rather uncomfortable. But it was not too serious a project anyway, judging by the other buildings he put up for his livestock – a Gothic cowhouse and another Egyptian pyramid for his pigs, about as unlikely as the Grecian temple piggery at **Fyling Hall** in Yorkshire which was featured in *Timpson's England*.

While some wealthy eccentrics were building dovecotes which looked like something totally different, others were building something totally different which might or might not have been dovecotes. At **Bawburgh** in Norfolk are two seventeenth-century structures which at one time had flightholes, and which are often referred to as dovecotes, but they are known officially as the Slipper House and the Hermit's House. The Slipper House, with four ornate gables topped by pinnacles, may have been the place where pilgrims shed their shoes as they walked to the nearby St Walstan's Well; the Hermit's House may have been just that, though it seems a bit large for the average hermit. Whatever their original purpose, they now stand in the middle of a modern housing estate, looking thoroughly

Eccentric dovecotes, or somebody else's pigeon? The Slipper House (left) and the Hermit's House (below) at Bawburgh are now marooned in a modern housing estate.

The seventeenth-century cockpit at Lydbury North has obviously seen better days, though the cocks may prefer it the way it is.

nasty shock if it got inside. Instead of nesting boxes around the walls there is a circular arena in the centre, and the birds which occupied it were not billing and cooing, but knocking the living daylights out of each other.

This was a cockpit, built about 1680 when cockfighting was re-introduced after being banned by Cromwell. In common with horse-racing it was a sport of kings, but a lot more bloodthirsty. Henry VIII, for instance, had his own cockpit opposite Whitehall Palace and another at Hampton Court. And again like horse-racing it attracted heavy betting. At Lydbury North it is said that the Walcot family who owned the estate gambled it all away in this arena.

Cockfighting was considered in fact very respectable and above-board. By the nineteenth century it operated under the poultry equivalent of the Queensberry Rules, which set an official size for the arena – twelve feet across with a surround eighteen inches high – and the weights of the contestants. It also had its own system of enforcing the honouring of bets; if a loser tried to decamp without paying, he was put in a wickerwork cage and hung from a beam above the arena – no doubt to the delight of the birds fighting underneath, who must have felt they were getting a little of their own back on the human race . . .

Queen Victoria, not surprisingly, was not at all amused by cockfighting, and it was made illegal for a second and final time in 1849. The cockpit at Lydbury North still

embarrassed and no doubt wishing they had been demolished at the same time as the manor house which they once served.

While pigeons are hardly likely to mistake either of these buildings for their ancestral homes, they could well be deceived by the octagonal brick building with the conical roof at Red House Farm in **Lydbury North**, Shropshire. It certainly looks like a dovecote, and an unsuspecting pigeon might head for it like, well, a homing pigeon, but it would have had a

Wentworth Woodhouse, the elaborate mansion built by the first Marquess of Rockingham. A later Marquess created a bearpit in the ground which looks almost as imposing.

survives, but its thatched roof was replaced by cedar shingles in the 1960s, and it has manifestly seen better days. The local roosters, I imagine, are quite happy to keep it that way.

At the other end of the scale is the weird henhouse at Elton Hall, near **Ludlow**, also in Shropshire. It is on private land but easily visible from the road. It looks like one of those strange houses at Portmeirion where 'The Prisoner' in the television series got so confused, as did we all; a white structure with tall windows and a double front door, and a curving roofline coming to a series of points, with balls on top. Anything less like a poultry house is difficult to imagine; it looks more like a sanatorium for slightly deranged hens.

However, this bizarre henhouse is no more unlikely than the grand accommodation provided for some of the larger animals which were popular among the gentry in earlier times. A bearpit sounds as if it must be unprepossessing, especially as most of it is underground, but on the Marquess of Rockingham's estate at **Wentworth Woodhouse** in South Yorkshire, the entrance to the bearpit is a Jacobean ornamental gateway, which the bears must have appreciated enormously. The pit was created on the site of an old quarry in the early nineteenth century, and as well as accommodation for the bears it has two retiring chambers and a viewing gallery. There was a bear in the bearpit within living memory, and the bear-keeper lived in what is now Lady Rockingham's Tea Room.

There was much more scope for extravagance in building deerhouses, which were occupied by much more elegant animals anyway. Most people who visit **Sudbury Hall** in Derbyshire go to see the Museum of Childhood, which even offers a chimney climb for more adventurous youngsters, but *aficionados* of animal houses head for the Gothic deerfold, with its crenellated walls and four towers. It was built for the Vernon family in the early eighteenth century, a few years before another crenellated deerhouse, more like a deer-castle, was built in 1760 by Bishop Richard Trevor in his park at **Bishop Auckland**, County Durham.

The deer 'castle' at Bishop Auckland – elegant, but draughty.

To be more accurate it is a deercote, which seems to put it on a par with a dovecote, but the only point of resemblance is that it offers shelter – of a sort. It is in the form of a grass quadrangle surrounded by open arcades, which provided a certain amount of protection from wind and rain, if not from the cold, for the fallow deer which once roamed the eight-hundred-acre park. The only cosy corner of the deercote is inside the pinnacled tower, where there is a comfortable room on the first floor – not for the deer, of course, but for the Bishop and his sport-loving friends, while the deer shivered below. Personally, I would rather be a dove . . .

You may think that the days of fanciful animal houses have long since passed, but the idea is being revived by at least one designer, albeit on a smaller scale. A Norwegian-born, Norfolk-based architect, Mette Farmer, designs luxury accommodation for small pets. Her portfolio so far includes a brick and thatch canine cottage (she doesn't talk about kennels) with underfloor heating, internal lighting, antique water pump and a window box; a Norwegian log cabin with genuine turfed roof, for guineapigs; and in the tradition of those elegant deerhouses, an eighteenth-century style stables – sorry, luxury home for horses – with mahogany stalls and marble columns, a snip at £100,000. Her most dashing design is a butterfly house – whoops, butterfly palace – which is actually shaped like a butterfly. Lord Snowdon never went as far as that.

Mrs Farmer calls her enterprise Dolittle Designs, in honour of the good Doctor. When I first met her, Dolittle had done very little indeed, but more recently she has had orders for a Georgian dog-house, a canary cage with a Gothic spire, and a chinese pagoda for chinchillas. So happily there are still a few individualistic animal owners around with a few bob to spare; the spirit of the Rockinghams, the Vernons and the Bishop Trevors lives on . . .

The shape of insect houses to come? Mette Farmer's butterfly palace.

'Man is practised in disguise . . .'

'Man is practised in disguise . . .'

'Man is practised in disguise, he cheats the most discerning eyes,' wrote a disillusioned eighteenth-century poet, and perhaps I can add another couplet: 'He does it too with bricks and mortar, even though he didn't oughter.'

All through the centuries the English have designed buildings to look what they are not, sometimes with the laudable intention of making them blend better with the landscape, more often because it happened to suit their own purposes, and occasionally, as in the case of all those follies that the English enjoy so much, they built them just for the hell of it. This is not about follies, however, but about buildings which have been disguised for a specific purpose, or have had their appearance altered to suit a different use – or have been put to a different use without being altered at all, so the building's original appearance is now a disguise in itself.

Disguises can be adopted to conceal the most prosaic activities, and you cannot get much more prosaic than the function of the **Christleton** sewage lift near Chester in Cheshire. It was built at the turn of the century when sewers were provided in the village. There was no difficulty laying the pipes; the problem was what to do with the sewage. Christleton is separated from the Chester sewerage system by rising ground, so it was originally proposed to discharge the raw sewage into a nearby brook which ran into the River Dee. Unfortunately it would have reached the river very close to the intake of Chester waterworks, and thus enter the city's water supply. True, it would eventually flow into the Chester sewerage system, but this was hardly the ideal way of getting there.

The waterworks company was understandably appalled, and agreed to do a deal with the council. It would provide a free water supply for a powerful hydraulic lift, which would suck the sewage out of a collecting tank in the village, force it over the rising ground, and discharge it into the city's sewers on the other side.

This process was quite as unfascinating as it sounds, and very reasonably the council wanted to draw as little attention to it as possible. They therefore designed the sewage lift to look like something else, and the something else turned out to be an outsize version of an ornamental pigeoncote. The waterpipe formed the central column, and on top of it the tank was covered with a conical roof.

It pumped away happily for nearly half a century, but after the last war it began to need too much maintenance, and an electric pumping station took its place. However, it had become such a familiar landmark that the council continued to give it the odd coat of paint, and it still stands beside the main road from Chester to Whitchurch, Nobody would suspect that 'The Pigeoncote', as it is still affectionately known, was actually an enormous lavatory flush!

Traditional-shaped dovecotes have often been adopted as a disguise for unsightly machinery too. Sometimes an original dovecote has been adapted, like the one at **Sherborne Park** in Gloucestershire. When

Deceiving the eye: (above) the Christleton sewage lift which looks like a decorative dovecote, and (right) a dovecote at Sherborne Park which is now an electricity sub-station.

the Hall was converted into luxury flats the octagonal dovecote found a new use as an electricity sub-station. The National Trust believes it was a meat-store rather than a dovecote, but dovecote buffs disagree. At **Lytes Cary Manor** in Somerset the process was the other way round; when a new water system was installed in the manor at the turn of the century, a circular 'dovecote' was built to act as the pumphouse. More recently, a brick 'dovecote' was built at **Dilwyn** in Hereford & Worcester, to conceal an oil tank. And to end where we began on this subject, there is a Victorian 'dovecote' at **Pembridge**, not far from Dilwyn, which was actually a privy . . .

Water towers can look pretty ghastly on the English landscape, particularly those modern ones disguised as giant mushrooms, and the Duke of St Albans had understandable misgivings in 1873 when he was asked to have a water tower on his land at **Bestwood**, near Nottingham. Only if it doesn't spoil the view, he insisted, and the engineers did their best. They built a brick tower 140 feet high with ornamental balustrading round the top, and laid out the surroundings like a flower garden, with the cooling pond disguised as an ornamental lake.

Towers of one kind or another have been involved in many disguises and adaptations over the years. For instance, a former pele tower at **Rothbury** in Northumberland, one of the fortifications erected in the north of England for protection against the marauding Scots, was converted into almshouses in 1845.

Tower windmills have frequently been converted into living accommodation in more recent times, but it is rare to find a converted mill which was disguised to look

More disguises: (left) a pumphouse at Lytes Cary built to look like a dovecote, and (below) a water tower at Bestwood built to look like – well, what's *your* guess?

like a castle. The original ironstone tower mill at **Finedon** in Northamptonshire was built in 1818 by the local squire, Sir John English Dolben, and it functioned as a mill for about forty years. Then one of his successors, the splendidly-named William Harcourt Isham Mackworth-Dolben, decided to convert it, not merely into a house, but a castellated house, with imitation battlements round the top of the tower.

Mr Mackworth-Dolben rather fancied battlements, and he added them to quite a number of buildings on his estate – it is perhaps no coincidence that his first four initials spell WHIM. All five initials appear on the former mill, together with another set, REST, for which I have found no explanation – unless they simply spell what he hoped to enjoy there. The name he devised for the converted building is easier to understand: Exmill Cottage.

It was the home of his gamekeeper for several years, and it has been occupied ever since. Part of the parapet collapsed in 1914, and it was replaced by a rather smaller one, while the two extensions to the tower have also been rebuilt, but it still remains an odd mixture of windmill, castle and cottage.

Finedon must have been a popular area for tower-converters, because in the adjoining parish of **Burton Latimer** is the Wellington Tower, round and fat and rather stubby, with a viewing platform on the roof, which has also become a private house. It was built after the Duke of Wellington had visited his friend General Arbuthnot at nearby Woodford House. As he stood where the tower stands now, the Duke observed that the view around him resembled the battlefield at Waterloo. It may have been just a passing remark, but it was seized upon locally, and the tower was built in 1820 bearing the inscription: 'PANORAMA. WATERLOO VICTORY. June 18, 1815'.

The man who built it was the Revd William Alington, and with the best of intentions he allowed it to be the headquarters of the Waterloo Victory Social

Tower transformations: a crenellated tower mill at Finedon (above) and a commemorative creation at Burton Latimer (left) have both been incorporated in private houses.

Club, known locally as the 'Pam' – short for Panorama. Unfortunately the club did not turn out quite as he had planned. As one historian put it: 'To this isolated place of entertainment, men from the surrounding towns and villages resorted for the purposes of drinking, dog-racing, gambling, and other probably illegal activities.' This went on until 1895, when a new headquarters for the club was built, but the club itself became even more notorious than before, and it must have been good news for the neighbours when it eventually closed. The bad news was that the building became a tannery instead . . .

Meanwhile the Wellington Tower shook off its unfortunate reputation, and it has now been extended and converted into a home. It might have been called Expam Cottage, but no doubt the new owners preferred to forget its seamy past. Instead they can offer their guests a visit to the viewing platform, to fight the Battle of Waterloo over again.

It is easier to visualise a famous battle from the top of another commemorative tower, because it is actually set on the battlefield. On the centenary of the Battle of Edgehill in Warwickshire a famous architect and local landowner, Sanderson Miller, built the tower on the spot where King Charles I raised his standard on 23 October 1642, to launch the first major encounter of the Civil War. Thirty thousand men fought at **Edgehill**, and about fifteen hundred of them were killed. These days the site has a different military significance and much of it is owned by the Ministry of Defence, who do not encourage visitors, but the tower still welcomes them, since it now forms part of the Castle Inn – an octagonal bar has been fitted inside it. Originally, as well as marking an historic site, it was also the gatehouse for Mr Miller's estate. It passed through various hands before it became a pub in 1924.

The Castle Inn is one of the many pubs and hotels which started life as a castle,

Crenellated conversions: a tower built on the spot where Charles I raised his standard at Edgehill is now part of the Castle Inn.

Black Castle at Brislington (above) was never a castle, just a fancy set of stables; now it too has joined the licensed trade. Clearwell Castle (above right), after being restored by the son of one of the gardeners, is now an hotel.

or part of one. **Clearwell Castle** in Gloucestershire was built in 1727 as the family home of the Wyndhams, and remained so until 1907. The period after that saw its decline and fall, and then its fairytale restoration. First a disastrous fire destroyed much of the interior. The owner did his best to repair it, and in 1946 the castle was acquired by the County Council, but unfortunately they could find no use for it, and sold it to a house-stripper. Off went the lead roof, out came the floors and other woodwork, and by the mid-1950s the place had become a shell, ripe for demolition.

Enter a knight in shining armour, in the unlikely guise of a family grocer from Blackpool. Frank Yeates's father had been a gardener at the castle, and he had grown up in one of the lodges. He now had a wife, two children, and a well-established grocery business; then he heard that Clearwell Castle was nearly a ruin and up for sale, along with the lodges and eight acres of neglected parkland.

Yes, you've guessed. Frank Yeates sold up his home and his business, came back to Clearwell and sank his money into buying the castle. He and his family devoted the next twenty-five years to restoring the old place to something approaching its former glory.

It was a formidable task for a semi-retired grocer. As one of his admirers put it: 'Think of the task of restoring an ordinary house that has become derelict, then multiply the number of rooms by five and their average size by four, and you will have some idea of the task that faced the Yeates family.'

As an example there was the main hall, fifty feet long and twenty feet wide, with a lofty ceiling to match. The floor had been ripped out and much of the ornamental ceiling had collapsed. 'Now Mr Yeates has laid a splendid oak floor, while his wife has restored the ceiling. The fact that the flooring had already seen service in a large chain store, and that Mrs Yeates graduated to ceiling plaster by way of cake-icing, adds fascination to the work without apparently harming its efficiency. . .'

In spite of all their efforts there was still work to be done when Mr Yeates eventually sold the castle in 1981 – I hope at a handsome profit. For a while it looked as though its future was still in doubt, but it has since been converted into a sixteen-bedroomed hotel. Interestingly, Mr Egon Ronay seems rather overwhelmed by its size. 'Guests' footsteps may echo in its enormous halls,' he observes. Fortunately Frank Yeates had no such qualms, or today there would be no halls in which to echo.

Another building which finished up in the licensed trade also looks like a castle, and is indeed called the Black Castle, but originally it was just a fancy set of stables. It was built in **Brislington**, on the outskirts of Bristol, by an eighteenth-century Quaker copper-smelter called William Reeve, who lived at Arnos Court and wanted somewhere to house his horses. Why he should have chosen such an ostentatious design seems rather odd for a Quaker, but the building made quite an impact on Horace Walpole, who christened it 'The Devil's Cathedral'. The locals just called it the 'Black Castle', because of its purple-black stonework, and the brewery that eventually acquired it could think of no better name.

There are in fact a number of castles which still look like castles after changing their careers, but there is one genuine castle which does not look like a castle at all. If you only gave **Woodsford Castle** in Dorset a casual glance, you might think it was just a very large thatched house, but Edward III granted a licence to crenellate it in 1337, and that makes it an authentic castle. It therefore holds the unusual distinction of being the only thatched castle in England. The inside, I am told, looks rather more martial than the exterior – it even has a guards' chamber – but it is not open to the public because it is a private home, and an Englishman's home, of course . . .

It might be argued that Node Court, near **Codicote** in Hertfordshire, is also a thatched castle, because it looks just like one of those circular turreted affairs which beautiful princesses used to wave from in fairy-tales. It is in fact a private house combined with an up-market furniture showroom, but at one time it was the most elaborate cowshed in England. Although it looks so terribly English with all that

Confusion under the thatch: Woodsford Castle (above) really is a castle, in spite of its lack of towers and turrets . . .

. . . while Node Court (below) does have a turret, fit for a fairy-tale princess, but the place was built as an elaborate cowshed, and the 'turret' was just a silo.

Spire Farm at Greystoke was one of three castle-like farmhouses built by the eleventh Duke of Norfolk; he added the spire for the benefit of a tenant who did not believe in churches.

thatch, even on the turret, the Node Dairy was actually built by an American, based on a French design.

Marie Antoinette created a model dairy at Versailles and, when an American millionaire called Carl Holmes bought the Node estate in 1929, he created a luxurious home for his pedigree Jerseys on the same lines. He made one or two practical adjustments – the central courtyard, for instance, provides the exact turning space required by a 1926 Foden lorry – but Marie Antoinette would still recognise it. Four curved wings project from the circle, and the main entrance is through an archway under a high, steeply-pitched gable. Originally there was a matching archway at the rear. The 'medieval turret' is in fact a cunningly-disguised silo.

When the Second World War came, Carl Holmes went back to America, taking his Jerseys with him but leaving their extraordinary home behind. Nobody could think what to do with it, and over the years the

thatch was stripped off and it became nearly derelict. In 1973 an attempt was made to convert it into craft workshops, without success. It nearly became a health farm, then it nearly became a restaurant, and after that it nearly became flats, but it was not until the mid-1980s that the fairy castle was rescued – in fairy-tale fashion.

A couple saw it, and fell in love with it. Other couples had doubtless done so as well but could not do much about it. Brian Hayhurst, however, had been building homes in Hertfordshire since 1959, and he and his wife not only knew what to do with it, but had the magic wand to do it with, in the form of his building company. They converted part of the old dairy into a six-bedroomed, four-bathroomed home, with a kitchen where the rear archway used to be. The rest of the building houses a furniture showroom, Mr Hayhurst's offices and a caretaker.

An overhead monorail used to run from one of the wings, carrying the sweepings from the cowsheds to another thatched building known as the Dungery. Mr Hayhurst waved his magic wand, and the wing became a dining-room, the monorail became a covered walkway, and the Dungery was transformed into a covered swimming-pool. The fairy castle was complete – and I hope that everyone is living happily ever after.

Viewed from the air, Node Court has been likened to something between an Oxo advertisement and a thatched spaceship, but most people only see it from the ground, and the Ovaltine company bore that in mind when they copied Carl Holmes's idea on their farm at **Abbots Langley**, some twenty miles away. They called it 'Antoinette Court', in deference to the original designer, though 'Holmes Court' might have been fairer. It stands alongside the main London–Birmingham railway line, and to passengers looking out of their Inter-City windows it looks just as much a fairy castle as Node Court; it even has some extra half-timbering which Carl Holmes never got around to. But at Antoinnette Court the builders have been economical with the thatch – they only used it where it is visible from the railway. Ovaltine's fairy castle, in fact, was erected as an elaborate advertisement hoarding. So over there in America, Carl can rest in peace – there is still no place like Holmes' . . .

The eleventh Duke of Norfolk was very well off for castles; he had Arundel in Sussex and Greystoke in Cumberland. In addition to these genuine ones he built four imitation castles on his estate at **Greystoke**; three of them are actually farmhouses and the fourth was a shooting box, but they all have an assortment of towers and battlements and turrets.

The Duke was a larger-than-life character who produced several illegitimate offspring. He once asked the butler at Greystoke: 'Whose are all these children?' The butler replied 'Some of them are mine, Your Grace, and some of them are yours.'

He was a Whig and a strong supporter of the American colonists, so to annoy his Tory neighbours he named two of the castle-cum-farmhouses Fort Putnam and Bunkers Hill, two of the battles in which the British were defeated in the War of Independence.

In each case the farmyards are surrounded by curtain walls embellished with thin towers and blank arches. Fort Putnam also has circular buttresses, and Bunkers Hill has arched windows under a crenellated roof. The third, Spire Farm, is equally castle-like but as a bonus it has a short lead spire on its central tower. It was designed for the benefit of a tenant who belonged to an obscure religious sect and did not believe in churches; the Duke got fed up with hearing about it and put a church spire on his roof in retaliation.

The shooting box, named Lyulph's Tower after a Saxon hero who gave his name to nearby Ullswater, is large enough to be used these days as a summer retreat by the Howards. The place has been modernised and made comfortable, but I gather an old black claret bottle dated 1772, the approximate year it was built, still stands on the dining-room mantelpiece.

Spire Farm was not the only private house with ecclesiastical trimmings built around that time. In 1770 the second Earl of Strafford had the same theme in mind when he built the gatehouse at the entrance to **Boughton Park** in Northamptonshire. It looks exactly like a church tower with an oversized vestry on the side.

The chapel on **St Aldhelm's Head** in Dorset really is a chapel, even though it hardly looks like one, with its square layout, but it is thought that when it was built in the twelfth century it was primarily intended to be a lighthouse. The story goes that a pair of newly-weds were sailing away on their honeymoon when the boat hit the rocks just off the Head, and both of them were drowned. The bride's father was on

St Catherine's Chapel (below) was built to serve as a lighthouse, but the light on the roof was replaced by a cross. There is still a hole in the central pillar (below left) where young women dropped in a pin and wished for a husband.

the Head to wave them goodbye, and he had to watch helplessly as the boat went down. He put up this building on the site where he stood, and arranged that a light would always be kept burning on the centre of its pyramid-shaped roof, so that other mariners would be saved from the same fate.

It is not known how long the light was maintained, but a quite different tradition grew up over the centuries, which may or may not be connected with that tragic bridal couple. Young women used to drop a pin into a hole in the central pillar and wish for a husband, 'or at least the happy consummation of whatever they have most at heart', as one historian delicately words it. This hint of the supernatural led to it being called the Devil's Chapel, something which its founder could hardly have foreseen. For a period in the last century it fell into disuse, except as a store and even as a

A reminder of Brunel's Biggest Boob: a pumping station at Starcross for his ill-starred 'atmospheric railway'.

stable, but the pin-dropping continued, to the obvious disgust of a 1901 correspondent of the *Church Times*:

'When visiting the building on two occasions last August, about a dozen pins were noticed in the aperture, which is not to be wondered at, since all the cheap guidebooks exploit its fame in this direction. On my last visit a young lady, apparently of some refinement and education, entered the fabric, at once proceeded to the pinhole and deposited her contribution, at the same moment closing her eyes with a rapt expression of countenance, whilst her lips moved as she mutely made her wish.'

Happily the chapel has now been restored to its original purpose as a place of worship and regular services are held in it. The round stone on the centre of the roof, originally intended for a beacon, is now surmounted by a cross.

Further along the coast, at **Starcross** in South Devon, is a prosaic-looking building which has also been used as a chapel in its time, but recently it had a depressing period as a coal depot, and is currently a museum. Originally it was part of a disastrous project dreamed up in one of his off-moments by the great railway engineer Isambard Kingdom Brunel. His plan was to build a railway system from Exeter to Totnes on which the trains would be powered by atmospheric pressure. It sounded marvellous – no smoke, no smell, very little noise, and economical to run. Go ahead, said the bosses of the Great Western Railway, and here is a quarter of a million pounds to pay for it . . .

In the 1840s that was enough to cover the laying of the track and the erection of ten large pumping stations along the route. A pipe ran between the rails, connected to the pumping stations, with a slot along the top covered by leather flaps. A piston under the train fitted into the slot, and this was literally sucked along the pipe. After it had passed, the leather flaps would close the gap again and make it airtight. Or so said Isambard Kingdom Brunel.

The trials were a great success. Trains reached speeds of seventy miles per hour hauling a load of twenty-eight tons. Back in the boardroom of the Great Western Railway, the cigars began to circulate – and no doubt, down in Devon, Isambard had a puff or two as well.

Alas, the celebrations were premature. It was the leather flaps which caused the problem; they just could not make the pipe airtight after the train had gone through. So Isambard put out his cigar and spent another quarter of a million trying to sort things out. The leather was affected by climate and the salt sea air, so he employed scores of men along the track to keep the flaps greased. Even if it had worked, it would have obviously been impractical to keep them there indefinitely, but in any case the grease proved a great attraction for the local rat population, and they added to the confusion by gnawing away the flaps.

In 1848 Mr Brunel finally admitted defeat. The puffing of smoke returned – not cigars, but steam engines. The rather gloomy building at Starcross, once a pumping station on England's only atmospheric railway, is about all that remains of his ill-starred adventure – 'a shabby memorial,' as one writer put it, 'to a great man's expensive failure.'

Most buildings with dual careers have experienced them one after the other, but a few have combined two different careers simultaneously. All Saints' Church at **Dale Abbey** in Derbyshire, for example, is claimed to be the only church in England which shares its roof with a farmhouse which was formerly a pub. This cosy arrangement dates back to the fifteenth century, when half the building was the abbey infirmary and the other half was its chapel. There were connecting doors on both floors; the upper one led into the chapel gallery, so that patients on that floor could be carried through to join in the service taking place below.

There was a rather jolly period long after the abbey was dissolved, when the infirmary was transformed into a pub called the Blue Bell. On Sundays the clerics robed in

The church building at Dale Abbey is part church, part farmhouse. Originally the house was the abbey infirmary; patients were carried into the church through connecting doors.

the pub and entered the church through the downstairs door. No doubt after the service the congregation would have liked to follow them back through this handy short cut to the bar, but I suspect they had to take the long way round, so the vicar could get in the first pint.

Even if the Blue Bell were still functioning, the temptation is no longer there – the door was blocked up in the 1920s. The church, however, is still in regular use, and apart from the lighting and heating, the interior has hardly altered for more than three hundred years. A Jacobean cupboard

It may look like a terraced cottage, but the little arched window gives a hint . . .

. . . Inside is the Buckler's Hard chapel, with an altar donated by Lord Montagu of Beaulieu, and an epitaph composed by Sir James Barrie and Winston Churchill.

is still used as the Communion table, the slightly askew pulpit dates from 1634, and some of the old box pews still face in the other direction, a convenient arrangement for parishioners inclined to drop off during the sermon.

At **Buckler's Hard** in Hampshire there is a similar combination on a smaller scale, a chapel inside an eighteenth-century cottage. The cottage saw several other activities during its long existence, first as a cobbler's shop, then reputedly a smugglers' den, and after that, more respectably, as a dame's school. When the school closed in 1885 the Vicar of Beaulieu held services there from time to time, and one room was consecrated to become a chapel dedicated to the Blessed Virgin Mary.

It had some powerful patrons. Lady Poole of Bucklerswood House did much to beautify it in the 1920s, and Lord Montagu of Beaulieu donated the altar from his private chapel at Ditton Park. A statue of the Virgin Mary, made in France in the seventeenth century, was the gift of Sir Forbes Lancaster, and presumably it was Lord Montagu again who presented a block of wood from Beaulieu Abbey, reputed to be the monks' chopping block. That may sound a little gruesome, but they used it in the kitchen, of course, not for executions. The chapel has another distinguished connection: the inscription on the memorial to Lady Poole and her son was written by Sir Winston Churchill and Sir James Barrie.

Another cottage which fulfils an ecclesiastical role stands outside the churchyard at **Penshurst** in Kent. It is raised on posts between two other cottages to form a lychgate; everyone entering the churchyard has to pass beneath it. It dates back to the sixteenth century or earlier, and is somewhat on the small side for a cottage, but the infallible architectural historian Pevsner certainly refers to it as such, although more recent experts call it just an archway. Either way, it provides a unique and attractive entrance to the churchyard. In fact, the little enclave in which it stands, known confusingly as Leicester Square, provides what Kent County Council describes with unusual lyricism as 'a desirable pause for contemplation between the common thoroughfare and the consecrated ground'. It adds rather coldly, however, that 'advertisements and other paraphernalia are particularly obtrusive on the Post Office, and some could be removed to advantage'. Nothing's perfect . . .

A cottage acts as a lychgate at Penshurst . . .

. . . and the ground floor of Luddendon's old school acted as a lock-up. Instead of 'Boys' and 'Girls' the doorways are inscribed 'Warley' and 'Midgley' – a cell for each parish.

'The Ramsgate Home for Smack Boys' – not nautical whipping-boys, but homeless youngsters who worked on the fishing smacks. This was the only establishment of its kind in England, and the only home they knew.

The lock-up, consisting of two cells, was on the ground floor and the school was above. The cells were mainly used to accommodate Saturday night drunks until they came before the magistrates on Monday. There is a word carved over each door opening off the road, and as they are just below the schoolroom one rather expects them to be 'Boys' and 'Girls', but they actually say 'Warley' and 'Midgley'. The boundary between these two parishes ran through the middle of the building, and presumably Warley wrongdoers were put in the Warley cell, and Midgley miscreants went in the other. No doubt they had a reciprocal arrangement if one parish had a particularly wild Saturday night.

With the building of a new school in Luddendon, this one was due to come on the market in the summer of 1993. There ought to be a prize for anyone who can think what to do with a disused school-room with cells . . .

The notice on the castellated building by the quayside at **Ramsgate** in Kent does refer to boys, though they no longer occupy it. These days it houses two firms of shipping agents, but when it was opened in 1881, next to the Sailors' Home, it was, as the sign still says, 'the Ramsgate Home for Smack

There is no doubt about the dual identity of the building which stands near the church at **Luddendon** in West Yorkshire. I am not sure if the idea was to disguise a lock-up as a school, or disguise a school as a lock-up, or just to save space and expense, but both functions were catered for when the joint establishment of correction and education was built in 1825.

Boys'. The name can be confusing, not only because the last of the smack boys left during the First World War, but because non-seafarers may think that a smack boy is the nautical equivalent of a whipping boy. The smack in this case, of course, is not a clip around the ear but a clipper round the fishing-grounds, on which the smack boys did the odd jobs while the men did the fishing. Not that the other kind of smack was unknown. The boys had a tough time at sea, and before the Home was built, they had a tough time ashore as well. Most of them were homeless and slept where they could. The Ramsgate Home for Smack Boys, the only one of its kind in the country, was the only home they knew.

After buildings with double lives, a born-again boat. There are examples in other chapters of bits of boats which have been converted into pulpits and memorials, and any number of boats have become floating restaurants or hotels, but a complete narrowboat from the Shropshire Union Canal has finished up on dry land as the bar of a pub. Alongside the canal at **Audlem** in Cheshire is an eighteenth-century mill which itself has undergone a change of life; it has been combined with the narrowboat to become the Shroppie Fly.

The name has no connection with insects or aviators. Shropshire fly-boats, or Shroppie flies, were narrowboats designed for speed, so they could get perishable goods to their destinations as fast as possible. The mill was one of the loading points, and the old loading crane still stands on the waterside. The fly-boats went out of business when the railways arrived with their much faster freight trains, but this is one of the few flies to land, as it were, on its feet.

Finally a building in Lincolnshire which has beggared description ever since it was built, so elaborate is its disguise. It has been called 'a sham castle . . . spidery and vegetable-like', 'a very singular but tasty and handsome residence', 'grotesque but

A Shropshire fly-boat finds a final safe harbour; in the Shroppie Fly Inn at Audlem.

not inelegant', 'a gnarled and scrunched-up facade', or more simply, 'ugly and grotesque – the place gives me the creeps even to look at it'.

You could argue that all these descriptions are accurate. The Jungle, near **Eagle** in Lincolnshire, might be mistaken for a ruined abbey, a prison, or just another extravagant folly. The one thing it does not look like is what it actually is – a luxury mansion originally built for a man who preferred the company of animals to people. Samuel Russell Collett kept a private zoo of kangaroos, deer and buffalo, and he may well have chosen the site for the Jungle because it lay between villages called Eagle and Swinethorpe.

Collett probably designed it with the dual purpose of embellishing his zoo and discouraging visitors, and it must have been highly effective on both counts. Gnarled wooden window frames made from oak branches formed into Gothic arches, over-burnt bricks built in forbidding black blocks, jagged outlines and uneven walls, the whole thing smothered in ivy – when you knock on the lozenge-shaped door you expect it to be opened by Quasimodo. Yet beyond that door is a sumptuous mansion, far more luxurious than its original owner could ever have imagined when he built his own house behind this bizarre facade in 1820. It became a farmhouse after his death, then lay derelict for years until it was bought by Dennis and Audrey Houlston in 1965. They demolished the old house, all except for its astonishing front wall.

By 1976 they had built nine projecting bays and two towers behind it, and by 1984 a swimming-pool wing had been added, with a jacuzzi, sauna and solarium, and a snooker room upstairs. City dwellers are all too familiar with the concrete jungle, but this is a lap-of-luxury Jungle, just as over-whelming in its own way as Samuel Collett's original frontage. I think his animals may have suited it rather better.

It might be straight out of a Grimm's Fairy Tale, but it was built like that by a man who preferred animals to people. He called it The Jungle and kept a private zoo. The house itself has been rebuilt, but its bizarre façade remains.

Buildings that moved with the times

Buildings that moved with the times

Moving house is something that most of us have done at some stage in our lives, and a very traumatic business it can be, but on 12 December 1961, the phrase acquired a much more literal meaning for the towns-folk of **Exeter**. They were able to watch a house actually being moved bodily for a hundred yards up Edmund Street – and not just any old house but a very old house indeed, a timber-framed veteran dating back to about 1430 and believed to be one of the oldest of its kind in the world.

There is, of course, nothing new about the idea of moving houses, or even entire villages. In *Timpson's England* I quoted a number of early examples, where the Lord of the Manor decided he did not like the village where it was. But their idea of 'moving' a building was just to demolish it and build a new one elsewhere. Occasionally they used bits of the original structure, but mostly they started from scratch.

The removal of a building in one piece had in fact been done before the Exeter operation. Back in the 1860s, when a new Methodist chapel was built at **Melton** in Suffolk, a neighbour established that it infringed his rights of ancient lights, and rather than demolish it, the enterprising Methodists jacked it up on tree trunks and rolled it down the road for eighteen feet, until the neighbour was satisfied. While the chapel was being trundled along to its new site, one of the more experienced chapel-shifters stood in the pulpit, as if on the bridge of a ship, to help direct operations – and perhaps augmenting his technical expertise with a few well-chosen prayers.

The chapel was brand-new and appar-ently had no difficulty in standing up to the journey. The Merchant's House in **Exeter**, however, was a very different proposition. As well as being over five centuries old it stood three storeys high, each storey over-hanging the one beneath it, and it was already in a semi-derelict state. The Tudor workmen who erected it could hardly have expected it to be still standing after so long, let alone fit enough to undergo a transplant. The operation was a triumph of ingenuity over gravity, and the fact that it happened at all was a triumph of conservation over the march of progress.

The old house stood in the path of Exeter's new inner bypass, and the City Council planned to demolish it, but the preservationists went into action. Among them was a Mr Henry Budd of Tedburn St Mary, who wrote a letter to the local paper so eloquently phrased that even the most materialistic councillor must have felt a twinge of conscience.

'Sir,' it began, 'Because man's upward march is not axiomatic, and must be planned, worked for, and aspired to, and because man is readily responsive to his environment, it is in the interest of society that the preservation and creation of beau-tiful things should be fostered, and perpetu-ation of the ugly and vulgar discouraged.'

Even in decay, wrote Mr Budd, the house was a thing of beauty, making a mute appeal for aid. 'It is possible that the requirements of modern traffic demand the few paltry square feet on which this fugitive from a previous century now stands, but re-erection elsewhere would present no insu-perable difficulty.

'Somewhere in the ancient city of Exeter there is a board, a committee, or maybe a person responsible for the preservation of the historic and the beautiful. If this little house is allowed to disappear, there is a strong case for the setting up of a gallows on the site . . .'

The gallows was not required. Mr Budd's appeal, backed by many others, was heard, not only locally, but by the then Minister of Housing and Local Government, the redoubtable Dr Charles Hill, remembered affectionately by many Home Service listeners as the BBC's Radio Doctor, and renowned for his solicitous breakfast-time enquiries about the state of our bowels. Dr Hill was later Lord Hill of Luton, and there was little he could do to save Luton, but he slapped a preservation order on the Merchant's House, authorised a government grant of £7,000, and told the City Council to go ahead and move it.

The City Council was not entirely over-joyed. One councillor described it as 'a gigantic waste of money'; another said that,

'The House that Moved' – all in one piece. It travelled on a timber chassis from its original site in Exeter where it had stood for over five hundred years.

Cirencester's domed lock-up, known irreverently as the Dumpling House, was moved piece by piece to the workhouse to serve as a 'refractory ward'. Now it is a mini-museum.

even after it was moved and restored, hardly anyone would bother to go and see it. But Dr Hill was not a man to be thwarted, and the project went ahead.

It was quite a project. First the house was shored up and enclosed in an enormous wooden packing case. Then it was lifted on to a timber chassis on wheels, which had hydraulic legs so that the house could be tilted to remain vertical as it went up the hill. The gradient was one-in-ten in places, and with its overhanging storeys the house was so top-heavy it could well have tipped over. As it was hauled off its site on the corner of Frog Street the wheels were set into iron channels which had been laid the length of Edmund Street, to its new location near the line of the old city wall. In case passers-by could not believe their eyes an explanatory notice was hung on it: 'House Moving'. As it set off, a dazed mouse was observed peering out of a hole in its unexpectedly mobile home . . .

Two winches were used to haul it at first, but it was found that the old structure was travelling too fast for safety, and rather than risk the first speeding ticket to be issued to a house, one winch was disconnected. The pace slowed to a gentle twenty yards an hour, and apart from sawing off a projecting piece of timber which caught in the kerb, the journey was completed without further incident. The Merchant's House was safely installed on its new site, in due course it was fully restored, and it

still stands there today, a dramatic example of how even a five-hundred-year-old Tudor house can move with the times . . .

It set a precedent which has been followed more than once since. A medieval house in **Sudbury**, Suffolk, was also pulled up a hill to a new location, not to avoid demolition, but simply to give its owner a better view over the top of a new estate. Another wooden building, an old granary at **Goodwood** in West Sussex, was lifted bodily by crane on to a trailer and taken to a museum several miles away. As the granary was twenty-five feet long and weighed over five tons, it could well have won the title for the Most Unlikely Abnormal Load.

The more popular method of physically moving a building, however, was to take it to bits and put it together again. For instance, yet another timbered house, but this time an imitation Tudor mansion built in 1891 for Robert Hudson, the soap manufacturer, was moved from Birkenhead to **Frankby** in the Wirral, after it was bought by Sir Ernest Royden some forty years later. It was several times too big to fit on any trailer, and no winches could have budged it, so Sir Ernest had it dismantled, transported in pieces, and re-erected. In more recent years, of course, Americans have done much the same thing with all manner of ancient English structures – not least, London Bridge.

One of the earliest instances of a building being moved in this way happened in **Cirencester**, Gloucestershire, in about 1837. It was not a house, nor a bridge, but a lock-up – though a much more imposing one than those little village green lock-ups, designed to hold just one malefactor with a tight squeeze for swinging his cat. This was a more substantial affair, sixteen feet long and eight feet wide, with walls eight feet high and a curious curved roof like a very large bowler hat, prompting the locals to christen it irreverently 'The Dumpling House'. It had a couple of two-inch-thick doors leading into separate cells and iron-grated, barred windows at each end.

The lock-up was built near the centre of Cirencester in 1805 at a cost of £60, including £4.10s for the two oak doors, 'with iron studs, hinges, and locks to ditto', and it functioned there for the next thirty years. At first the town only had watchmen, but in the 1820s they were upgraded to constables, their numbers were increased – and the criminal fraternity increased too. The Town Commissioners decided that the lock-up was not big enough to cope, 'and cannot be improved without still being a nuisance or annoyance to the public'. It recommended removing the building to a timber yard, but a better idea cropped up. A workhouse was being built in the south-west of the town, and the Board of Guardians agreed that the lock-up would make an admirable 'refractory ward' for the inmates – in other words, a punishment cell.

The blocks of limestone forming the walls were dismantled and rebuilt next to the workhouse, a fairly straightforward task, but the domed roof must have presented problems. With its bowler hat shape, I like to visualise a little army of workmen marching down the street with the roof resting on their heads, like a multi-legged commercial for Homepride . . .

The Dumpling House served as a refractory ward until the workhouse was smartened up a bit after the last war and renamed a geriatric hospital. The little domed building then began a new career as a boilerhouse, but in 1975 it became redundant and started to deteriorate rapidly. In 1979, however, the old workhouse became the headquarters of Costwold District Council, and new brooms swept in. An inspection of the ageing ex-boilerhouse, ex-refractory ward, ex-lock-up, showed that the stonework had decayed, repairs had been carried out with the wrong materials, and some of the original blocks of limestone had actually been re-laid in the wrong positions when the building was moved. The Council shook its head sadly and shored it up, pending demolition.

But the demolition never took place; the Council was refused permission to knock it down because it was a Grade II listed building. So they decided to restore it instead, and in 1984 it began a new and more up-market existence as a miniature museum. These days, to keep in the fashion, it is called a heritage centre, which might raise a wry smile among its former inmates, let alone all those who knew it as the Dumpling House.

At the other end of the moved-building spectrum are the quite considerable number of churches which, for one reason or another, have been transported either entirely or partly to a new site. According to ancient ecclesiastical law, a church could be moved but not its chancel, and one illustration of this is Selsey Parish Church in West Sussex, which started off in **Church Norton** but is now mostly in **Selsey** village

The chancel of Church Norton church was left behind when the rest of the building was moved to Selsey. It is back in business again as St Wilfred's Chapel.

The chancel of Sidmouth Church was going to be demolished, until Peter Orlando Hutchinson bought it and attached it to his own house.

– just the chancel was left behind. Its original site was always fairly remote, from the days when Rudyard Kipling's seventh-century priest Eddi held a midnight service there on Christmas Eve, and only the animals turned up. In Victorian times only a few big landowners lived in that area, while most of the parishioners lived in the village, over two miles away, and in 1864 the congregation decided it was fed up with this lengthy pilgrimage to church each Sunday, and rebelled.

Happily the rector, the Revd Henry Foster, was entirely on their side. He reckoned it was this long trek which kept his congregation down to a hundred, out of a total population of nine hundred. It is a percentage that any rural parson today might envy, but in 1864 it put him near the bottom of the league table. He and his flock therefore decided to raise £600 towards moving the church to a more convenient site. Even in those days, £600 would hardly have moved one wall, but the remaining £3,000, plus a new site at the top of the village, was donated by the Lady of the Manor, the Hon. Mrs Vernon-Harcourt, heiress to the last Lord Selsey. This was

extremely civil of her, since presumably all her land-owner friends at Church Norton had the long journey to church instead of the villagers, but no doubt they could manage the odd carriage between them.

The demolition began straight away, and as the walls came down the stones were carried on farm carts to the new site, and re-erected. A new chancel was added and the church was consecrated in 1886. Back at Church Norton the chancel, now just a chapel, was forsaken by its congregation and allowed to deteriorate – 'derelict, unhappy, a home for bats and owls'. However, in 1905 a church in Chichester was pulled down and its rector gave twelve oak pews and a Communion table to refurbish the little building. The roof was repaired and the walls painted, and by 1917 St Wilfred's Chapel was back in business again. Services are still held there about six times a year, including one on St Wilfred's Day, October 12. So, in effect, Selsey acquired two churches for little more than the price of one.

Quite the reverse happened at **Sidmouth** in Devon in 1859. Sidmouth Church's medieval chancel, containing some fine

fifteenth-century glass, was due to be demolished as part of a restoration plan. A local archaeologist and historian, Peter Orlando Hutchinson, came to its rescue.

Mr Hutchinson was an enterprising as well as a determined campaigner. When his local efforts failed, he petitioned Queen Victoria to grant the chapel a Royal Pardon. It is even said that when he heard the Queen and Prince Albert were in residence at Osborne House on the Isle of Wight, he donned his uniform of an officer in the Devon Artillery Volunteers, made his way to Osborne, and managed to get into the Royal presence. Perhaps his unfamiliar uniform confused her entourage into thinking he was a visiting ambassador from a distant corner of the Empire. Alas, Queen Victoria was not amused, and he returned to Sidmouth a frustrated man.

But not for long. Just as the local council had appointed a demolition contractor to knock down the chancel, Peter Orlando Hutchinson played his last card. He put up the money himself to buy the chancel, lock stock and fifteenth-century window. His offer was accepted and he had the chancel dismantled, each stone was numbered, and

it was re-erected in his garden just up the road, forming a new wing to his house. From then on he had a high old time refurbishing it, even adding a bell-pull which, instead of ringing a bell, produced the notes of an organ. Today the Old Chancel, as it is called is still a private house, but its owner often opens it to the public.

The most common reason for moving a church is because its congregation has moved already. For instance, St Andrew's Church in **Kingsbury**, Middlesex, was originally built in 1847 just off Oxford Street in London's West End. Most of the local residents, however, moved to the suburbs after the First World War as the area became more commercialised, and in 1933 the church followed them.

In that case the church moved fairly promptly after the congregation, but in Norfolk, where most things take a little longer anyway, some five centuries passed before the parish church at **Edgefield** caught up with the rest of the village. The Black Death of 1349 caused many rural communities in Norfolk to evacuate their villages and build new homes some distance away. The church, often the only

Edgefield Church was moved a mile to be more convenient for the village – and the rector . . .

solid stone building in the village and by far the biggest, was left behind. At Edgefield, therefore, the Church of St Peter and St Paul remained behind in a valley while the rest of the village was moved to higher ground about a mile away.

For five hundred years the villagers trooped back into the valley for their church services, just like many other Black Death villages, but this was not good enough for a remarkable Victorian rector called Canon Walter Herbert Marcon. He was born in Edgefield Rectory, returned as rector in 1875, and remained there until he died in 1937, in the same bedroom in which he was born. He had not been rector long before he decided that something had to be done about the church. It was not just the inconvenience of the site; the building itself was in a sorry state.

. . . only the original tower remains on the old site.

'Its broken and moss-covered walls, its miserable seating, its chancel arch with a threatening bend in it, the wretched altar old and stained, its font with only its Early English bowl remaining, without pedestal or foot-space, were enough to try the stoutest heart,' he wrote. Many other rural rectors must know how he felt.

Two years after his induction as rector he applied for a faculty and started raising the money to move and restore the church. The Marchioness of Lothian gave him a new site near the centre of the village, and a notable Victorian architect, John Dando Sedding, was put in charge.

However, the project was not without opposition. A quite inaccurate rumour was spread that the graves and headstones would be damaged if the church was removed – and few things rouse the passions of Norfolk villagers more than the possibility of a tombstone being tampered with. A written objection was sent to the Bishop, but as is often the case in such protests, many of those who signed it were not villagers, none of them belonged to the church, and according to Canon Marcon, several of the signatures were in the same handwriting. They had also omitted to give a name and address to reply to. The Bishop, who was doubtless just as shrewd about such things as the Canon, disregarded the objection, and the work went ahead.

The main body of the church, with its fourteenth-century piers and arches, was dismantled and re-erected; only the chancel and tower were left behind. The medieval rood-screen and parclose screen, the monuments on the walls, and the oldest item of all, the font bowl, were all reinstated. Sedding built a simple new chancel and designed a new altar to replace the 'wretched' one. The rebuilt and restored church was consecrated in 1884.

There have been further additions since. A square-sided tower was built twenty-five years later, in contrast to the original octagonal one which still stands on its old site, next to a farmyard. The pews came from a redundant school chapel and the local schoolmaster designed new churchyard gates, incorporating the keys of St Peter and the sword of St Paul. For me, though, the most delightful feature is the stained glass window which was installed in 1984 to mark the centenary of the consecration. It

features Canon Marcon himself, in his long black cassock and neat little hat, riding his old bone-shaker bicycle to the church. The window is a reminder, among other things, that few have achieved such a dramatic method of reducing their mileage to work, as the man who moved Edgefield Church.

Most moved churches have retained their identities, but a very strange metamorphosis took place in a church which was moved from Wareham to **Dorchester**, Dorset, in 1907. It started its life as a monastery church, built by a Roman Catholic sect called the Passionists, a name derived from the theme of their preaching, Christ's passion and death. They arrived in Wareham in 1888, and two years later the church was opened and dedicated to St Michael. They actually got the building for nothing; a wealthy London couple who were friends of the Order paid the bill.

The Passionists, however, did not arouse much passion in Wareham, and in 1906 they decided to move on. They put their premises on the market, and a Catholic priest in Dorchester, whose congregation was growing, heard that a church was going spare and asked if he could have it. The building was duly dismantled, and the stones were numbered and transported by horse and cart to Dorchester, sixteen miles away. They were reassembled on a site in the main street, and the church was re-dedicated to Our Lady, Queen of Martyrs, as well as St Michael, in memory of six local Catholics who were put to death during the Reformation.

There it served the Catholic community for nearly seventy years, but the congregation continued to grow, and by the 1970s this church too had become too small. The current Catholic priest struck lucky again.

A Wareham church (above left) was transported by horse and cart to Dorchester for use by the Roman Catholics. Since then it has moved through time instead of space: its interior has been converted into a replica of the Tomb of Tutankhamun, complete with a copy of the Ancient Egyptian king's mummy (above).

Part of the Tutankhamun
exhibition in the former
catholic Church of Our
Lady, Queen of Martyrs,
and St Michael.

A local Anglican church, Holy Trinity, became redundant, and he took it over. Our Lady, Queen of Martyrs, and St Michael was left empty and forsaken, far from its original home, and its days, like its stones, seemed to be numbered. It might have ended as a crumbling ruin, in a corner of some foreign Dorchester field that would be for ever Wareham, but after eleven years the old place found itself transported again, not through Dorset but through time.

The building was taken over by a body called World Heritage, and its interior was converted into a complete replica of the Tomb of Tutankhamun. Instead of entering a Catholic church visitors find themselves following in the footsteps of Howard Carter, who discovered the real tomb in 1922 – except that Howard Carter did not have the benefit of a running commentary.

The exhibition opened in 1987, and in 1992 World Heritage added the final touch, an accurate facsimile of Tutankhamun's mummy, made from a real skeleton filled out with organic-substitute flesh and covered with animal skin. Anything more

unlikely in a former Roman Catholic church is difficult to imagine, and what the Passionists would have thought of it, goodness knows. But they would have been forewarned by the notice outside; instead of 'Prepare to Meet Thy God', it says, 'Come Face to Face with the King's Mummy'. I suspect the old church rather wished it had never left Wareham.

A commemorative cross may seem difficult to justify as a moved building, but the Bristol High Cross qualifies on three counts. First, it is not just a cross but a substantial monument. Second, it is very high indeed, much higher than most ordinary buildings, so the problems of moving it were just as great. And third, it did indeed move, for quite a considerable distance; in 1765 it was transported piece by piece to the famous Stourhead Gardens at **Stourton** in Wiltshire, after four hundred years in its home city.

The High Cross was erected in 1373 to mark the granting of a charter by King Edward III, and its design is reminiscent of the Eleanor Crosses which his ancestor

King Edward I erected along the route of his wife's funeral procession. The tall pointed spire has niches containing statues, not of Queen Eleanor, but of other assorted sovereigns who had connections with Bristol, from King John to Charles I. The Cross had to have an extra section added to accommodate the last four, and if the practice had continued, then our current Queen would be perched high enough to be a danger to low-flying aircraft.

So far as its neighbours were concerned, however, the Cross was already too high for comfort. In 1733 a silversmith who lived opposite complained to the authorities that it shook so much in high winds that his

was dismantled and dumped in the Guildhall cellars.

It lay there for three years, until some local dignitaries raised funds to re-erect it on College Green, near the cathedral. But it still had its enemies, in this case a Mr Wallis, who wanted it moved so he could 'make well the footpaths'. Another fund was opened, this time to improve the footpaths and move the Cross to 'any unexceptional place', but unexceptional places were apparently in short supply, and in 1762 all the money was spent on the footpaths, while the Cross again finished up in pieces. As the sympathetic historian put it: 'It was obliged to lay low its spiral summit, and the

The High Cross started its career in 1373 in the heart of Bristol; now it has found a more peaceful home at Stourhead Gardens.

house and life was threatened. One historian notes sadly that 'from this and other trifling objections, this beautiful memorial of gratitude' and antiquity was taken down and thrown aside as useless lumber'.

The deciding factor, it seems, was that it created a traffic hazard at a principal crossroads in the City. The council had no compunction about removing what it called 'a ruinous and superstitious Relick which is at present a public nuisance', and the Cross

disjointed fragments were thrown carelessly aside' – this time inside the cathedral.

This was hardly a satisfactory arrangement, either for the Cross or the cathedral, but happily a new Dean was appointed who knew Henry Hoare, creator of the Stourhead Gardens. Hoare agreed it would make a pleasant addition to the gardens, and it was rescued once again, taken to Stourhead in two wagons, and re-erected in its original form, except that the base was

The Wandering Windmill of Lacey Green used to stand in Lowndes Park, but the Duke of Buckingham may have thought it spoilt his view. It is the oldest smock mill still standing – but it stands in a different place.

made solid and an iron bar was inserted from top to bottom to strengthen it. That kindly historian should have the last word:

'Notwithstanding its repeated dilapidation and removals, it is surprising to behold it all in existence. So beautiful and captivating is its appearance, that I wish I could assume the authority of a prophet and exclaim: "Esto perpetua!" '

Its existence may not be perpetual but that was written 170 years ago, and the Bristol High Cross stands at Stourton still.

It might be stretching things a bit to include old windmills among buildings that moved, if it were merely on the grounds

that a large part of them, the sails, were constantly on the move, and postmills did move in their entirety to face the wind, albeit on the same spot. But there are one or two which really did move completely from one site to another. At **Thorpeness** in Suffolk, for example, just opposite the disguised water tower known as the House in the Clouds, there is an old postmill which started life at Aldringham, a few miles away. Stuart Ogilvie, who created one of the earliest and certainly one of the most unusual holiday camps at Thorpeness in 1922, acquired it partly to pump water and partly as an attraction for his guests.

Another old wooden mill was moved in Buckinghamshire, for a rather different reason. It was built in 1650 in Lowndes Park, Chesham, the home of the Dukes of Buckingham, and it is the oldest smock mill still standing – but it no longer stands in Lowndes Park. In 1821 the current Duke ordered it to be moved, some say because it needed extensive repairs and might as well be moved to a windier site before being restored, while others hint that he just thought it spoilt the view. It was replanted in a field at **Lacey Green**, about ten miles away, and the locals christened it the Wandering Windmill.

It functioned there for nearly a century, but when the First World War started it fell into disuse, and it stayed in the doldrums until the 1970s. At one time it served as a weekend cottage, during the last war the Home Guard used it as a watch-tower, and later it was a store for farm implements. Meanwhile all but one of its sails disappeared, the fantail went missing too, and finally the whole structure became so dilapidated it seemed likely to collapse. Then the Chiltern Society came to the rescue, strongly supported by Sir Bernard Miles, who lived nearby, and after twelve years' work the restoration was completed in 1983. The Wandering Windmill now looks as elegant as it did nearly 350 years ago when it started life in Lowndes Park.

Drivers entering East Anglia from the north-west, on the A17 trunk road, will be familiar with the sight of one of England's most remarkable windmills, the eight-sailed tower mill at **Heckington**. Only seven mills were built in England with that many sails, and this is now the only place you can see one. But if you had been travelling before

1891 you would have had to turn on to the Boston road and continue for another twenty-odd miles to enjoy that experience. While part of the shell of the Heckington mill has always been there, the entire mill machinery, including the eight sails, was brought from another mill at Skirbeck, on the outskirts of Boston.

The original Heckington Mill was built in 1830 with only five sails. After passing through various hands it was put up for auction in 1890, but shortly before the sale a violent storm smashed the sails, tore off part of the tower and wrecked the machinery. The auction went ahead, but understandably nobody showed much interest; the bidding only reached £340, and the last bid came from the Nash family, who already owned it. The Nashes no doubt did a little gnashing themselves, then cut their losses and abandoned the place.

Meanwhile the eight-sailed mill at Skirbeck was also falling on hard times. It was built in 1813 by a family whose firm made ironwork for mills and farm machinery. The business declined and was sold up in 1891, including the mill, and this was bought by an enterprising young baker called John Pocklington for £72 10s. It was a very low price, even for those days, so for John Pocklington that was the good news; the bad news was that he had not the remotest idea what to do with it – and part of the deal was that it had to be cleared from the site.

By a happy coincidence, one of the Nash family bumped into him soon afterwards at Boston market, and the two of them talked windmills. By the end of that day Pocklington had bought the shell at Heckington, along with the bakehouse and a parcel of land, for £250. He and his wife and three children moved into a rented cottage while he stripped down the Skirbeck mill, transferred all the parts to Heckington, and rebuilt everything there. He was just twenty-six years old.

Even today a complete set of mill machinery and eight massive sails would rate as an abnormal load. On rough Victorian country roads, using horse-drawn

More like a Catharine wheel than a windmill, perhaps: Heckington's eight-sailed mill. The massive sails and the mill machinery were hauled from Skirbeck on double waggons.

drays, it was very abnormal indeed. The 'Iron Cross', the main chunk of machinery, weighed five tons and was nearly twelve feet across. The traffic was stopped in Boston to allow it through, and when it got out into the country the dray sank axle-deep in the mud, and the horses had to stop every hundred yards for a rest. When darkness fell, Pocklington's men had to stay overnight with a friendly farmer, and next morning an extra horse was brought to add pulling power.

The sails presented a different problem. They were thirty-four feet long and needed two drays to carry them. Boston's narrow streets were not designed for double-harness drays, and on one sharp corner there was just an inch of clearance on either side, but Pocklington and his sails got through. In due course the Skirbeck machinery was installed in the Heckington shell, the Skirbeck cap was fitted above the Skirbeck machinery, and the Skirbeck sails were put on the Skirbeck cap. When John Pocklington set it all going in 1892, to all intents and purposes it was Skirbeck mill back in action again.

When he died in 1941 his son took over, but business had declined. The shutters were taken off the sails for the duration of the war, and were not replaced. The County Council bought the mill in 1953, and in due course it was restored, with the help of the Friends of the Mill. The founder of the Friends was Ron Pocklington, grandson of the man who brought it to Heckington a hundred years ago.

Incidentally, its removal from Skirbeck did not leave the Boston area bereft of mills. It has the five-sailed Maud Foster Mill, the tallest working windmill in Britain, and further north is **Sibsey** Trader Mill, one of the last six-sailed mills. At one time there were 350 tower mills in Lincolnshire alone, but these days, instead of elegant shuttered sails set on stone or brick towers, these much-loved landmarks of the English countryside are being superseded by 'wind-farms', clusters of gaunt metal poles surmounted by over-sized propellors.

Yes, windmills have moved with the times – and in many ways, more's the pity.

Sibsey Trader Mill, one of the last six-sailed mills in the country.

Their home is their castle – but preferably with knobs on

Their home is their castle – but preferably with knobs on

An Englishman is not always content for his home to be just his castle; he often adds personal touches to make sure it is quite a different castle from everybody else's. Even in these days of vast, anonymous housing estates, we still like to add a bit of trellis here, a false window-shutter there, and perhaps an instant wishing-well out the front. In the days before planning permissions and conservation areas, however, owner-occupiers were able to make much more dramatic additions to their properties. In some cases the results were quite appalling, but many of them provided an entertaining variety to the English scene,

Some say it is three miles long, but a cyclist who made the complete circuit, lifting his bike over a kissing-gate, three stiles and a field-gate en route, clocked it at just on two. Even so, it still holds the record, which is all the more remarkable because it is reputed to have been built by just one bricklayer; he finished the task a very old man.

Nobody is certain who started building walls like this, but one theory is that they originated on the Continent and were introduced to England by French prisoners during the Napoleonic war. The great merit of crinkle-crankles is that, although they

The crinkle-crankle wall around the Easton estate is said to be the longest wiggly wall in the world.

and even the appalling ones have taken on a certain quaint charm as the years have passed by.

Take walls, for example. Most people are content to have walls which are straight, or for extra elegance perhaps gently curved. The twelfth Duke of Hamilton, however, liked his garden wall to be wiggly. In Suffolk they call it a crinkle-crankle wall, and crinkle-crankles can be found in various parts of East Anglia, plus a couple in Kent, but the Duke of Hamilton liked his to be long as well as wiggly, and the one that encircles his former estate at **Easton** in Suffolk is the longest of its kind in the world.

are only one brick thick, the design makes them very strong. It also makes them very tricky to build. They should form perfect reversed semi-circles, but according to the cycling statistician the 'waves' in the Easton wall vary considerably in length, depth and height. Maybe that lonely bricklayer needed a little variety to keep going as he walled on, walled on, with hope in his heart . . .

Over the years the Easton crinkle-crankle has had its ups and downs as well as its ins and outs. In 1978 Easton Nurseries got permission from the local council to demolish fifteen feet of it, but that was overruled by the County Council. In 1991 Suffolk Preservation Society lamented that

A Whitchurch ironmonger fronted his shop with cast-iron (far left), perhaps hoping it would make the business a cast-iron certainty – but it was sold in 1972.
The Hermitage in Bicton Gardens (left) is a bit too fancy for most hermits – the walls are covered with thousands of wooden shingles (below) . . .

'lack of maintenance for years, and the growth of shrubs, trees and undergrowth, have taken their toll, and gales too have played their part.' But the wall is now Grade II listed, making it the longest and wiggliest listed building in the country. I hope this status helps, as it were, to get it straight.

Then there are the walls of houses. Some individualists are not satisfied with the normal materials of brick and stone and stucco; how about fronting your premises with cast-iron? One of the last buildings to be adorned in this way stands in the High Street at **Whitchurch** in Shropshire. It was originally two establishments, Joyce's Clock Works (lucky old Joyce, I can't help thinking) and the Alexandra Hotel. They were both bought by an ironmonger, the front section of the hotel in 1896 and the whole of Joyce's Works in 1902. He had them rebuilt with a frontage of cast-iron extending over them both, the ironwork being transported by rail from Glasgow and erected by a local builder. He opened the business in 1904, and it remained in his family until his grandson, Mr Philip Birchall, sold the business and the property in 1972.

Mr Birchall still has the original accounts, which show that the frontage cost all of £280. After he sold the property it passed through a number of hands, and for the past seven years it has been 'empty and unwanted', as he sadly describes it.

'The Hermitage' at **Bicton** Gardens in South Devon is not a hermitage. No frugal hermit would go to all the effort and expense of facing the outside walls with thousands of tiny wooden shingles, each one pinned on separately to overlap the one

below, so they look like the scales of a massive square fish. This hermitage was built by Lady Louise Rolle in 1839 as a

. . . while the floor of the Hermitage in Bicton is made from deer's knucklebones. Parquet might have been simpler.

However, just outside Henley-on-Thames in Oxfordshire, near **Harpsden** Church, there are two barns with very exotic wooden panelling in the walls. Each panel has a different design on it, squares or diamonds, leaves or flowers, all of them very un-barnlike. A notice beneath the panels gives the game away: 'Please do not touch these old wallpaper blocks'.

They were indeed used to print wallpaper patterns, and when the paperhanging public got bored with these particular designs the blocks were made redundant. They found a new career as wall panels on a hunting lodge, and when the lodge was demolished an enterprising farmer incorporated them in his barns.

In a way these wall-blocks are a wooden version of the old art of pargeting, the decorative plasterwork which brightens up many old walls, particularly in East Anglia. There is a spectacular display of pargetry work on the rather obviously-named Ancient House in **Ipswich**, Suffolk, a town where the planners have not allowed many ancient houses to survive, so Ipswich makes the most of this one. Amidst an amazing assortment of angels, animals, coats of arms and saints – including a gentlemanly St George, wearing a top hat while he slays the dragon – there are symbolic representations of the continents. An elegant lady with an open book

rather exotic summer-house, and she didn't stop at fish-scales on the walls. The roof is made of shaped shingles too, and it has a rather impractical chimney made of oak. The inside walls are lined with basketweave wickerwork, the windows are of salvaged stained glass, and the floor consists of knucklebones of deer. There must be easier ways . . .

An ornamental garden house might be expected to have eccentric touches like this, but barns are generally much more prosaic.

Another unlikely building material: wallpaper blocks used as wooden panels in a barn wall at Harpsden.

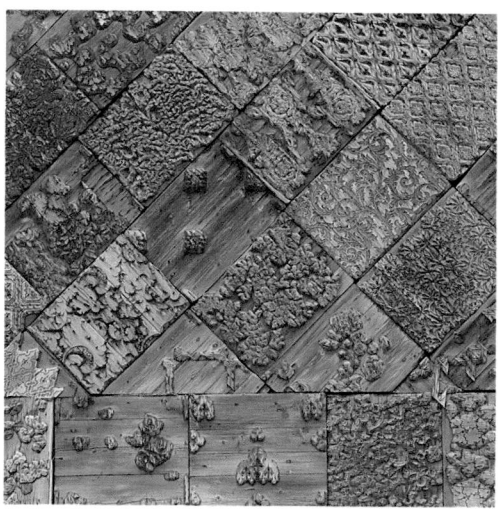

The pargetry work on the Ancient House at Ipswich includes symbols of the only four continents they knew about in 1567. (far left) This one represents Asia.

represents sophisticated Europe, another not-so-elegant lady under a palm tree represents Asia, a naked man on a tree stump symbolises Africa, and a not-quite-naked man – he has a loincloth and a feather head-dress – is America.

So what symbolises Australia, you cry? Could it be a man in shirt-sleeves and a big floppy hat, holding a can of lager? Alas, no. The Ancient House may not be all that ancient – it was built in 1567 – but even then, nobody had got around to discovering Australia, so the pargeters had to make do with the other four. These days the old place is much more knowledgeable about such things; indeed it is packed with information. It houses a bookshop . . .

For a really ancient wall decoration I commend the former school, now a private house, in **Rochester**, Northumberland. It has a porch made of stones which were originally used by the Romans to build the nearby fort of Bremenium; you may spot that some of the stones were hollowed out to use as gutters. Not all the fort was dismantled; there are still bits of it *in situ* on the village green.

As well as the porch, it is said that two round stones, weighing about a hundredweight, in the gable of the house were originally ammunition fired from a Roman spring-gun catapult. It seems unlikely that the Romans retrieved their catapult-stones like golf-balls, but maybe these came from an ammunition dump, and were never fired in anger.

Another wall decoration with Roman connections is on Llwyd Mansion, a timber-framed building in **Oswestry**, Shropshire. It is a double-headed eagle, the emblem of the Holy Roman Empire, and it originates from warfare in a rather later era. The family was granted the right to use it as

their coat of arms, as a reward for services in the Crusades.

Much more difficult to date – or indeed to spot – is a tiny heart within a diamond, carved high up on the wall of a building in

Long-term recycling: stones in this porch at Rochester were originally used by the Romans to build the fort of Breminium.

the Tuesday Market Place, **King's Lynn**, Norfolk. There are various stories attached to it, each one more bizarre than the next. The Tuesday Market was the execution place for women condemned as witches, and a favourite venue for Matthew Hopkins, the notorious Witchfinder-General. Not surprisingly, therefore, most of the stories about the heart involve witches, whether they were hanged, burnt at the stake, or in one gruesome instance, boiled. It is said that, as one woman died, her heart leapt from her body, 'refusing to submit', and embedded itself in the wall.

The name of Mary Smith crops up most frequently, sometimes as a servant girl who killed her mistress, sometimes as a glove-maker's wife who was empowered by the Devil to put curses on her neighbours. The second version seems more authentic, because there are many details handed down of whom she cursed and why. There was a sailor called John Orkton, for example, who got cursed for striking her

The heart that would not burn: it is said that when an innocent woman was burnt at the stake in the Tuesday Market Place at King's Lynn, her heart burst from her body and ended up at this wall.

son. She said his fingers and toes would drop off, and nine months later they very nearly did – they had rotted away to such an extent that they had to be amputated.

After a few more experiences of this kind the neighbours got fed up with losing bits of their anatomy and accused Mary Smith of witchcraft. She put forward the rather unhelpful defence that she had only imposed these curses because the Devil had told her to. This hardly seemed a very good excuse, and Mary was condemned to the stake. It is said, however, that she repented

overnight and went calmly to her fate, so calmly in fact that, instead of the customary catcalls and jeers, the crowd sang Psalms as the fire was lit.

The story has two alternative endings. One is that her heart burst from her body and lay beneath the wall on which a carved heart miraculously appeared. The more romantic version, and the one I prefer, is that she continued to proclaim her innocence as the flames rose, and as proof of it she predicted that her heart 'would fly forth and perch above the window of the magistrate who had condemned her'.

The carved heart perches there still. These days the building contains the offices of a firm of solicitors, so the heart may be a reminder to them that the legal system can sometimes get things wrong . . .

There is a much more prominent emblem of crime and punishment, whether deserved or not, against the wall of a building in Church Hill, **Coleshill**, in Warwickshire. It is a combined pillory, whipping-post and stocks, with the two-man pillory section perched seven feet up in the air, no doubt to offer an easier target for missiles. It originally stood in front of the Market Hall, but when that was demolished in 1865 it was moved to its present position, and it has not been used in anger since. Its last official occupants were two labourers being punished for drunkenness, two years before it was moved, but in 1885 a photographer managed to persuade a tramp to insert himself into the pillory for a picture. The close proximity of the wall must have made it even more uncomfortable than its original designer intended.

Old notices and plaques are often a revealing form of wall decoration. Sometimes their message is plain, like the name-plate on the Green Dragon Hotel in **Hertford**, preserved from the early days of motoring. In addition to offering good stabling for horses, it notes the availability of a 'motor pit'. But sometimes the story behind a name-plate can be very obscure but quite fascinating, as with the IOU cottages at **Kelveden Hatch** in Essex.

The name resulted from a bitter village feud in the early 1900s between the squire, Charles Royds, and his neighbour, a Mr Roebuck. Royds lived at Brizes Park and also owned a small piece of land opposite the park itself. Roebuck shot a pheasant

The lofty two-man pillory used to stand by the Market Hall in Coleshill. The building was demolished in 1865 and the pillory went to the wall.

which fell on this land, sent his dog to retrieve it, and the trouble began. Royds complained to Roebuck, and Roebuck retaliated by building two houses outside the park to spoil Royds's view. In response Royds planted fast-growing fir trees to obscure the houses and put up a notice saying: 'This is the King's own plantation. Anyone found trespassing will be prosecuted.'

Roebuck, further incensed by this, then built two terraces of rather plain bungalows, along the main road facing the Park. One row was called 'The Thorns' – in Royds's side, he hoped – and the other was 'The IOUs', symbolising the grudge that he owed him. The bungalows were built with second-hand bricks to make their appearance worse, and indeed they were condemned almost as soon as they went up. Roebuck was not too worried, because the more derelict they became, the more depressing they looked from Royds's house.

The Green dragon at Hertford (above) makes its message clear; the IOU Cottages at Kelveden Hatch (left) are rather more discreet.

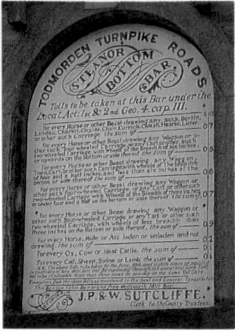

Every window tells a
story; well, this one
does, on the tollhouse at
Steanor Bottom . . .

. . . and so does this
doorway on the village
smithy at Claverdon.

However, they were brought into use for
housing troops during the First World War,
and later put into a more habitable condition. They stand there today, but I am sad
to report that the name 'The IOUs', which
Roebuck carved on a stone in the wall, has
been blacked out and covered by a new
name-plate bearing the name 'The Briars' –
perhaps to match 'The Thorns', though the
point is rather lost. I confess that if I lived
in a row of bungalows called 'The IOUs' I
would treasure the name and the story
behind it.

Even a simple window can tell a story,
and a window at **Steanor Bottom**, near
Bolton, does so literally. On the old tollhouse a blocked-up window is still
inscribed with the tolls that were charged to
users of 'Todmorden Turnpike Roads'; the
amounts ranged from a penny to seven-
pence. But generally you have to dig a little
deeper to discover a window's significance.

The Wreckers' Window is in a cottage
looking out to sea near **Shaldon** in South
Devon. It looks like an ordinary circular
window, but when a lantern was placed

The George and Dragon
at Batheaston has an
ingenious revolving
door . . .

Warwickshire goes one better; the entire doorway is in the form of an enormous horseshoe, not for luck or for knocking, but for symbolism. It must be one of the best advertising gimmicks in the smithy business. The George and Dragon Inn at **Batheaston** in Somerset has just as symbolic an entrance, a thousand-gallon beer barrel converted into a revolving door.

However, the doors of the Dooley Inn at **Lower Walton** in Suffolk, on the fringes of Felixstowe, look perfectly normal these days; it is the former multiplicity of them that makes the story. Long before the giant container terminal was built close by, the Dooley was the haunt of smugglers and other dubious characters. It was popular with them because of all its doors; every room had at least two of them, so if the Excisemen or the Press Gang came in one way, it was easy to depart through another.

In case you are wondering about the Dooley's name, it has no connection with England's distinguished rugby forward. The mundane explanation is that 'dole', locally pronounced 'doole', was the grass edging round a ploughed field. It produced a coarse hay, called 'doole hay'. However, there is another explanation which I rather prefer, though the experts discount it. At the turn of the last century a group of local sailors returned from a voyage to India and rechristened the taproom of the Ferry Boat Inn the 'Doali Tap', an Indian phrase for anyone who was slightly dotty.

. . . while the Dooley at Lower Walton had enough doors for the customers to do the revolving, to dodge the Excise men.

behind it the impression given to seafarers was of a lighthouse, and if they were unfamiliar with that coast they might well steer on to the Ness rocks, where the wreckers awaited them. It was also used to warn smugglers if the Revenue men were on the way, and as an 'all clear' when they had gone – one hopes for the smugglers' sakes that the signals did not get confused. Details of the wreckers' activities are understandably vague, but there is no doubt that a number of ships were wrecked and plundered at Shaldon – and the Wreckers' Window got the blame.

Doors may have stories to tell also, and again it may be fairly obvious, albeit rare, like the toll charge window at Steanor Bottom. For instance, many thousands of front doors have a horseshoe on the lintel for luck, or on the door itself as a knocker, but the village forge at **Claverdon** in

Even a humble doorknocker can have a tale to tell. There is a cottage by the green at **Beck Hole** in North Yorkshire which was formerly the Lord Nelson Inn, and on its white-painted door is an iron ring, quite a substantial affair weighing about five pounds. Originally it was not a doorknocker at all, but one of the quoits which are still used in a traditional Eskdale game. It is rather like American horseshoe throwing – and indeed it may have been the original version. The idea is to throw the iron quoits on to an iron pin about twenty-five feet away. It is all taken very seriously, and there is a keenly contested world championship each year, with entries from as far afield as Whitby.

Once the walls, the windows and the doors have been given some special characteristic, only the roof remains. Sometimes it is the roof itself which is designed to impress the passer-by, like the one on the Umbrella Cottage at **Lyme Regis** in Dorset. This former tollhouse has been given a round, overhanging thatched roof which looks as though it can be furled as soon as the rain stops.

However, the more common way of making a roof distinctive is to add something unusual on top of it. It may be a curious-shaped chimney, and as well as those mentioned in *Timpson's England,* there is, for instance, a cylindrical one on the Norman House at **Christchurch** in Hampshire, once part of Christchurch Castle, which is reputed to be the oldest domestic chimney in England. That was not, of course, a curious chimney when it was built, but the one on a pub at **Lemsford** in Hertfordshire would be considered curious in any era. Which pub? The Crooked Chimney, of course . . .

Chimneys can be useful, whatever their shape, but the metal spikes on what looks like a private house at **Pevensey** in Sussex seem to be, as it were, rather pointless. This was, however, the old Court House, once claimed to be the oldest and smallest town hall in England, and the spikes are over the little lock-up which formed an integral part

At Beck Hole they enjoy a spot of quoit-tossing on the green – but one of them finished up as a doorknocker.

of the building. In spite of its small size, it housed all manner of prisoners, including some condemned to death in the court-house above, but its most interesting occu-pant, and one of its last, was a woman called Betty Breach. In the early 1880s her husband spent every evening at the New Inn, and one night, fed up with waiting for him, she went to the pub, poured his drink over his head and smashed his glass. She was put in the lock-up, but there was such a local outcry, no doubt from the wives of other New Inn regulars, that the magistrate ordered the door of the lock-up to be left open, as a discreet way of dropping charges. Mrs Breach, scenting a rare victory, refused to leave her cell until the magistrate person-ally apologised to her. The hapless fellow eventually did so, and she emerged from the lock-up in triumph.

During the early days of the Second World War the lock-up found a new use: the wooden bunks were lined with zinc so it could act as a mortuary if the Germans invaded. Happily it was never needed.

Spikes may be suitable for a lock-up, but most people prefer something less forbid-ding on their property – a weather-vane

A chimney-sweep's nightmare! This pub at Lemsford could only be the Crooked Chimney.

The spikes are not to deter burglars; this was Pevensey's court house and lock-up.

Rooftop residents. Sir William de Postlip (right) is said to climb down at midnight to drink from Postlip's Holy Well. The figures on the Image Barn at Wood Norton (far right) are rather more static.

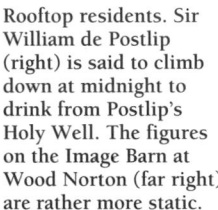

perhaps, or a plastic peacock. Occasionally the rooftop decoration can represent a real person, like the stocky figure of Sir William de Postlip, which stands on a medieval tithe barn at **Postlip** in Gloucestershire. Legend has it that Sir William rouses himself at midnight, climbs down from the roof and refreshes himself at the nearby holy well. The story remains unconfirmed, but there is no doubt about the authenticity of the entertaining tale of the Image Barn at **Wood Norton** in Norfolk, which has two carved stone figures on the gables.

They were put there by the farmer, a Mr Phillips, after he had fallen out with Sir Jacob Astley, later Lord Hastings, and William Norris, squire of Wood Norton Hall. It seems that Sir Jacob persecuted a friend of Mr Phillips for poaching a pheasant – a gamekeeper had seen him taking it out of a trap. The man was brought before the local Bench, of which

William Norris was chairman. Phillips paid for a defence lawyer, who claimed it was a frame-up and the gamekeeper had put the pheasant in the trap to tempt his client. The Bench was unconvinced and found him guilty.

What happened next was recorded years later by Norris's great-nephew. 'Phillips was so angry at the conviction that he pilloried the prosecutor and the chairman of the Bench by putting their effigies on a new barn he was building, close to the road along which they constantly passed to visit each other. Sir Jacob was furious, but William took all his friends to see it . . .'

These days one rarely finds such an enterprising form of roof decoration, but the outstanding exception, which has achieved considerable fame in recent years, can be found near Oxford. It is the **Headington Shark**, an eighteen-foot monster made of fibreglass which Mr Bill Heine inserted

Layer Marney has the highest Tudor gateway in England . . .

. . . and this terraced house at Headington must have the highest shark.

nose-first into the roof of his small terraced house in 1986. He claimed it was a work of art, but the council took a different view. They said it was a traffic hazard and a blight on property values, and told him to take it down. The legal battle that followed went on for six years, ending in victory for Mr Heine and what he called 'a triumph for art in public places'.

An enlightened inspector from the Department of the Environment ruled that 'this was one case where a little vision and imagination is appropriate'. He added, with the sort of genial benevolence rarely attributed to planning inspectors: 'Any system of control must make some small space for the dynamic, the unexpected and the downright quirky, or we shall all be the poorer for it.'

In years gone by, of course, the dynamic, the unexpected, et cetera, did not have to depend on the goodwill of planning inspectors. Anyone with money and influence could add whatever they liked to their properties, and if they had a big house in big grounds they could make the entrance big too. Entrances do not come much bigger than the gateway of **Layer Marney**, near Colchester in Essex; at eighty feet it is the highest Tudor gateway in England. It is so high, in fact, and took so long to build, that Lord Marney died before it was

finished in 1523. What is more, he was so busy with the gatehouse that he never got around to building the mansion which was supposed to go with it. However, with its eight storeys and four towers it is quite a mansion in itself.

Layer Marney may have the highest gatehouse, but **Thornton Abbey** near Scunthorpe, in what is now Humberside, undoubtedly has the bulkiest. A seventeenth-century traveller was dumbfounded when he came across such an enormous structure in this remote countryside. 'There is all the gaithouse yet standing of a vast and incredible bigness, and of the greatest art, ingenuity and workmanship that ever I saw in my life.'

The centre block is 66 feet wide, 44 feet deep and 66 feet high, with four turrets on the back and front, and screen walls with more turrets on each side. It was built in 1382, two hundred years after the foundation of the abbey itself, and it was designed as a fortress as well as a residence for the Abbot, who presumably preferred to get away for a little privacy after work rather than live, as it were, over the shop.

The abbey is in such a lonely spot, on the way to nowhere in particular, that one wonders why the Abbot needed such a massive fortification. However, a successor must have shared his fears, because a formidable brick barbican was added two hundred years later. It has been suggested that, as the gatehouse was built just after the Peasants' Revolt, the Abbot feared the locals might try it on again – though the total population of that corner of Lincolnshire could hardly have besieged a henhouse, let alone this towering mass of brick and stone. More likely the Abbot was worried about pirates, who often patronised this stretch of the coast.

In the sixteenth century, when the barbican was added, there was much greater cause for worry, with Henry VIII on the rampage, far more dangerous than any pirate. In the days before the Dissolution, when abbeys were in favour, he did actually visit Thornton, and enjoyed himself so much that he stayed for several days. But

Thornton Abbey must have the bulkiest gatehouse in the country; nobody is quite sure why . . .

come the Dissolution that did not stop him knocking the daylights out of it – or more literally, into it – and Thornton Abbey was dissolved with all the rest. Only the gatehouse survived intact, and in more recent years an Earl of Yarborough, whose family acquired the abbey and its estates, put it in the care of the Ministry of Works. It remains one of the least known ancient monuments in England; one custodian commented: 'We get very few visitors now. It seems too far off the map for Lincolnshire people.' But he did add more cheerfully: 'Yet Americans will always find it.'

That was in 1948. I suspect it still applies.

At the other end of the gatehouse scale are a couple of curiosities in Suffolk. The sixteenth-century Erwarton Hall, on the **Shotley Peninsula**, has a Tudor brick gatehouse with nine tall, thin protuberances on the roof, almost as unlikely as Bill Heine's shark. I like to picture the gatehouse turned upside down, so that the nine turrets act as legs. It would look like an enormous brick sideboard . . .

Erwarton Hall still stands behind its curious gatehouse, but Rendlesham Hall near **Wickham Market**, did not fare so well. It was burned down in a disastrous fire in 1833, and only a ruined pinnacle and a gateway remain. It is the gateway, however, which catches the eye of travellers on their way to the nearby American air base at Bentwaters. Woodbridge Lodge, as it is called, was built in 1806 by Lord Rendlesham as an adjunct to his remodelled Hall. His father, Peter Thellusson, was reputed to be the richest man in England, so there were no problems about indulging in the odd architectural quirk, and Woodbridge Lodge is as odd as they come.

Instead of Erwarton's nine turrets it has three flying buttresses on the roof, rising to a central tower which is in fact a chimney. Pinnacles stick up all around. If this gatehouse were turned upside down it would resemble, not so much a sideboard as a square spinning-top; it only needs a little spire to spin on.

Happily, instead of being up-ended, the long-deserted lodge is now in caring hands

. . . while Rendlesham Hall has one of the strangest – all pinnacles, buttresses and turrets; the central tower is actually a chimney.

Scrivelsby Court, home of the Hereditary Grand Champion of England. The Hon. John Dymoke was still challenging all claimants to the throne at the coronation of George IV.

Sacred to the Memory of
The Hon.ble JOHN DYMOKE,
of *Scrivelsby* in this County,
Champion of *ENGLAND*,
who performed that Service at the
Coronation of His Majesty GEORGE 3.d
and whose Body lieth interred
in a Vault near this Place;
He departed this Life March 6th 1784
Aged 52 Years.

again, and I have seen plans for restoring it with a few extensions to make it a more commodious, if still unorthodox, residence. The owners say in all modesty that they intend to make 'an important contribution to both the Historic and the Current Architecture of Suffolk Coastal, East Anglia, the United Kingdom and Europe' – and short of adding 'the World, the Universe', you can't say fairer than that. At least it will not be taken home as a souvenir by one of those American airmen up the road.

The two lodges at **Scrivelsby Court** near Horncastle, in what is still Lincolnshire, are much more luxurious affairs, and one of them is now the home of the Hereditary Grand Champion of England. The original title, along with Scrivelsby Court, was granted by William the Conqueror to the Marmion family, but in 1350 the Hereditary Champion failed to produce a male heir, so the title and manor passed all the way down to the husband of the last male Marmion's great-grand-daughter. On the face of it a blatant example of sex discrimination, but in this case there seems to be a good excuse, because the main job of the Champion of England was to challenge anyone who contested the King's right to the throne, which might well finish up in a rather unpleasant punch-up. That sort of thing happened rather more frequently in

the Middle Ages than it does today, so it was felt this was no job for a woman, and who can blame them.

The man who inherited the title from the Marmions was Sir John Dymoke, and it has stayed in the Dymoke family ever since. King George IV still took the title seriously, and at his Coronation the Champion of England rode his horse into Westminster Hall, wearing full armour and flanked by esquires carrying his shield and lance. The challenge was read by a herald, and it started off rather like the banns of marriage:

'If any person of what degree soever, high or low, shall deny or gainsay our Sovereign Lord, George the Fourth . . .'

But after this mild opening there came the medieval equivalent of 'put your money where your mouth is':

'Here is his Champion, who saith he lieth, and in the quarrel will adventure his life against him, on what day soever he shall be appointed.'

At this point the Champion threw down his gauntlet, and everyone held their breath. To the great relief of George IV, and probably of his Champion, nobody picked it up.

Life is a bit quieter for the Hereditary Grand Champion of England these days. He moved out of Scrivelsby Court by 1980 to live in the lodge, which was designed by Humphrey Repton and is still a very nice place to live. But I wonder if his sleep is ever disturbed by a nightmare, in which he hears that challenge being read in Westminster Hall, he throws down his gauntlet – and somebody picks it up . . .

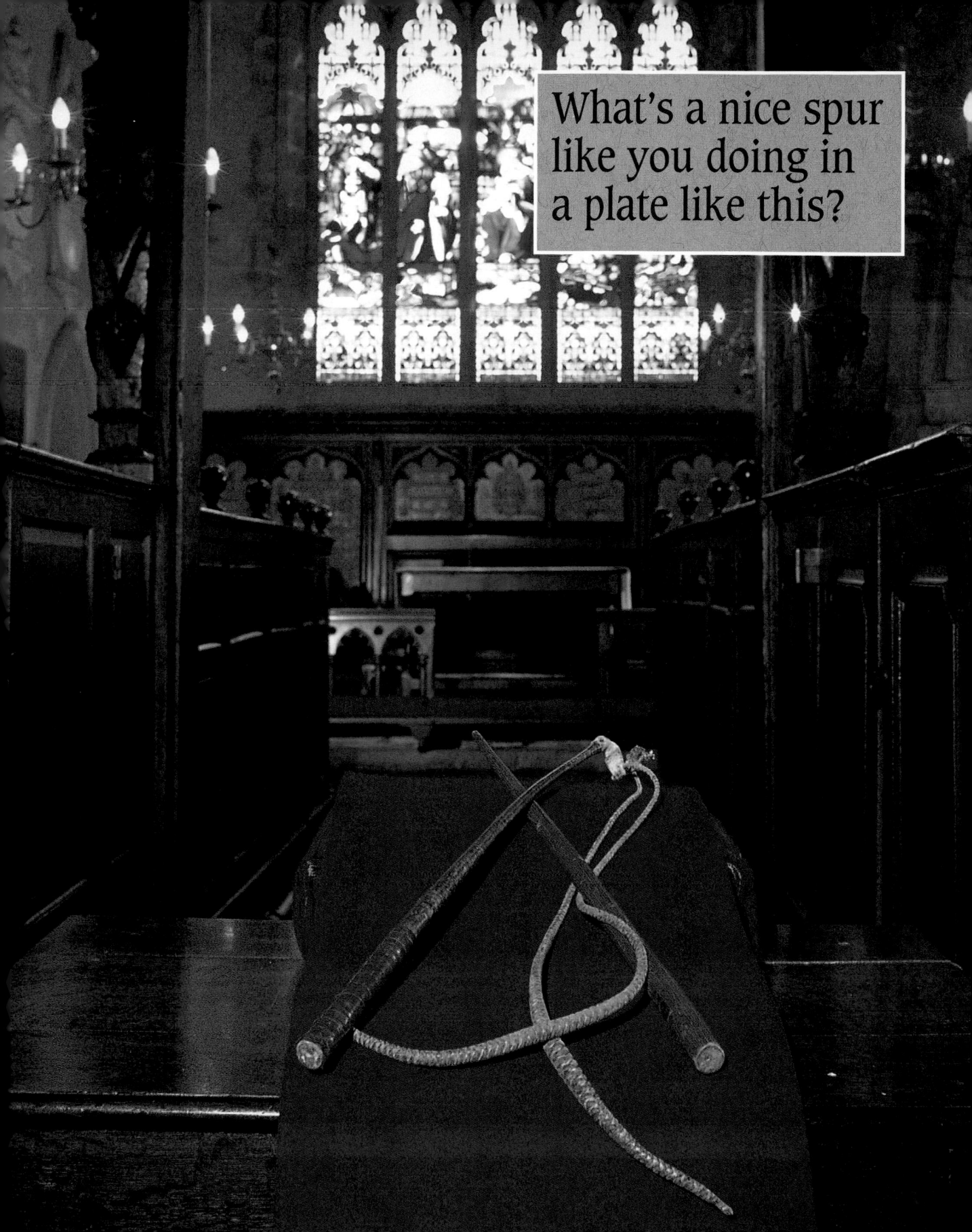

What's a nice spur like you doing in a plate like this?

Sometimes the most ordinary objects can take on a bizarre flavour because of their incongruous surroundings. There is no point in my mentioning them if they are inaccessible to the public, but these days many of our great houses and stately homes are open at certain times, and there is often an unexpected oddity which hardly gets a mention in the official handbook.

For instance, how about the familiar domestic scene of a devoted wife serving lunch to her husband, but instead of roast beef and two veg. on the plate, it's a spur? You will find this depicted at Wallington, the seventeenth–century mansion near **Cambo** in Northumberland. The handbook

Not so much a light snack as a heavy hint. 'The Spur in the Dish' is one of William Bell Scott's paintings at Wallington.

goes on about its plasterwork and porcelain, and its collection of dolls' houses, and it does mention William Bell Scott's paintings in the central gallery, but for me it is one particular painting which gives Wallington a special appeal. Why the spur on the plate?

You may guess that it is the medieval equivalent of a hostess bringing in the coats of her guests – a gentle hint that it is time to go. One famous lady actually fetched a broom and started sweeping the floor. In the case of the spur, however, the hint is being given to the husband, and I doubt even the lady with the broom would have gone as far as that.

Instead of being outraged, however, the husband looks quite resigned. He knows lunch is over, not because his wife wants to get on with the washing-up, but because the meat supply has run out and it is time to 'ride and rieve', as cross-border rustling was called. The spur on the plate was the traditional way of telling him.

Not far away near **Rothbury** is Cragside, the great house created by the first Lord Armstrong in the 1860s. Sir William, as he then was, combined shrewd business acumen with an inventive mind, and made a great deal of money as a result. Cragside is not only a splendid house in beautiful grounds, it was the first private house in the world to be lit by electricity derived from water power, and this is duly emphasised in the brochures, which also draw attention to the hydraulic lift. However, it is the kitchen which contains, for me, Sir William's most unexpected device, and it is the one most often missed – a hydraulic spit.

The water comes from lakes in the hills above the house, and Sir William piped it down into a gadget called a Scotch mill, a tiny water-wheel which turned a rod, which turned other rods, which eventually turned the spit. Cynics point out that, while this was as ingenious as anything by Heath Robinson, it was almost as useless, because there were plenty of servants to turn the spit by hand. Indeed, compared with the world's first hydraulic crane, which Sir William invented in 1840 for Newcastle Docks, it was no big deal – but I reckon it's a lot more fun.

If the staircase in the Talbot Hotel at **Oundle**, in Northamptonshire, strikes you

as rather grand, it is because it started life in Fotheringhay Castle. It was the one which Mary Queen of Scots walked down on the way to her execution, and inevitably it is said that, when the Talbot acquired it in 1625, her ghost accompanied it to the hotel, and can still be seen wafting down it. These days it leads to the lounge bar instead of the execution block, so Mary's ghost should get a pleasant surprise.

Another pleasant surprise awaits any visitor who hasn't been warned about the murals in what used to be the schoolhouse

Not just a pretty house. Cragside has hydro-powered electricity, a hydraulic lift, and in the kitchen the meat is roasted on a water-powered spit.

at **Ford** in Northumberland, and is now the village hall. It still looks a fairly typical Victorian school, built in 1860 by the Lady of the Manor, Louisa Ann, Marchioness of Waterford, and used as such for over ninety years. Inside, however, the walls were not merely used for blackboards and coat hooks; they were decorated with the most elaborate Biblical scenes by Lady Waterford herself. She used the villagers as models, so in the first mural, for instance, featuring Cain and Abel, Cain was a local fisherman and Abel was the son of the village stonemason.

A village schoolroom is not an ideal place for preserving such splendid paintings. As a local historian wrote: 'The rigours of school life over almost a century have not been particularly kind to the pictures: smoke from the open fires in particular has discoloured the south wall, rain has penetrated the gables, and over the years no

Is this England's most lavishly-decorated village hall? The Marchioness of Waterford (above) painted the walls of Ford's hall (originally the village school) with a series of Biblical scenes, using the villagers as models.

doubt schoolmasters will have covered up with their own handiwork ink stains and damage . . .' Nevertheless they still provide a spectacular surprise for the unsuspecting tourist, and give Ford the distinction of possessing the most elegantly decorated village hall in the country.

One would expect to find this sort of thing in stately homes, but Browsholme Hall near **Clitheroe** in Lancashire has another kind of surprise among the more orthodox decorations in its main hall. In the midst of assorted antlers, crossed swords and pieces of armour, there is a strange circular device called a dog stirrup, a reminder of the days when sportsmen could be singularly unsporting if their activities were hampered. Nearly five hundred years ago the dog stirrup was used to test the size of dogs in the vicinity of the Forest of Bowland, a popular area for hunting deer. Only dogs below a certain size were allowed, to prevent the deer being harassed by anything except the deer-hunters. If a dog was too big to fit in the gauge, its deer-chasing days were ended forthwith; its front paws were cut off. I should mention that Browsholme is pronounced to rhyme with 'gruesome' . . .

Happily, the punishment for obstreperous dogs was not always so drastic; in general, a few flicks with a dog whip would suffice. Dog whips were therefore quite common in stately homes, but it is less common to find them in a church. There are two in St Andrew's, **Slaidburn**, which is also in the Forest of Bowland, but these whips have no connection with hunting. In the days when parishioners took their pets into church with them, a dog-whipper was employed to

deal with any fights that broke out among the canine congregation.

I gather that one dog was immune from his ministrations. A Slaidburn rector was said to have had a dog called Bounty, which

Little Basil would have fitted into the dog stirrup at Browsholme Hall, and thus avoid losing his paws.

The whips (right) that kept the dogs quiet during services in Slaidburn Church – except, of course, for lucky Bounty.

Bounty was so renowned for his barking that he was immortalised in the name of a Slaidburn inn.

The ducking-stool in Leominster Church, said to be the only one still in working order:
'No brawling wives, no furious wenches,
No fire so hot but water quenches . . .'

was allowed to make as much noise as it liked during a service. It took advantage of this concession to such a degree that passers-by were said to nudge each other and murmur, 'Hark to Bounty' – and that is one version of how the Hark to Bounty Inn at Slaidburn got its name. However, the parson was also the squire, a common combination in those days, and the more likely story is that, while out hunting, he and his party stopped at the inn, then known as the Dog, for refreshments. Outside the pack got impatient and started barking, with Bounty barking loudest of all. 'Hark to Bounty,' said its

owner benevolently as he refilled his glass – and the name stuck.

Some churches contain other instruments of correction, for people rather than dogs. Stocks are fairly common, but in **Leominster** Church in Hereford and Worcester there is a ducking-stool, said to be the last one in working order – and indeed the last one to be put to use. In 1809 a woman called Jenny Pipes was put in it for using bad language, and was paraded round the town in it before being ducked in the river. A witness commented that it seemed to do little good, as 'the first words uttered by the culprit on being unfastened

always the comfiest of the lot. **Minstead** Church in Hampshire had three such pews, each belonging to one of the important families in the parish. They had their own outside entrance, an open fireplace and pleasant furnishings, so not surprisingly they were known as parlour pews. The most opulent was the Minstead Manor pew, occupied by the squire himself, who even installed a sofa. It has since been merged with the rest of the church, and the Minstead Lodge pew now houses the organ. The Castle Malwood pew still resembles a private sitting-room, and is used as a place for quiet meditation and prayer.

In Lakenheath Church they liked their comforts; they used tussocks of sedge (left) to kneel on – later known as hassocks – and even the tigress on the pew-end (above) seems to have kept cosy with a warming-pan but it's actually a mirror.

The gentry liked their comforts too. In Minstead Church each important family had its own parlour pew.

from the chair were oaths and curses on the magistrates'. A few years later another offender was given the same punishment, but when they reached the river the water was too low to duck her. In that case, perhaps it was the magistrates who cursed!

I will stay now with oddities in churches, which should be easily accessible, although far too many churches are locked these days, for fear of vandalism or theft. But if you can get into them, there are many more curiosities to be found – and not all of them were designed for punishment or discomfort. For instance, one or two churches in Suffolk still have the original version of what we now call hassocks. To start with, they were just tussocks of sedge, brought into church to lessen the wear and tear on knees during long periods of prayer. The two in St Mary's, **Lakenheath**, now appear almost as uncomfortable as the bare floor, but as one writer observes: 'Now harsh and prickly as a week-old beard, they must in their youth have been balm to the knees.'

Pews have also been adapted for comfort, and in Georgian times the squire's pew was

Meanwhile the parson at Donington (right) was keeping dry inside his hude at funerals . . .

. . . while at Odcombe (far right) Thomas Coryate may have had an ill-shod rector in mind when he gave the church his walking shoes.

these days only a plaque remains. It notes that 'in this church for many years hung the shoes of Thomas Coryate, as a thank offering for his return from five months' touring, mostly on foot, of the Continent, 1608'. It was a curious thankoffering – the church would probably have preferred hard cash – but Thomas Coryate was a curious man. As well as hiking through Europe he was the first European to walk from the eastern Mediterranean through Persia and Afghanistan. Everywhere he went he made notes, and the result was *Coryate's Crudities*, not a collection of questionable foreign jokes but titbits of unusual information. As Coryate put it himself, the Crudities were 'hastily gobbled up in five months' travelling . . . newly digested . . . and now dispersed to the nourishment of the travelling members of the kingdom.' It is a recipe which somehow seems strangely familiar . . .

In one or two cases it was the parson who got the personal fireplace. In **Salton** Church, near Helmsley in North Yorkshire, a little Victorian grate has been set in the wall by the priest's chair, with the result that a very incongruous chimney emerges from the ancient chancel roof.

Other churches catered for the comfort of their parsons in other ways. **Donington** Church in Lincolnshire has a hude, or hood, a kind of portable sentry box which was put by the graveside at funerals if the weather was inclement. The parson conducted the committal from inside the hude, while the mourners got drenched.

There is another hude, this time equipped with carrying handles like a sedan chair, in **Walpole St Peter** Church in Norfolk, and hanging in the church porch are a pair of pattens, the wooden-soled forerunners of Wellington boots. A faded notice requests parishioners to remove their pattens before entering; a clean floor was presumably more important than warm feet.

There used to be a pair of shoes hanging inside **Odcombe** Church in Somerset, but

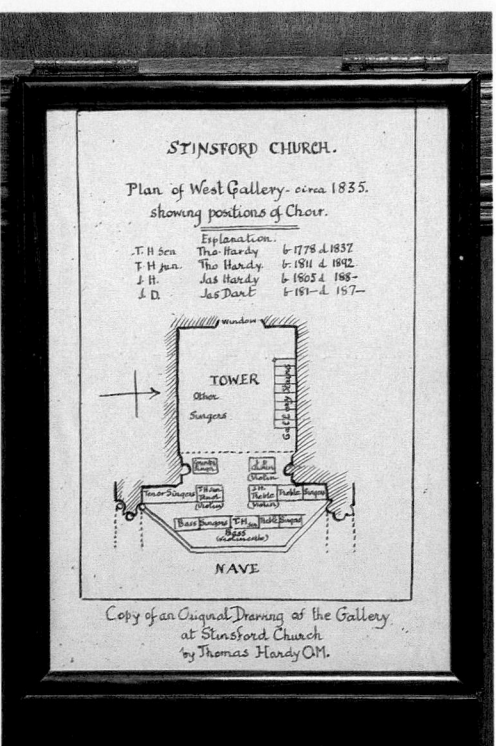

Musical memories:
Thomas Hardy drew a
plan of the players
(above) in the church
gallery at Stinsford . . .

century, and were basically just speaking trumpets which amplified a singer's voice. Presumably it was easy to improvise a tune on a vamp horn, and musicians still do a little vamping when they can't think of anything else.

. . . while Charing Church remembers vamping it up on this original vamp horn.

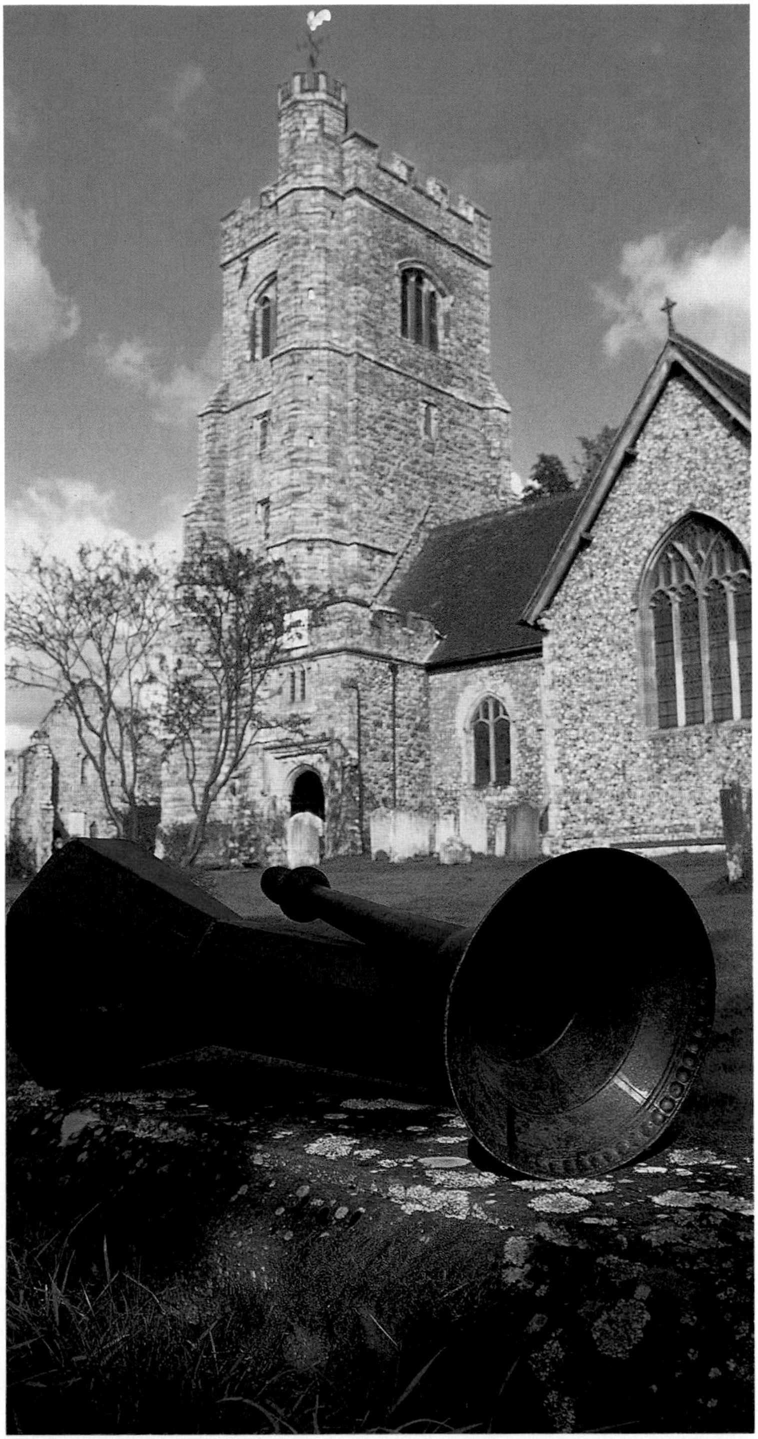

Thomas Coryate was considered by some to be one of the outstanding figures of seventeenth-century literature, although his name seems little known outside his home village. Thomas Hardy, on the other hand, was a nineteenth-century literary giant whose fame has spread worldwide, but like Coryate he took the trouble to leave a personal memento in his local church in Dorset. He was christened in St Michael's, **Stinsford**, he attended it for much of his life, and some of his family were in the church band, which performed in the west gallery, now long since gone. What remains, however, is a plan he drew of the gallery, showing the positions of the players, and beside it is a tablet he designed to commemorate the Hardys who took part.

I am not sure if the Stinsford band had the use of a vamp horn, but it was a device popular among church musicians, and **Charing** Church in Kent still has one, with its original oval mouthpiece. Vamp horns were introduced in the late seventeenth

St Michael and All Angels at **Hawkshead** in Cumbria is another church associated with a notable literary figure. William Wordsworth went to school in the village, and the Wordsworth connection overshadows almost everything else in Hawkshead, but inside the church is a fascinating piece of writing which has nothing to do with the great man – unless he happened to be buried in a woollen shroud. Near the vestry door hangs a 'Buried in Woolen' affidavit, one of nearly two hundred preserved in the church records.

In 1666 the Government devised a macabre way of boosting the woollen industry. It passed an 'Act of Burying in Woolen onely', which decreed that all burials must be in cloth or clothing made entirely of wool. For three years nobody took the slightest notice, much to the irritation of the wool lobby, so another law was passed, saying an affidavit must be produced within eight days of a death, confirming that the body had been interred in something woolly. That did the trick, for a few years at least, and Hawkshead has preserved the evidence. These days, perhaps, there should be a new law saying that every coffin must be accompanied by a hundredweight of coal . . .

Another church linked with a famous figure is at **Colsterworth** in Lincolnshire, which retains a rather odd personal memento. Sir Isaac Newton was born at the nearby manor house at Woolsthorpe, and I would love to report that he donated to the church the famous apple which started him off on the laws of gravity, but the Colsterworth keepsake is in fact a sundial. Young Newton was rather keen on sundials, and made a couple which were let into the south wall of the manor house.

More ecclesiastical mementos: a 'Buried in Woolen' affidavit in Hawkshead Church . . .

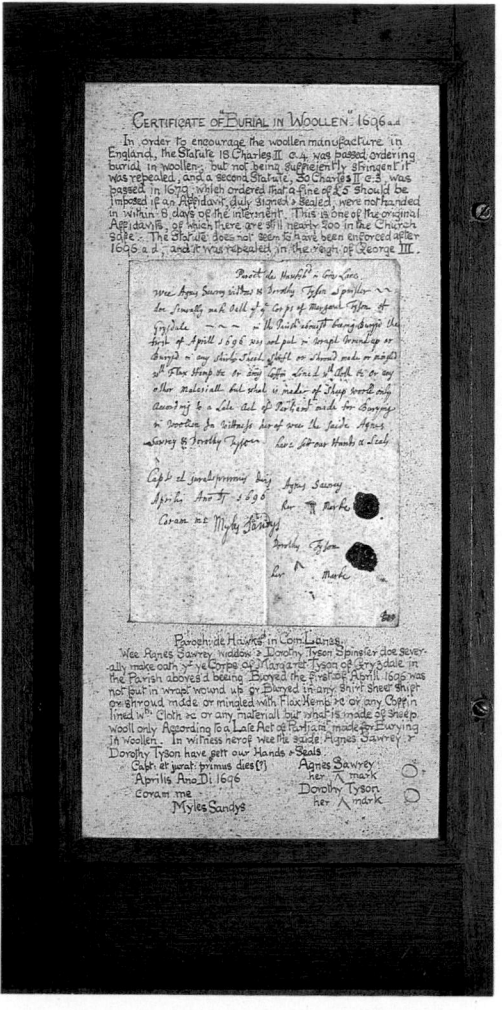

. . . and the youthful Isaac Newton's sundial at Colsterworth.

Low Ham Church (left) has the spear (below) which rid the locality of a flying serpent – or was it just used in church pageants? Either way, it gets some interesting visitors. 'Julie Coombes, Traveller, looking for and found the Green Man,' wrote one; 'James Ravenscroft, Nomad, in search of the Godhead,' wrote another. Just travellers' tales?

They were both removed in the nineteenth century; one finished up in the library of the Royal Society, the other is in Colsterworth Church.

It is unusual to find a sundial inside a church, rather than outside. It is even more unusual to find one made by Sir Isaac Newton. But what adds the final distinction to this one is that it is mounted on the wall upside-down. Experts are rather scathing about the dial itself – 'the positions for the hour lines are completely incorrect . . . the dial is neither true nor approximate seasonal-hour, but appears to be an erroneous hybrid pattern . . .' – but young Isaac was only nine when he made it, and the experts' wrath should surely be directed at the chap who installed it in the church the wrong way up. Perhaps the rector was so embarrassed at this very unscientific slip that, when an organ was installed in 1897, twenty years after the sundial was put on the wall, it was placed slap in front of it, and it is still hiding it today.

Finally, a couple of curiously tangible relics of very intangible legends. Propped against the wall in **Low Ham** Church, near

Langport in Somerset, is a long spear or halberd, said to have been used by a fearless fellow called John Aller to kill a flying serpent in the locality. I am sure nobody would like to suggest that the spear was actually just a prop used in the old days in church pageants; the flying serpent is a much better story.

The Frensham cauldron – loaned by the fairies, used by a witch, or just a brewing-pot for church ale? . . .

any wish, but anything acquired in this way had to be returned at the appointed time, or no more wishes would be granted. The good folk of Frensham wished for a cauldron for some festive occasion, which proved so festive they forgot to return it in time, and they have been stuck with it – and with no more wishes – ever since.

It is much more probable, however, that the cauldron either originated from nearby Waverley Abbey, where it fulfilled some prosaic function in the kitchen, or it was used for brewing church ale. The present vicar has, in fact, done his best to dispel the superstitions attached to it, and the church guidebook only gives it the briefest of mentions. So perhaps Frensham should follow the example of **Stoke Dry** in Leicestershire, which also has a witch legend. A previous vicar is supposed to have sealed up a witch in the little room over the church porch, and starved her to death. One of his twentieth-century successors got so tired of this story that a notice is now displayed in the church saying, in effect, 'Don't believe that load of rubbish!'

It seems a pity, because I rather treasure the strange tales that have been handed down through the centuries, but in some cases perhaps we need reminding that they should not be taken too seriously.

. . . Whatever use was attached to it, at Stoke Dry they would add a pinch of salt.

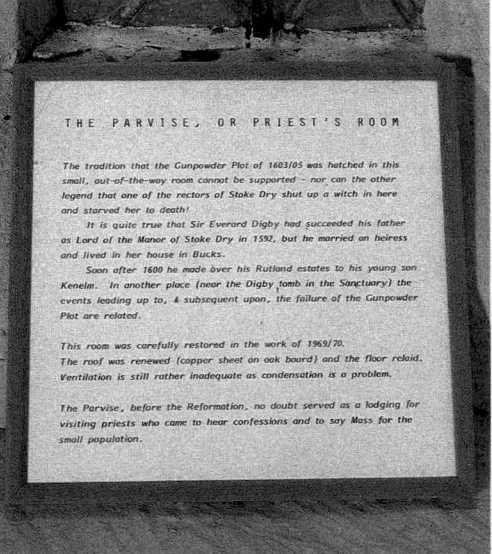

At **Frensham** in Surrey, however, they are getting rather fed up with the equally fanciful story that an old copper cauldron which has been in the church 'from beyond the memory of man' was once the property of Mother Ludlam, a local witch who used it to brew her magic potions. Since the cauldron is eight feet eight inches in circumference, she must have mass-produced the stuff for a very large clientele. There is another story, more romantic but even less likely, that a nearby hill was crowned by a flat stone which, when tapped, would grant

Slabs in the pulpit, a sow in the roof and a potty on the font

Slabs in the pulpit, a sow in the roof and a potty on the font

Churches can so often contain striking features that catch the eye – the memorials, the brasses, the stained-glass windows – that the routine furnishings may be taken for granted. The pulpit could be considered just a platform to preach from, the font just a basin to baptise in, the choir stalls a place to sing in, the pews a seat to sit, or pray, or doze in. But thanks to the ingenuity, and sometimes the sense of humour of our early craftsmen, these standard fittings can often be the most fascinating items in the church. And if all these prove unrewarding, there is always the roof . . .

Happily there is still some ingenuity about, even in the design of pulpits, and one of the most unusual modern designs is in **St Leonard's** Church, near Hastings in East Sussex. Many seaside churches have monuments with maritime associations and one or two, like St Mary's at **Maryport** in Cumbria, have ships' beams as part of their fabric, but St Leonard's has a pulpit which is shaped like the prow of a boat – and a very special boat at that, with a remarkable story behind it.

In 1944 the original church was destroyed by German bombs, and the following night – which presumably wasn't so noisy – the rector was able to get to sleep, and had a dream. He saw Jesus preaching from a boat on the Lake of Galilee.

No, the pulpit is not part of that boat – there is a limit to the extravagance of these stories – but it came from the same place. It was made by a Jewish carpenter on a kibbutz close by the scene that the rector saw in his dream. The boat-pulpit was incorporated in the new church, and to add

Maritime connections in St Leonard's Church: a binnacle for a lecter and a boat's prow for a pulpit.

Castle Donington's pulpit is lined with memorial slabs; some carvings still survive.

taken up anyway, and they would have been thrown out if they had not been saved by the man who built the pulpit, the Revd John Dalby's son-in-law. His name, confusingly, was the Revd Robert Dalby, but there is an explanation for that too; his name was originally Blunt, but he took his wife's surname when he married.

Fonts can be made of unexpected materials as well. **Cardington** in Bedfordshire

Fascinating fonts: Cardington has a genuine Wedgwood one (left), and on the next page . . .

another maritime touch from a rather different era, a brass-topped ship's binnacle was converted into a lectern.

In contrast to a boat, the pulpit at **Castle Donington** Church in Leicestershire is made from memorial slabs. It was built in about 1875 in memory of the Revd John Dalby, who was vicar for forty-five years. Its sides are made of alabaster – but the alabaster was second-hand. It came from slabs which had been in the floor of the church, and you can still see the name on one of them, William Oldburie, with a group of standing and kneeling figures. That particular slab is thought to be dated about 1480. On others you can see traces of Gothic patterns.

It may seem a little drastic to rip up fifteenth-century memorial stones to build a pulpit, but I hasten to pass on the explanation which is given by the Dalby family, who have been in Castle Donington for as long as those stones. Mr Gerald Dalby is currently churchwarden, as was his uncle, his grandfather, and other Dalbys before him. He says that when the pulpit was erected, the alabaster slabs were due to be

Ashover has the only lead font left in Derbyshire, preserved from Cromwell's men by a gardening rector.

features in all the guidebooks as the home of Britain's last giant airship, the ill-fated R101, but it was also the birthplace of Samuel Whitbread, founder of the brewing firm. He and his family did a great deal to refurbish their parish church, and their most striking contribution was the font, given by Harriet Whitbread in 1783.

It looks, not so much a font, as a pot on a plinth, but a very grand pot indeed. It is genuine Wedgwood, made of black basalt at Josiah's famous pottery near Stoke-on-Trent, and it stands on a fluted pillar, looking as though it ought to contain a few gallons of soup or a very large aspidistra.

Wedgwood may not be generally associated with fonts, but Josiah was an essen-tially practical man, and he made sure the font was practical too. Appreciating that a baby could disappear without trace inside this splendid bowl if it was filled with water, he also made a little basalt pedestal to go inside it, about ten inches high and decorated with one of his favourite patterns, bell flowers and acanthus leaves. At a baptism the pedestal was put in the bowl, and on the pedestal went a much smaller silver gilt bowl for the holy water.

The Cardington font is not in fact unique. The Whitbread family also had a home at **Essendon** in Hertfordshire, Bedwell Park, and a similar font is in the parish church there. A third was made for Melchbourne Church, where Samuel Whitbread's daughter Emma was married in 1780, but that one has since found its way to America. One cannot help wondering, with all these Whitbread commissions for Wedgwood fonts, whether Samuel and Josiah had some sort of reciprocal arrange-ment, involving basalt bowls on the one hand and best bitter on the other . . .

Lead is a rather more common material for fonts – or used to be until Cromwell melted most of them down for ammunition. Today there are about forty originals left, but in Derbyshire, once noted for its lead-mines, there remains only one. It was preserved from Cromwell's ministrations by the shrewd foresight of the Rector of **Ashover**, near Matlock in Derbyshire, the Revd Immanuel Bourne.

Ashover Church has a wealth of little oddities, from the top half of a Bronze Age beehive grindstone found in the church-yard, to a heart-shaped lead tablet from a stone coffin. It also has the only bell in England which bears the name of Napoleon – not because it was shipped across from France, but because it was recast with his name on it after being rung over-energeti-cally to celebrate his abdication. But the lead font is my favourite, a veteran dated about 1150 which might have been turned into bullets if Immanuel Bourne had not taken it home to Eastwood Hall and buried it in his kitchen garden.

Eastwood Hall was the only house in Ashover to be blown up by the Roundheads, and they made quite a mess of the church as well, smashing all the stained glass and burning the registers, but Immanuel and font happily survived unscathed. One lived on to complete forty-eight years as rector, the other is still functioning today.

The font at **Castle Combe** in Wiltshire has been missed by countless tourists as well as Oliver Cromwell. They are far too busy admiring the rest of what has been described all too often as 'the prettiest village in England'. Its prettiness is marred these days by the double yellow lines down the village street and the hordes of cars which make them necessary, but that is the street where most visitors congregate, to admire the old weavers' cottages, long since weaverless, and the bow-fronted shops full of cream teas and souvenirs.

I went to Castle Combe to track down the story of the Blanket brothers, said to have been local weavers who gave their name to the well-known bed-covering. I should have checked in the dictionary first: 'blanket' comes from the French *'blanchette'*, or white cloth, and nobody I could find in Castle Combe had ever heard of the Brothers Blanket. So I took refuge in the church, tucked away off the main street and quite deserted, and I came upon this most unusual font. The ingenious stonemason who constructed it some five hundred years ago provided a stone book-rest on the side of the bowl, so the parson can put down his prayer-book and have two hands free to cope with the baby.

The guidebook in the church says it is unique, which is always a dangerous claim – I have since heard of another one in Norfolk – but if that stonemason had been a good marketing man, and there had been such a thing as copyright in 1450, he could have made a fortune.

I think my favourite font, though, is in the Church of St John the Baptist at **Badingham**, near Saxmundham in Suffolk. It is the only one I know which features a chamber-pot. Like many other fonts, particularly in Suffolk, the Seven Sacraments are portrayed on it, but in the carving of a priest at a bedside, administering the last rites, underneath the bed of the dying man, can clearly be seen his slippers and his pot. As one historian comments, the sight of these homely objects carved on the side of a church font 'jolts us into recognition of universal humanity'.

Fonts with user-friendly features: Badingham (below) has a potty for the patient . . .

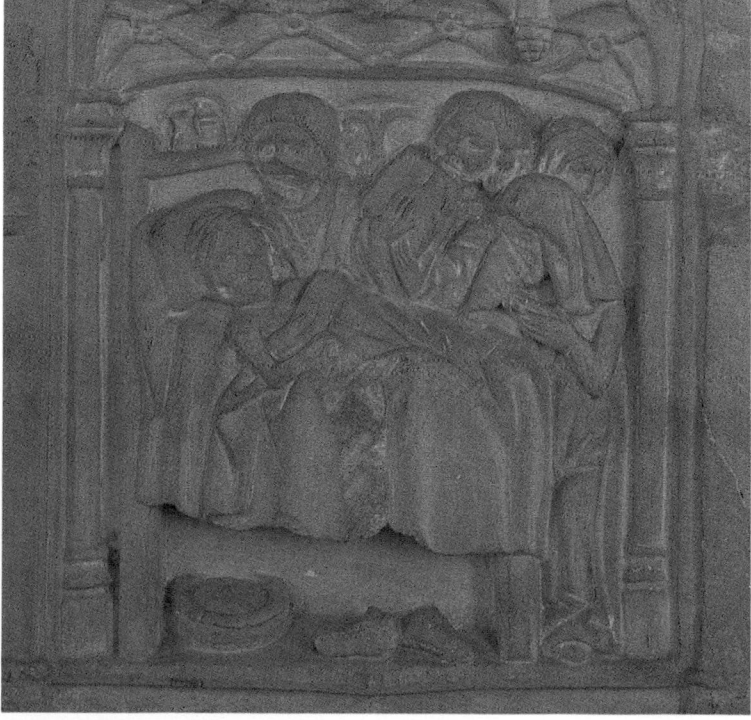

. . . and Castle Combe has a bookrest for the parson

There is another doctor and patient carving in **Malvern** Priory Church, Hereford and Worcester, but in this case they are in wood, beneath one of the monks' stalls or misericords. It is thought to be the only example in such surroundings of a human physician carrying out a urinoscopy, the testing of a urine specimen. I stress 'human', because a similar scene is depicted in **Stratford-upon-Avon** Church, but the physician and the patient are both monkeys. The monkey patient is actually using the glass urinal flask most realistically, and one distinguished writer admits that it was seeing this which made him realise what was happening on the misericord at Malvern. The carving there is much more discreet, and the doctor and patient could be mistaken for just raising their glasses to each other . . .

The woodwork in **Plemstall** Church in Cheshire looks as venerable as that misericord, even though the medical flavour is missing. Remarkably, most of it was carved during this century; and more remarkably still, it was all created by one amateur craftsman, the Revd J. Hooker Toogood. One of his admirers, a cabinet-maker himself, wrote: 'He spent thirty-seven years of his life preaching on the seventh day and carving on the other six – a quiet country parson whose dedicated hand worked so long to the glory of the Master Carpenter.'

Mr Toogood came to Plemstall as rector in 1907, enlisted during the First World War to lecture on mathematics to artillery officers, and returned to the village in 1919. One of his first actions was to add a workshop to the Rectory; his second one was to add a workshop to the church. Here he designed and carved the main altar and four smaller ones, the reredos with its thirty-eight figures, the square box-pews with linen-fold panels, the choir stalls, the sanctuary panelling, the cladding for the chapel pillars, the baptistry screen, the lectern, the war memorial, the font cover – you name it, he made it. The rood screen was his greatest achievement, with its eighteen figures standing on the cross-beam and the

One of Malvern's misericords (top left) might look like a drinks party, but it is actually an early urinoscopy. Plemstall's woodwork (bottom left) looks almost as venerable, but it is all the work of a twentieth-century rector.

Crucifixion scene in the centre. Every item is intricate, elegant, and quite amazing.

The Revd Henry Cockayne Cust, Rector of **Cockayne Hatley** in Bedfordshire early in the last century, also filled his church with remarkable woodwork, but he was no great shakes at carving. Instead he had a great deal of money, being the squire as well as the rector, and rather than make the woodwork himself, he just went out and bought it – on quite a grand scale. What is more, he bought it in Belgium, which makes it the only example of its kind, so the experts say, in an English parish church.

When he arrived in 1806 he found the church 'in a most lamentable state of neglect', and it was the last straw when snow fell on his head at the altar on Christmas Day. In the next twenty-odd years he rebuilt much of the church, and filled the chancel and half the nave with

The carved dignitaries in Cockayne Hatley Church (above) started life in a Belgian abbey. The rector picked them up from a dealer in Charleroi. A couple of cherubs (left) came too.

elaborately decorated stalls from the Belgian abbey of Aulne. The abbey was ruined in the French invasion of Flanders, and the stalls were acquired by a dealer in Charleroi. He must have thought it was Christmas when the parson of an obscure Bedfordshire village turned up and bought the lot . . .

Cockayne Cust continued his shopping in Malines. He bought a magnificent communion rail from the church there to put in front of his now snow-free altar, and when he discovered it was too long, he put the rest of it round the organ loft. His final purchase was in Louvain, where he picked up the oak folding doors which now separate the nave from the tower.

It was those heavily decorated stalls, however, which must have made the greatest impact on his parishioners. They found themselves being stared at by some of the most distinguished saints and writers of the Roman Catholic Church – and the saints and writers must have been somewhat bewildered by their company too, after a century and a half with Belgian

Braunton Church was built where a sow was suckling her piglets; now they are all in the roof.

monks. The parishioners were able to avoid their eye and stare at each other, because the stalls in the nave, like those in the chancel, face each other in collegiate style. Between them on the floor are brasses in memory of assorted Cockaynes, though the memorial to Henry Cockayne Cust is elsewhere, on the north wall. However, if you look very hard at the roof, you may see in the centre of the beams his initials, HCC.

Looking hard at church roofs can often be well worthwhile. You may not see initials as such, but in **Norwich** Cathedral, for instance, you can spot another kind of signature, a series of gold wells on the bosses of the presbytery. They are the rebus, the pictorial punning signature, of the man who restored the cathedral and erected its splendid spire in the fifteenth century, Bishop Goldwell. And in **Braunton** Church in Devon, one of the roof bosses has a more obscure form of identification, a sow feeding her litter, the unlikely emblem of a sixth-century saint called Brannoc, to whom the church is dedicated, and who is reputed to have had it built.

It is one of those legends which you can't help thinking might just possibly be true. Brannoc was a holy man who came and preached to the villagers, and inspired one of them, a wealthy farmer, to say he would build a church on the hillside he owned above the village. It seemed a generous gesture, and Brannoc happily accepted, but the farmer knew that, instead of the bleak hillside a good league from the village, which was little use to him anyway, he should have offered a fertile field close by.

He may not have been too surprised, therefore, when a mighty storm came one night when the church was half-built, and blew it down. Work started again, and they were nearly up to roof level when, without even a storm, it fell down again. Still he kept his qualms to himself, and Brannoc urged the villagers to have another go, but this time they kept watch to see if the church would be destroyed again.

They soon got the answer, in the form of what one chronicler describes as 'a spirit tall, with mighty wings outspread, swinging a golden censer in his hand, who cried in a voice like surge on the rocky coast: "Down, down, ye walls! Why stand ye proudly here? The Lord has spoken; His House shall be elsewhere".'

Brannoc, grasping the situation at last, enquired where the Lord had in mind. The spirit's instructions were clear: 'It is not His pleasure to dwell on this mount, but in the fair valley amidst His children. Go, seek the spot below where thou shalt find a humble sow with seven young. There build the church – the House of God.' Whereupon he departed, but not before making sure the half-built church fell down again – all except for the wall near Brannoc and his flock, who remained unharmed.

Sure enough, they found the sow and her litter, and sure enough, it was the field the farmer should have given in the first place.

Rowlstone in Hereford and Worcester. The church is mainly decorated with cocks, which is fair enough in view of Peter's well-known connection with the one that crowed thrice, but alongside a cock on the arch are these two saints, one holding a book and scroll, the other a short cross, and while the cock stands belligerently upright, the saints are perched on their heads.

The reference books either record this without comment, or just make a guess. An 1892 writer observes casually that the church contains 'quaint references to its patron saint, whose effigy we observe is represented head downwards upon the

The acrobatic saints in Rowlstone Church. Nobody is quite sure why they are standing on their heads – but the cock is not too bothered.

He was duly contrite, and confessed all. This time the church stayed up, and they finished it off with the carving of the sow and piglets in the roof, 'proving the legend to be truth', the chronicler ends. You may not entirely agree, but up on the hillside they will still point out the wall that the spirit left intact . . .

While there is a plausible explanation for the sow in Braunton's roof, it is not so easy to explain the upside-down saints on the chancel arch of St Peter's Church,

wall'. But why? And who is his friend? Later historians shared my doubts, one commenting dubiously: 'Two upside-down figures on the south capital are *said* to represent St Peter crucified head downwards.' Why two St Peters side by side, and why are they not on crosses, instead of just the wrong way up?

No, I go along with the great authority, Pevsner, who offers a much more practical explanation. In his view it was just careless-ness by the stonemason, who carved the

A touch of Eastern promise in Wickham Church – angels the colour of milk chocolate and an octet of elephants. They actually came from Paris.

figures the wrong way up by mistake, and couldn't be bothered to throw the stone away and start again. I suppose with the cock on the same block of stone, it was either they who had to be inverted, or the cock – and we know the mason was very fond of cocks.

His master, apparently, let him get away with it, and Pevsner approves. 'Such indul-

gence is attractive,' he writes. It has also caused some fascinating speculation over the centuries . . .

The roof decorations in **Wickham** Church, near Newbury in Berkshire, offer a different kind of surprise, not only in the form they take but in the material they are made of. The roof of the nave is supported by eight coloured elephants in full ceremonial dress, while the angels supporting the chancel roof are the shade of pale milk-chocolate. As one visitor commented: 'They give the church the air of an Eastern temple.' The elephants did not come from India, however, but from the Paris Exhibition. A nineteenth-century rector, the Revd William Nicholson, followed the example of his colleague at Cockayne Hatley, and went to the Continent to embellish his church. When he spotted four of these elephants at the Exhibition, he was so taken with them that he acquired the lot, and ordered four more to complete the set.

What makes these elephants and angels more fascinating is that they are not wood or stone, but papier-mâché. This only came into use in the eighteenth century, and one of the first churches to have ceiling mouldings made from it was St Michael's, **Great Witley**, near Tenbury Wells in Hereford and Worcester. The mouldings were installed by the second Lord Foley in 1755, a century ahead of those at Wickham, but they are rather overshadowed by the Belucci ceiling paintings, which came from the Duke of Chandos's mansion in Edgware.

Church ceilings have had paintings on them since long before Belucci, but the results have not always been so universally

The paintings are by Belucci, but the mouldings are papier-mâché; a ceiling full of surprises in Great Witley Church.

You name it, Bromfield Church ceiling has got it – and all for seven pounds!

acclaimed. **Bromfield** Church in Shropshire has a painted ceiling in the chancel by a seventeenth-century artist called Thomas Francis, which has been variously described as 'a splendid piece of ecclesiastical pop-art', 'a display of robust naivety', and 'not a great work of art, not Gothic, but no doubt the best that could be done at the time'. Personally I think it's rather jolly – lots of billowing clouds and angels flying around, some carrying Bibles, others consisting only of heads and wings. There are texts flying about too, on the lines of 'Thus sayth the High and Lofty One that inhabits eternity', which perhaps we could have done without, but Thomas Francis was only paid seven pounds for all this effort, and I reckon the church got its money's-worth. It could hardly have covered the cost of the paint . . .

Monumental
mysteries and
other tales from
the tombs

Monumental mysteries and other tales from the tombs

Tombs and memorials have presented some pretty puzzles over the centuries, but Sir Ralph Pudsey's memorial in **Bolton-by-Bowland** Church in Lancashire is more of a monumental marvel than a mystery – as indeed is the prolific Sir Ralph himself. He was a distinguished fifteenth-century knight who sheltered King Henry VI in 1463 after an unpleasant encounter with the Yorkists at the Battle of Hexham, but his principal claim to fame is the size of his

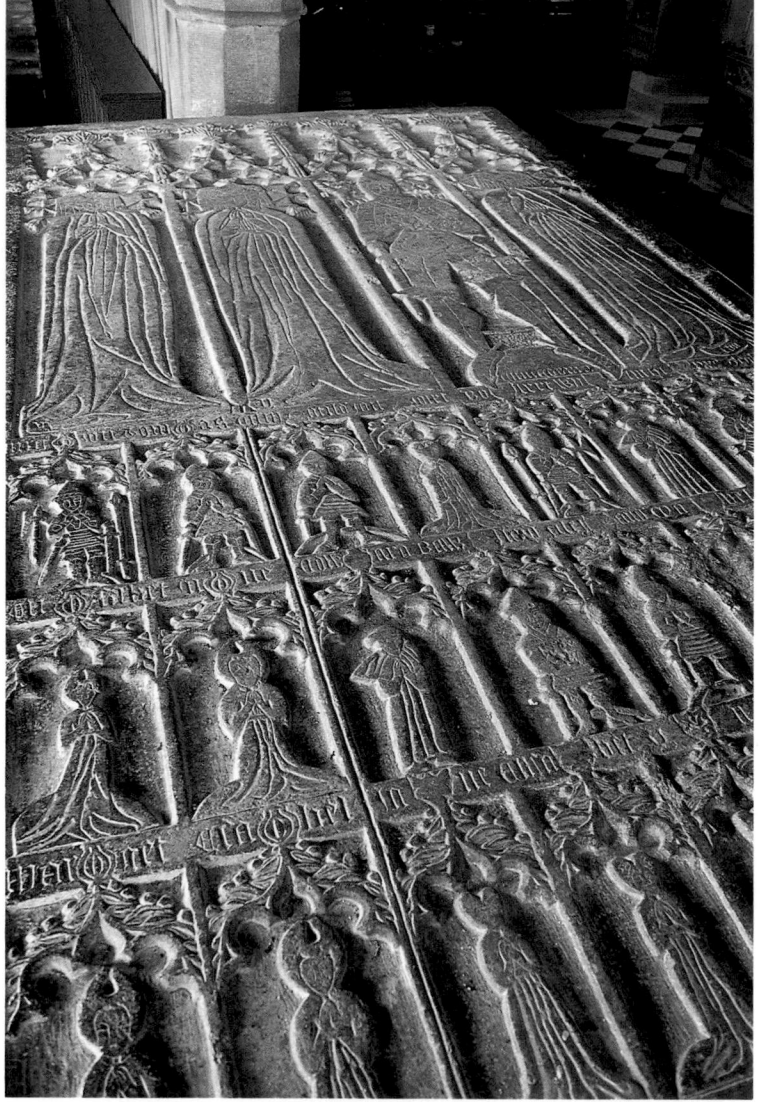

Sir Ralph Pudsey and his family, all twenty-eight of them, lying down to be counted on his tomb in Bolton-by-Bowland.

family. With the help of three successive wives he produced a total of twenty-five children, and all of them are portrayed, row by row, on his tomb.

Wives and offspring are set out systematically beside and beneath him. His first and second wives, Matilda and Margaret, are on his right, and Edwina, who survived him, is on his left. Very helpfully, each wife has been given a sort of score-card, in the form of a Roman numeral set in the folds of her dress, stating how many of the children in the three rows below were her progeny. Matilda, the opening bat as it were, scored only two; Margaret did rather better in the middle-order with six, but the star was undoubtedly the tail-ender, Edwina, with a spectacular seventeen not out.

It was quite usual, of course, for entire families to be portrayed on a tomb, but I often wonder who put them there. Was it the last surviving offspring, or was it done when the father died, in which case it must have been rather eerie for the surviving family to see themselves portrayed on a tomb which was not yet theirs. In the case of the Pudseys I have a sneaking suspicion that Edwina was responsible. As the surviving wife, with by far the most children, my bet is she set them all out on the tomb so people who saw them would think: 'Didn't she do well . . .'

The sixth Earl of Rutland was not nearly as prolific, nor as fortunate, as Sir Ralph. He only had two sons and one daughter, and both sons died in their infancy, while the daughter fell seriously ill too. This in itself was not remarkable, such was the infant mortality rate in the seventeenth century, but his misfortune was blamed on six women who were accused of witchcraft. On the family tomb in **Bottesford** Church, near Belvoir Castle in Leicestershire, is the only epitaph in England which mentions sorcery. The Earl's inscription reads: 'In 1605 he married ye Lady Cecelia Hungerford, daughter to ye honble knight Sir John Tufton, by whom he had two sons, both wch died in their infancy by wicked practise and sorcery.'

The Earl of Rutland's family tomb at Bottesford has the only epitaph in England which mentions sorcery – his children fell foul of the Witches of Belvoir.

The story of the Witches of Belvoir, and what became known as the Witchcraft Tomb, is so bizarre it needs no elaboration from me. A Bottesford woman called Joan Flower and her two daughters, Margaret and Phillipa, worked for the Earl at the castle, but they were slovenly, lazy and dishonest, and one after another they were dismissed. Joan Flower decided to have her revenge and, with her two daughters and three other women, she acquired a glove belonging to the Earl's elder son Henry, plunged it into boiling water, pricked it with a knife and rubbed it on the back of her cat Rutterkin, accompanied by a few appropriate curses. The unfortunate Henry duly died.

Then they tried the same trick with a glove of the younger son, Francis. Perhaps the water wasn't hot enough, or the cat was feeling uncooperative, but Francis survived, though distinctly off-colour. Undeterred, they buried the glove and left it to rot – and sure enough, Francis wasted away and died too. Joan and her colleagues finally had a go at the daughter, Katherine, using her handkerchief instead of a glove, and

The chancel of Burford Church, where Edmund Cornewall's heart was interred . . .

. . . and the effigy at Giggleswick of Sir Richard Tempest, 'buried with the head of his favourite charger.' But was he?

Katherine fell ill with the same mysterious malady.

By now, however, the activities of this sinister sextet had got around. All six were arrested in 1617 and brought before Lincoln Assizes, where each one gave evidence against the others, and the whole story came out. As a further act of revenge it was learned that Joan had put an extra curse on the Earl to prevent him having more children, and this seemed to work too – he died without further issue. However, the arrest came in time to save Katherine, because she recovered from her illness and lived happily ever after.

Not so the six defendants. In spite of all turning King's evidence, all were sentenced to be hanged. It was left to Joan Flower to give the story a final twist. As she awaited execution she still pleaded her innocence, and asked for some bread to prove it. If she were guilty, she said, God would strike her dead as she ate it. The bread was brought, she took a bite – and choked to death . . .

While the story of the Witches of Belvoir is well documented, there is remarkably little information about a rather curious burial in **Giggleswick** Church, North Yorkshire. It contains the battered sepulchral effigy of Sir Richard Tempest, who was knighted at the Battle of Wakefield in 1460, attainted for treason a year later but pardoned by Edward IV, and his death is recorded in 1488. So far, so good, but every reference book then adds the throwaway line: 'He was buried with the head of his favourite charger.'

No explanation is given for this bizarre interment. We do not even know the name of his horse, let alone why Sir Richard wanted his head for company. Did it die with its master, or was its body dug up for the head to be retrieved, or was the unfortunate animal slaughtered to suit Sir Richard's whim?

I was relieved to learn from Mr A.V.B. Norman of the Church Monuments Society that all this macabre speculation is probably unnecessary. Sir Richard's effigy has its head resting on the head of an animal, which was probably intended to be a goat, representing the Tempest crest. But it could easily be mistaken for the head of a horse – so could some early chronicler have assumed that it belonged to Sir Richard's charger, and another legend was born?

Interring a human heart was more common than a horse's head, if the deceased had died abroad; conveying bodies for long distances had its problems in those pre-freezer days. Sometimes it was placed in a heart tomb, like Edmund Cornewall's in the chancel of **Burford** Church in Shropshire – though the church guidebook records, without explanation, that the heart itself disappeared from the tomb in 1819. But some experts say that, when a heart is buried, the place is marked by a miniature effigy of the person involved, and they quote the little figure of a cross-legged knight, only two feet long, which is carved on the piscina in the south chapel of **Long Wittenham** Church, in Oxfordshire.

However, there is no evidence of any heart, nor of the identity of the figure. Some say he was Gilbert de Clare, but he died at

his castle in Monmouth, no great distance away, and his body at any rate is buried in Tewkesbury Abbey. One expert says simply: 'Nothing remains on which to found a conjecture.' But all agree that this is the smallest and least conspicuous sculptured monument in any church in England; it could also be the only one on a piscina.

The carvings on the tomb of Piers Shonks the dragon-slayer are an example, like Sir Richard Tempest's headrest, of how stonemasons can cause confusion for later generations. Piers was Lord of the Manor of **Brent Pelham** in Hertfordshire during the thirteenth century, and is credited with killing a local dragon by sticking a spear down its throat. The Devil, it is said, disapproved of this and vowed he would take

The village may be Long Wittenham, but the slumbering knight is very short – the smallest sculptured monument in any English church.

Piers Shonks, the dragon-slayer of Brent Pelham, was buried in the church wall to thwart the Devil.

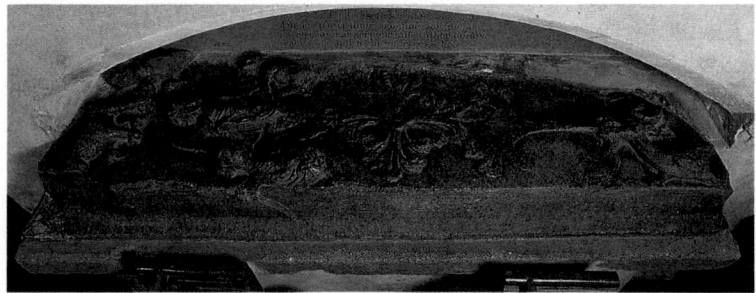

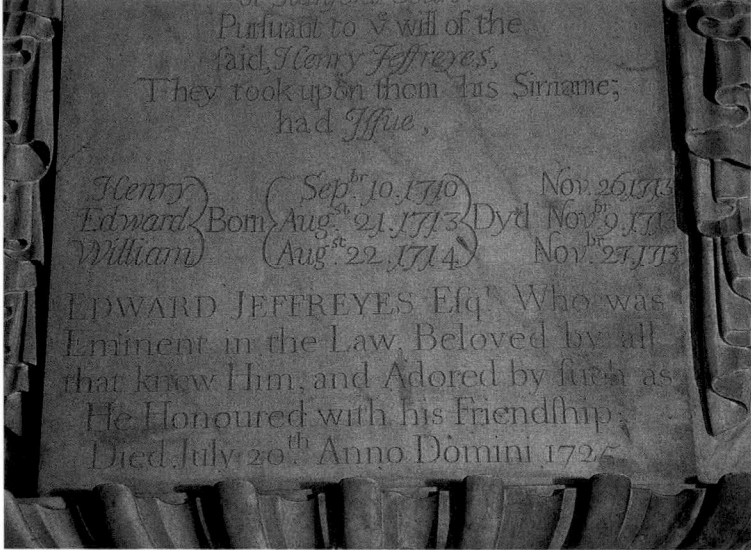

Little William Jeffreys of Clifton-upon-Teme seems to have died nine months before he was born (above) but there's an explanation.
The gravestone at Northchurch (right) refers to Peter the Wild Boy, but by the time he died he was Peter the Tame Old Man.

Shonks' soul after his death, whether he was buried inside or outside the church. So Shonks very shrewdly elected to be buried in the church wall, a ploy which the Devil hadn't thought of, and one hopes his soul rests in peace.

The story seems to be corroborated by the carvings on his tomb. There is a dragon apparently with a spear in its mouth, and a figure, perhaps the Devil, carrying Shonks' soul. But the spear could well be a cross, a symbol of right vanquishing evil, and the figure carrying the soul could just as easily be an angel. However, a seventeenth-century vicar perpetuated the tale by adding a verse on the tomb which ends: 'Shonks one serpent kills, t'other defies, And in this wall, as in a fortress, lies.' It is difficult to argue with that.

Confusion over carvings and inscriptions on old tombs cannot always be blamed on the mason. There is the matter of dates, for instance. Inscription-spotters get great delight from contradictory dates on tombstones, and in some cases it can be a genuine error. I cannot think of any other reason, for instance, why Jane Smith, who was buried in **East Adderbury** Church in Oxfordshire in 1508, should have had her date of death recorded as February 30th. But there is an entirely logical explanation for a floor tomb in Norwich Cathedral recording that a baby girl was born on April 13th and died on February 20th in the same year, 1736. It is probably the same reason why a baby boy called William Jeffreys,

buried in **Clifton-upon-Teme** near Tenbury Wells in the same period, apparently died nine months before he was born, and it also explains why Sir John Dutton's memorial in **Sherborne** Church in Gloucestershire records that he died in 1742/3 – as if the mason could not decide which year it was.

These and other similar 'mistakes' came about because until 1752, when England switched from the Julian to the Gregorian calendar, the beginning of the legal year was Lady Day, March 25th. So in 1736, for instance, according to the legal calendar, April really did come before February, and the mason who put 1742/3 was complying with both the legal and the standard calendars. However, I cannot let him off with a mistake he really did make over the name of Sir John's grandfather; he inscribed it first as John, then he, or the master mason, blatantly crossed it out and carved 'Peter' above it . . .

The engraver of the brass plaque in St Mary's Church, **Northchurch** in Hertfordshire had no doubts about the Peter in that inscription. 'Peter the Wild Boy' was a name familiar to most people in England during the eighteenth century, from the Queen down, and the inscription gives some details of his strange story.

In 1725 he was found wandering in the forest near Hanover, wearing only the remnant of a shirt, eating acorns and living mostly in trees. Word reached the Princess of Wales, later Queen Caroline, and she had him brought to the English court as a novelty. The novelty, alas, soon wore off, and as he showed no signs of saying anything interesting or improving his table manners, he was sent to Harrow. No, not the School, where he might have fitted in rather well, but a private boarding house. He still failed to improve, so he was put in the care of a Berkhamsted farmer, Thomas Fenn, and to the credit of Mr Fenn – and to be fair, to Queen Caroline, who sent an annual allowance – he lived there reasonably happily for the rest of his long life.

As the years went by, Peter the Wild Boy became the Peter the Tame Man, but he still wandered in the woods, sometimes for days at a time, and on one occasion got as far as Norwich, which still has a pub called the Wild Man. It was near the head office of the newspaper for which I once worked, and I always assumed the Wild Man was named after my editor, but it must date back to Peter's brief visit. When he died in 1786, aged about seventy-two, he had still not been forgotten in the corridors of power, and the Treasury paid for the brass plaque in St Mary's, with its engraving of a bearded, rather melancholy figure.

My connection with Peter and that brass plaque is somewhat remote – just the odd pint in the Wild Man – but I feel much closer to another memorial erected more than two centuries later, in 1993, in **Broxted** Church, Essex. It consists of two pairs of windows designed by the artist John K. Clark, one pair grey and bleak showing a pair of hands tied together, the other a bright blaze of colour, featuring the dove of peace and glasses of champagne – perhaps the first time a champagne glass has appeared in a memorial window. The windows symbolise captivity and freedom; they are in honour of the Beirut hostages, one of whom, John McCarthy, is a local man and used to read the lessons in church. The congregation had toasted him in champagne when he was freed, hence the glasses.

Brian Keenan and Terry Waite were there also, and like many others who admired and respected all the hostages, I wish I could have been there too. But I also had a more personal reason. I had met Terry Waite a number of times in the *Today* studio, and he was there on my last day on the programme, Christmas Eve, 1986. He was about to set off on his final mission to Beirut, but he remembered I was leaving and gave me a glass paper-weight as a memento before we parted. 'Take care,' I said. 'I will,' he replied . . .

The Captivity Window at Broxted, epitomising the sufferings of the Beirut hostages . . .

It was over five years before he returned and I spoke to him again. While he was away, that paperweight was a constant reminder of what he was going through, while I was enjoying my return to Norfolk.

Now those stained-glass windows will be a permanent reminder, for a much wider public, of the fortitude and courage of the hostages of Beirut.

. . . and the Freedom Window at Broxted, celebrating their release. John McCarthy used to read the lessons there.

High church relics:
a cannon-ball,
a bed bug –
and hallo abseiler!

High church relics: a cannon-ball, a bed bug – and hallo abseiler!

St Clement's Church at Hastings (below left) has two cannon-balls embedded in its tower. Only one is genuine; the other was added to provide a balance. A number of church towers were bombarded with fives balls when the game first came to England, but at Montacute a succession of vicars eventually banned it and a free-standing fives wall (below right) was built at nearby Stoke-sub-Hamdon.

In most small towns and villages the church tower has become such a familiar feature, because of its prominence, that we are inclined to take it for granted. One square tower may seem very like another, and you often have to study them fairly closely to spot anything odd about them. The distinguishing feature may be no larger than a penny – and indeed it could actually be one, like the Beccles penny embedded in a plaque on the tower of **Beccles** Church in Suffolk. It is the eighteenth-century locally-minted coin which was handed over by the town council in 1972 when they bought the tower. On the face of it they got a bargain, but in the next four years it cost £67,000 to restore it.

The round objects on the tower of St Clement's Church in **Hastings**, Sussex, are much bigger than pennies, but they are set high up in the wall on each side of the belfry louvre, and even if you noticed them, you might not realise what they were. One is a cannon-ball which was fired at the church from a ship offshore, two or three hundred years ago, and the other one, made of stone, was added many years later by an architect with an eye for symmetry.

Just who fired the cannon-ball has never been established. The popular story is that it came from a Dutch ship during a four-day battle in the Channel in 1666, but another authority puts the date at 1720. It is also not clear whether the ball actually embedded itself in the tower, or was found lying in the churchyard, where it had bounced, and was stuck into the hole it had made to stop the draught. Either way, since St Clement's is hardly a military target, it must have been a rotten shot.

While on the subject of balls embedded in church towers, it would be appropriate to find a fives ball preserved in the tower at **Montacute** in Somerset. When fives was introduced into England, the only requirement for the early form of the game was

one large, flat wall, and a church tower seemed ideal. The vicar of Montacute was apparently a fives enthusiast, and removed all the projections on the wall of the tower so he could practise. His successors, however, took a poor view of turning the churchyard into a fives court, and the bulky stone base of the market cross was dumped against the wall to discourage players.

The vicar of Montacute was not the only culprit. Records have been found in other churches of items like 'To digging ditches across ye fives courts', and in one church-yard, trees were planted to prevent the game. At **Brewham** Church, also in Somerset, shutters were hung over the windows in case the players' aim became too wild; the hooks the shutters were hung from are still in the wall.

In recent years church towers have attracted another form of sport, which gets ecclesiastical approval because it generally raises money for the church. Amateur abseilers, sometimes including the vicar himself, have thrown themselves off church towers with happy abandon in the name of sponsored sport. This sort of thing, however, is not as new as it may seem. Back in the seventeenth and eighteenth centuries, travelling entertainers used to do much the same thing, though in their case they kept the money.

This was how Thomas Pelling came to find himself on the tower of **Pocklington** Church, in what is now Humberside, in 1733. Mr Pelling was an itinerant stuntman who made a living from flying off churches. He wore stiffened wings, Batman-style, and one ankle was attached to a pulley which ran along a rope. This was tied to a pinnacle on the tower, and the other end was attached to a windlass on the ground. The idea was to keep the rope taut and at a reasonable angle, so that Mr Pelling could zoom down it on the pulley, flapping his wings and no doubt looking forward to collecting a few bob from the spectators when he got to the bottom.

Alas, it didn't quite work that way. For some reason the rope went slack, and sagged so much that instead of giving him a clear run to the ground it bounced him into the chancel roof. A tablet inside the chancel preserves his memory, and the entry in the burial register sums up his sad little story: '1733, April 10th, Thomas Pelling from

The tower of Pocklington Church where Thomas Pelling, 'A Flying Man', made a fatal crash landing.

Burton Strather in Lincolnshire, a Flying Man, who was killed by jumping against the Battlement of ye Choir, when coming down ye rope from ye Steeple.'

Since those days, church towers have said goodbye to Flying Men and it's 'hallo, abseiler', but they are only temporary adornments, whereas the permanent deco-rations usually have a more ecclesiastical flavour. However, it is difficult to appre-ciate at first the ecclesiastical reason, or indeed any reason at all, for putting the letters of the alphabet along the north wall

The reason for the alphabet on Stratford St Mary Church (above left) is rather obscure, but there is a simple explanation for the extra clock-face at Thornton Hough (above right) – the squire couldn't see the lower one.

of **Stratford St Mary** Church in Suffolk. They were let into the flushwork, together with various Latin inscriptions, at about the time the north aisle was built by the Mors family in 1499. Nobody was quite sure why, until an old leaflet came to light which indicated that they were put there as a reminder to travellers on the nearby London road to say their prayers. 'By means of this alphabet,' said the leaflet, 'the whole of the Breviary is composed.'

The present vicar, the Revd Brian Ettlinger, comments that this reasoning is similar to that which applied when a person who asked for a library of books was given a dictionary and told to rearrange the words to suit himself. However, he has heard no other credible explanation for the letters, and a number of churches on the Continent have the same alphabet motif for this reason. It never seemed to catch on over here, perhaps because English travellers never recognised the writing on the wall.

A more common decoration on English churches is the church clock, and several have four clock-faces, one on each side of the tower, but I know of only one which has a fifth. **Thornton Hough** was once just another hamlet in the Wirral, until it was transformed by two rich men. A retired Yorkshire woollen manufacturer, Joseph Hirst, built himself Thornton House, plus the parish church, the vicarage, the church school, some cottages and shops. Twenty years later Lord Leverhulme turned the place into another custom-built workers' village, like Port Sunlight, but I trust that

by then Mr Hirst had enjoyed his declining years in peace.

In his own building operation, however, he had slipped up on one small point – the sort of error anyone can make in extending one's property, which only becomes apparent when the job is done. Having put up the church and installed a clock in the tower, Mr Hirst found that an intervening wall prevented him from seeing it. Most of us, I imagine, would have muttered something rude and left it at that, but Joseph Hirst was not a man to admit defeat. He had an extra little clock-face added above the one he couldn't see, and the two faces on that side of the tower have been ticking away in tandem ever since.

Another familiar decoration on church towers is the weather-vane, but **Kingsclere** Church in Hampshire has a distinctly odd one, which depicts a bed bug. It is a very elegant sort of bug, with six ornate little crosses for legs, and another one for its tail, but a bed bug it undoubtedly is, and it serves as a permanent reminder of an unfortunate experience which King John had after a hunting expedition. A thick fog prevented him returning home, and he spent the night at the Crown Inn at Kingsclere – in the company, so it transpired, of a bed bug. Considerably irritated, in every sense, he decreed that an effigy of a bug be erected on the church tower.

This seems a little hard on the church since, by rights, the bug ought to be perched on the Crown Inn as a warning to other wayfarers. Happily the beds are much purer these days, and Kingsclere is rather proud of its unlikely royal heirloom.

Towers and steeples can be unusual in their own right, without the addition of any odd decoration. **Chesterfield**'s twisted spire is the most famous example, and in *Timpson's England* I mentioned **Ermington** in Devon, which has the same distinction. There is a third, at **Cleobury Mortimer** in Shropshire, where the timber-framed spire has been put out of shape by wind and weather. It was not so much the twist as the sway which disturbed one investigator. He reported: 'The frequency of sway is about one cycle per four seconds, so that coming down to solid ground after a day's surveying in the top of the spire is like landing from a cross-channel ferry after a rough passage.' However, repairs were effected, and while the spire still tilts and probably still sways, it also still survives.

Needless to say, local legend offers quite a different explanation for the twist in the spire. It is supposed to have happened when a bride who was not a virgin arrived at the church. The spire's ability to detect virginity, however, must be sadly flawed, because the legend forecasts that it will only resume its original shape when a virgin comes to be married. I am sure the ladies of Cleobury Mortimer will confirm that it must have missed hundreds . . .

The spire at Cleobury Mortimer got in a twist, they say, when a bride came to the church who was not a virgin.

Kingsclere Church (below left) got its bedbug weathervane (below) after King John had an unpleasant experience at the local inn.

At Peterchurch the spire is made of fibreglass.

The spire that lost its church. When St Mark's, Horsham, (right) was demolished to make way for an office complex, the spire was left behind. Now it is used as a flower-shop.

When the parishioners of **Peterchurch** in Hereford and Worcester were faced with the problem of replacing their old spire, they decided to avoid such hazards by erecting one made of fibreglass. This was only after long debate: the original spire was declared unsafe and taken down in 1949, leaving an ugly stump, and it was nearly ten years later that a parishioner first advocated an aluminium replacement. After another eight years a parish meeting chose a design in openwork pre-stressed concrete, which happily was discarded too. Then in 1972 a prefabricated fibreglass spire, 110 feet high, was hoisted into position in three sections by a giant crane. The third section unfortunately didn't fit, but the vicar took a very Christian attitude: 'No one has done a job like this before, and we are meeting problems as they come.' It took a couple of days to meet this particular problem, but eventually all went well, the sceptics were silenced, and the fibreglass steeple is now a familiar and accepted feature of the Peterchurch skyline.

Certainly it does not look as incongruous as the lonely Victorian church spire which stands in the heart of a modern office complex in **Horsham**, West Sussex. The centre of Horsham has been virtually taken over by the insurance company Sun Alliance, which has its headquarters there, and its newest office-block, St Mark's Court, is the largest group-occupied building in England, able to accommodate a thousand staff. In the centre of this towering block, and almost dwarfed by it, is the 150-foot spire of St Mark's Church; the main body of the church has disappeared.

The company began to clear the area in 1988, and by a convenient chance, St Mark's was declared redundant in 1989. At the same time there was an increasing need for a new church to serve an expanding area on the outskirts of Horsham, so the company did a deal. It built a new church there in exchange for the site of St Mark's.

The old church was demolished, but its spire was left intact. The company's official brochure does not explain why, but the spire was, in fact, a memorial to a former vicar, Canon A.H. Bridges, which was erected by his daughter Mary in 1870, thirty years after the rest of the church. I imagine therefore that the family of the good Canon, and indeed the church authorities, might not have been too happy to see it bite the dust. The only comment in the brochure is that 'the spire was retained, becoming an integral feature of the new development'.

The idea of integrating a 120-year-old church spire into a brand-new office complex was novel, to say the least. Its principal effect seems to have been to block the view from some of the office windows. But the final touch to the integration came a year or so later. The double wooden doors at the base of the spire were replaced by glass ones, and Canon Bridges' memorial started a new career – as a flower shop.

How high is the
lychgate,
how steep is the
floor . . .

How high is the lychgate, how steep is the floor . . .

The Lost Church of Perranporth. St Piran's was buried first by the sands, then by courtesy of the Department of the Environment. Only its name survives.

The *Guinness Book of Records* has not been entirely good for us. It was all right when it just recorded the fastest mile, or the highest mountain, or the biggest car park (it's by a shopping mall in Edmonton, Alberta, 20,000 spaces), but then people started creating new sorts of records to get their names in the book, so that Mark Gottleib, for example, earned himself a mention by being the first violinist to play Handel's *Water Music* under water. I think the book's

proprietors have drawn the line now, but the damage has been done, and this enthusiasm for digging up unlikely records has proved catching. I confess I have caught it myself, and while I was delving into the many fascinations of our old English churches, I came upon a few obscure title-claimants which have escaped even the all-embracing grasp of Mr Guinness.

How about, for instance, the church with the steepest floor, or the smallest door, or the highest lychgate, or the thickest wall? But let us have a look first at the only church to be buried twice . . .

St Piran's Church at **Perranporth** in Cornwall suffered this indignity, once in the eleventh century through the forces of Nature, and again in the twentieth, much more thoroughly, thanks to the Department of the Environment. 'The Lost Church', as they call it locally, was the oratory of a monastic settlement founded by St Piran in the early sixth century. Piran was doubtless a splendid saint, and if he was looking for good surf-bathing he chose the right spot, but he was not too strong on erosion and sand drift. The oratory was far too close to the dunes, and over the years the dunes got closer still. By the twelfth century they had completely submerged it.

The lesson, however, had still not been learnt, and the replacement church was built close by. That was gradually buried too, and it was eventually abandoned in 1803, when a new parish church was erected on a less vulnerable site. That might have been the last we heard of the oratory, but in 1835 an archaeologist returned to the area and dug the ruins out of the sand. He published his findings about 'the little church in the dunes', and suddenly it became a tourist attraction.

In some ways the oratory was better off under the sand. Souvenir hunters removed chunks of it, amateur excavators dug out some more, and so much soil was removed that, instead of burial by sand, the oratory was in danger of submersion by flooding. Eventually the Ecclesiastical Commissioners sold the site, and the new owners

The rise of the floor ... adds to the uplift of the spirits.' A cheerful view of Burton Dassett's sloping church floor.

encased the oratory in a quite hideous concrete shell, in order to protect it. Services were held there until the Second World War, then in 1960 it was sold again, this time to the neighbouring Ladbroke's holiday camp. St Piran would have been intrigued to find that his ancient chapel was now linked to a firm of bookies . . .

To be fair, Ladbroke's did their best by the old place. They were advised by the Department of the Environment that the only way to preserve the ruin, ironically, was to bury it again, but before taking such a drastic step Ladbroke's called a public meeting to get local reaction. Perhaps surprisingly, most of the heritage organisations and the Church favoured burial. Ladbroke's handed over the site free of charge, and in 1980 the oratory disappeared for the second and last time. All that remains above ground is a rough stone bearing the name, St Piran.

There is a happier tale to tell of **Burton Dassett** Church in Warwickshire, which may hold the record for the church with the most sloping floor, but it shows no sign of sliding down the hill or into the ground. One estimate suggests there is a difference of fifteen feet between the east and west ends, but the official guidebook quotes a figure of ten and a half feet. 'The rise of the floor by sloping and steps,' it says cheerfully, 'adds to the uplift of the spirits.' It was built on the steep hillside in Norman times, and when it was extensively restored in 1890 the architect found seven different floor levels under the rotting floorboards.

There have been more problems since. The church walls were made of hard mud faced with stone, and in the 1930s the mud was not only washing away from the stone but also providing a healthy home for blackthorn roots. For a time Burton Dassett could have claimed another record, as the church with the largest blackthorn hedge on top of its tower. Happily the hedge no longer survives, and the church does, but the struggle continues. The last I heard, they were looking for £150,000 for more restoration work. I hope that impressive slope continues to uplift their spirits until they get it.

Not merely incomparable, but unique', says the vicar of Shrewsbury about his circular church (above and below). No wonder it is unique; it was built that way by mistake.

If Burton Dassett Church can be visualised sliding down the hill, St Chad's at **Shrewsbury** in Shropshire would be more likely to roll. The main part of the church is completely circular, and while this does not make it unique – there are a handful of round churches linked with the Knights Templar – St Chad's must be the only round church in England which was built that way by mistake!

After the old church collapsed in 1788 an architect called George Steuart put forward four alternative designs for a new one, one traditional, the others circular. The building committee plumped almost unanimously for the traditional one, which also happened to be the cheapest, whereupon Steuart worked a rather cunning ploy. From his office in London he sent a scale plan, which could be fitted over the site plan, so they could adjust its position as they wished. The committee became so engrossed in deciding how to site it that they apparently never noticed the plan was for a circular building.

They blithely returned it to Mr Steuart, indicating the position they wanted it but making no comment on its shape – and that was quite enough for the architect. He went ahead with detailed plans on that basis, and when the committee saw them and protested, he told them they had already approved the general principle. He did offer to re-draw all the plans using a traditional design, but pointed out gently that of course it would cost them a lot extra.

'Reluctant to venture into further expenditure,' the church guide records sadly, 'and, one imagines, exhausted by months of argument, the committee sullenly agreed to accept Steuart's design.' So Shrewsbury found itself, to its considerable surprise, with a circular church.

Murray's Guide of 1897 condemned it as 'in execrable taste', and the great authority Nicholas Pevsner avoided any comment on its shape and merely praised 'its uncommonly beautiful position', but views have mellowed over the years, and these days the church literature calls it 'perhaps the finest product of the last phase of the English Renaissance, that is, of the Grecian revival'. The vicar says firmly it is not merely incomparable but unique – and in spite of those Knights Templar churches, who can contradict him?

St Chad's is also claimed to be the largest round church in England, and this opens up a more familiar field of church statistics – the largest, the smallest, and so on. Like most statistics, they have qualifications; it all depends what you mean by 'largest', or 'smallest', or even 'church'.

Take 'smallest' as an example. In *Timpson's England* I went for **Culbone** in Somerset, but I have to qualify that by saying it is 'the smallest completed medieval church in regular use'. The palm is supposed to go to **Bremilham** Church in Wiltshire, which measures just twelve feet square, but it is not actually licensed to carry out services – they do have one on Rogation Sunday, but that is just for old times' sake. It was actually downgraded to a mortuary chapel in 1874, and it has not been a parish church since.

There are, in fact, plenty of other contestants. **Lullington** Church in East Sussex is just fifteen feet square and seats eighteen at a pinch, but it is actually the surviving chancel of a much larger church. **Fifield Bavant** in Wiltshire has a genuine Norman parish church, said to be the smallest in the

Two contenders for the title of smallest church in England: Lullington (above) is fifteen feet square, Fifield Bavant (left) is the smallest in the south.

Another contender for smallest church. Wasdale Head is tiny, but only a chapel-at-ease.

Ixworth claims a different title; it may have the smallest church door.

south, but it is all of thirty-three feet long. **Wasdale Head** in Cumbria has a church smaller than Culbone, but it was built as a chapel-at-ease, not a church. And so it goes on.

I think it is rather more fun to go for individual features rather than complete churches. For instance, I have two contenders for the church with the smallest door. **Ixworth Thorpe** in Suffolk has a Norman south door, thirty-three inches wide and sixty-one inches high, but **Newton Arlosh** in Cumbria has a rather more interesting history attached to its tiny entrance, barely the height of a man and just thirty-one inches wide. It could also be the only church which has virtually turned through ninety degrees: the altar was origi-

nally in the traditional position at the eastern end, in what is now the vestry, but when the church had a major face-lift in 1894 the box pews were removed and the new ones were turned round to face the re-positioned altar and sanctuary on the northern side.

The tiny door was built as part of the church's defences. St John's is as much a fortress as a church, designed for defence against the marauding Scots. The walls are enormously thick, the windows are little more than arrow-slits, and the doorway can take only one person at a time, which was very useful if that person was a rampaging Scot, but causes problems these days at weddings – the bridegroom has to leave the church ahead of his bride.

Bridegrooms used to have an easier time at St John the Baptist's Church at **Mamble**, in Hereford and Worcester, where the doorway was made high enough to accommodate a mounted Crusader. The gallant knight was presumably too impatient for

But the door at Mamble, now blocked up, was tall enough to take a mounted Crusader.

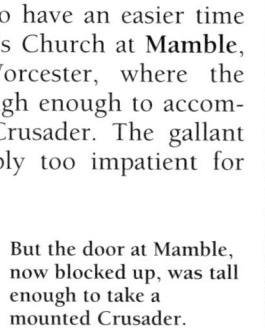

The long and the short and the tall . . . Newton Arlosh (above) was designed to repel marauding Scots, and only a very small Scot could get through this door . . .

The light at the end of the tunnel, in this case, is stained glass; Kirknewton (above) has one of the lowest chancels in England (right).

battle to waste time dismounting, so he rode into the church to be blessed. A knight lies cross-legged near the altar, looking reasonably peaceful, so maybe the blessing worked and he got safely home.

The door is now blocked, but Mamble lays claim to another kind of record as well. It has a wooden tower, erected before the rest of the church as a lookout tower, and at some stage it was given a stone surround, so the only part of it visible from the outside is the wooden spire with its oak shingles. However, the original tower still stands inside its stone casing, with a gap of a few feet between, and experts say it could be the oldest unaltered timber structure in the country.

Kirknewton Church in Northumberland could put in a bid for the lowest chancel. It looks more like a tunnel, with side walls only three feet high, joined by a low barrel-

by Roman Christians and its west wall incorporates Roman tiles, so it could claim to have the oldest church wall in England too. As one historian says, 'By comparison the Saxon doorway set into a chancel wall is quite modern!'

Finally, a title which must hold its own record as the one most hotly disputed. It is quite impossible to prove who holds it, because it depends entirely upon personal

Undisputed champion: St Martin's, Canterbury (below) is the oldest parish church in England still in continuous use. Boughton Monchelsea, however, may have the oldest lychgate (left), built in the fifteenth century.

vault roof. It also resembles the ground floor of a pele tower, and probably served much the same purpose, as a defence against the Scots. **Boughton Monchelsea** in Kent, on the other hand, may have the oldest lychgate in England, built in the fifteenth century, but my own money would go on **West Walton** in Norfolk, which could argue that its lychgate is not only the oldest but the highest. It is actually the tower of the church, erected quite apart from the main building on the place where a lychgate ought to be, so you enter the churchyard through the base of the tower. It could also be the only instance of a lych-gate being cared for by the Redundant Churches Trust, while the church still looks after itself.

The one record which everyone seems agreed upon is the title of the oldest parish church in England. Never mind all those chapels which have the occasional service as a gesture, the tiny church of St Martin in **Canterbury** has functioned continuously as a church in its own right since the sixth century. This gives it a considerable edge on its much larger and more famous neighbour, but most visitors to Canterbury head for the cathedral and ignore this venerable little place of worship, just a short step outside the city wall. St Martin's was used

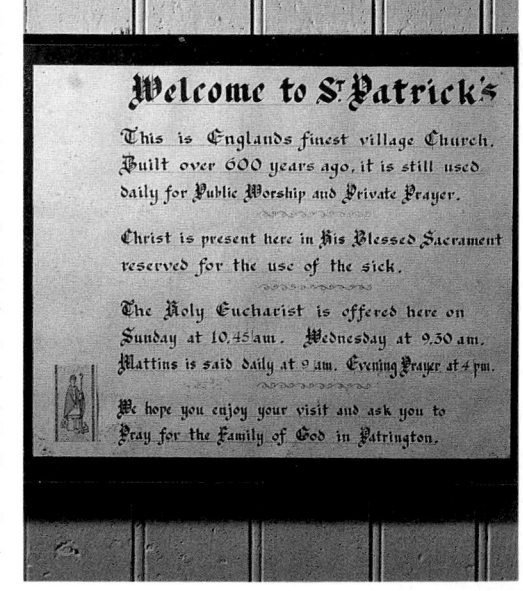

'This is England's finest village church', says the notice in St Patrick's, Patrington, and at least one archbishop agrees.

tastes, but St Patrick's at **Patrington** on Humberside claims it was awarded the title by Archbishop Garbett, and they will not part with it easily. He called it 'the most beautiful parish church in England' – and I can hear the sharp intake of breath from every parochial church council in the country . . .

The great Pevsner is rather more cautious: 'For sheer architectural beauty, few parish churches in England can vie with it.' More recently, Alec Clifton-Taylor toned it down a bit further: 'It should be included in any expert's list of the dozen finest churches in the land.' But Patrington prefers to stick with the archbishop; his comment is given considerable prominence in the church, and who can blame them. But I think they are going to get some challenges – including a few hundred from Norfolk!

Welcome to St Patrick's

This is Englands finest village Church. Built over 600 years ago, it is still used daily for Public Worship and Private Prayer.

Christ is present here in His Blessed Sacrament reserved for the use of the sick.

The Holy Eucharist is offered here on Sunday at 10.45 am. Wednesday at 9.30 am. Mattins is said daily at 9 am. Evening Prayer at 4 pm.

We hope you enjoy your visit and ask you to Pray for the Family of God in Patrington.

Did picnics start
with a pyx-niche
in the churchyard?

Did picnics start with a pyx-niche in the churchyard?

Graveyards in the main are sombre places, and probably rightly so, but often there is more to be found in graveyards than just graves, and some of the extraneous objects have strange tales to tell. Even the more routine items which crop up fairly frequently – a church cross, a sundial, a gardener's tool-shed – can have something rather special about them. It is remarkable what you can find if you look, as it were, beyond the grave.

You have to look very closely indeed to see anything fascinating about the churchyard cross at St Kenelm's, **Clifton-upon-Teme** in Hereford and Worcester. The cross itself is quite modern, but its base dates from medieval times, and cut into the base on the west side is a small niche. It was put there in the days when the rector carried the pyx, the little box containing the Host, at the head of a procession into the churchyard on Palm Sunday. When the procession stopped by the cross he placed the pyx in the niche. It is in fact a pyx-niche, and I like to think that, when the practice of taking bread outdoors for consumption spread into more general use, the pyx-niche developed into our modern picnic. The

dictionary says the word comes from the French *piquenique*, but admits that piquenique is 'of unknown origin' – so I reckon pyx-niche is as good a bet as any.

Most self-respecting old churchyards have a sundial, but none has one as old as **Bewcastle** in Cumbria. It is not immediately recognisable as a sundial because it is one of many carvings on the great pillar known as the Bewcastle Cross, erected some time in the seventh century – nobody is quite sure why. The sundial is a half-circle with thirteen radiating lines, three of

Bewcastle Church probably has the oldest sundial in England – but most people just know it as the Bewcastle Cross.

Not an outsize shepherd's crook but Ivinghoe's eighteen-foot thatch hook, used by very large firemen for pulling thatch off blazing cottages.

which have crossbars. One theory is that it was used to calculate the Spring equinox, and thus the date of Easter Sunday, but there is an ingenious suggestion that it was much more sophisticated than that, designed to suit both the Saxons and the Roman Britons, on the same principle that modern electric razors are designed to work off English and Continental voltages.

The Romans divided the day into twelve hours, so the thirteen lines were for their benefit, but the Saxons had a system of three 'tides' a day – this was before tides had anything to do with the sea – and the three lines marked with crossbars were for them. The Bewcastle Cross is mainly known for all the other carvings that it bears, but I like to regard it as England's oldest surviving sundial.

Of perhaps more practical value in its day was the long pole with a heavy iron hook on the end, which is still on the wall of **Ivinghoe** Church in Buckinghamshire. This is an ancient thatch hook for pulling thatch off the roof if fire broke out, to prevent it spreading. It must have been quite an operation; the handle is eighteen feet long, and I imagine it would take two or three men to lift it, let alone wield it at roof-height. I trust that the vicious mantrap just below it is a much later addition; otherwise, in their haste to grab the hook, they might well have lost the odd leg.

THIS BRASS WAS PLACED HERE BY THE PARISHIONERS OF IVINGHOE TO COMMEMORATE THE CORONATION OF KING EDWARD VII JUNE ST 9TH 1902

The churchyard pulpit at Tockholes, not for the benefit of overflow congregations but used at the annual outdoor service.

The churchyard at **Tockholes** in Lancashire has what looks like an ancient pulpit, built on to the ruined wall of the old schoolroom, but it is not as ancient as all that, and it was not required because the congregation grew too big for the church. It was actually the bright idea of the Revd A.T. Corfield as recently as 1910. It was the custom at the church to hold an outdoor service each year on its anniversary, and when Gerstaine Hall was demolished by Liverpool Corporation as part of a water-works scheme, the rector managed to acquire some of the old stone from the mullion windows, and built the pulpit to use on these occasions.

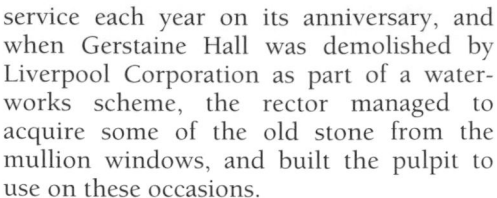

Open-air services might have been a boon for the ladies who made use of the Fainting House in the churchyard of St George's, **Shimpling**, in Suffolk. It was built in the 1840s, and it may have been originally intended as a Sunday schoolroom. It also came in handy for the rectors of Shimpling, who lived about a mile from the church and were able to rest in it between services. The little building was equipped with a fire-place and chimney, a fitted seat, a cloak-room and an earth closet, so it was ideal for the purpose.

However, it became known as the Fainting House because Victorian ladies in the congregation, laced up tightly in their stays, were sometimes overcome by the lack of air in the church – and possibly the surfeit of hot air coming from the pulpit. They were assisted across the churchyard into the Fainting House to recover.

A local benefactor paid for its restoration to mark the Queen's Silver Jubilee in 1977, after it had been derelict for some years, and it was last used as a robing room for visiting clergy when the present rector was inducted. I prefer to picture it, though, in its heyday, occupied by the languishing ladies of nineteenth-century Shimpling as they sought respite from the rigours of interminable church services.

About the same time that Shimpling acquired its Fainting House, the churchyard at **Morpeth** in Northumberland acquired a similar little building with a very different purpose. It was more Spartan than Shimpling's, with just a fireplace and very little else, and it was occupied, not by languishing ladies but by armed watchmen, keeping guard against the Resurrectionists – the fancy name for body-snatchers. That area was within easy range for body-snatchers servicing the surgeon-teachers of Edinburgh – Burke and Hare both had connections there – and it reached the point where watch clubs were set up to maintain an all-night patrol in the church-yard, particularly after fresh burials. At Morpeth the club built itself a watchtower,

This little building (above) in the graveyard at Morpeth was just big enough to house two watchmen, on guard against body-snatchers.

Shimpling Church (left) has a 'fainting house' in the churchyard, where Victorian ladies could recover if the service had gone on too long.

just big enough for two men doing two-hour shifts. These days it serves a more prosaic function as a tool-shed.

Just as watchtowers and fainting houses have become period pieces never likely to be repeated, so have the elaborate grave-stones which share the churchyard with them. Today there is a formidable document issued to all churchwardens, 'Churchyard Regulations', which bans, for instance, all those whimsical epitaphs that some of us enjoy collecting. Never again,

Sad memories. 'What am I doing in this place?' The memorial at Gravesend to Princess Pocahontas, who died of consumption after coming to England as a colonist's bride.

And ten other victims of the English coastal weather are commemorated by a boat-shaped memorial at St Mawgan. They were found frozen to death in a drifting boat.

for instance, will a dentist have on his gravestone anything like: 'Stranger! Approach this spot with gravity. John Brown is filling his last cavity . . .'

Apart from inscriptions, Churchyard Regulation Number 5 gives a list of prohibited items on graves, such as kerbs, railings, fencing, chippings, birdbaths, 'any stone in the shape of a heart or book', and statues. Luckily this was not in force when the lovely American Indian princess Pocahontas died of consumption as she was about to sail back home from Greenwich. She came to England as the bride of an early colonist, John Rolfe, who is credited with being the first successful planter of tobacco, and thus had much to answer for. Having sown this ominous crop he returned to Heacham in Norfolk, and the princess lived for three years at Heacham Hall as the squire's lady. She never got used to the climate, and her husband decided to take her back to America with their baby son, but she died before she could board ship, and was buried in St George's churchyard, **Gravesend**, Kent. Her statue still stands there, in full Indian dress, with arms outstretched and head thrown back, as if she is saying, with disbelief: 'What am I doing in this place?'

Back to the Churchyard Regulations. That one about statues and birdbaths does not specifically mention boats, but I suspect there would be short shrift these days for the memorial in **St Mawgan** churchyard, Cornwall, which commemorates ten men found frozen to death in a boat which

HERE LIE THE BODIES OF
JACOB WILLIAMS   DAVID ROBERTS
OWEN HUGHS   THOMAS COLLINS
CHARLES CAWLEY   RICHARD CUTLER
WILLIAM LOYD   WILLIAM ELIOTT
THOMAS BROWN   JEMMY
who were drifted ashore in a boat frozen to death at
Tregurrian Beach in this Parish on Sunday
13th December 1846

drifted ashore in 1846. It is an historic as well as an unusual headstone, because these men were the first to be buried under a law which made it compulsory for the bodies from shipwrecks to be buried at public expense, together with rewards for those who discovered them. The good news was that the bodies were guaranteed a decent burial; the bad news, I suspect, was that ruthless bounty hunters made sure that anyone washed ashore in bad shape finished up very, very dead . . .

If the compilers of Churchyard Regulations had baulked at the St Mawgan boat, they would have had a real tantrum over the **Mortlake** tent. The tomb of Sir

A tent that became a stone shroud: the tomb of Sir Richard Burton, pitched in Mortlake churchyard.

The thirteen little graves in Cooling churchyard which probably inspired the opening pages of Charles Dickens' *Great Expectations*. These tiny children had none . . .

Richard Burton, noted traveller and Arabic scholar, is made of stone, which is a plus; the minus is that it is shaped like a full-size canopied tent, with a crucifix perched on top, a most unlikely object to find in the churchyard of a Surrey suburb.

I think the complete antithesis of this extravagant monument can be found in a bleak churchyard by the Thames marshes in Kent, a sombre double row of little humped stones, thirteen altogether. They lie in **Cooling** churchyard, sharing one headstone between them, babies belonging to the Comport family, though three had the surname Baker. The Baker babies died at the ages of five months, one year and three years, the others were seventeen months or less. The reason for all these early deaths is not given, but in the 1770s, when they occurred, the infant mortality rate was pretty appalling. It was the sight of these graves that is supposed to have inspired the opening pages of *Great Expectations*; Dickens cut down the number of Pip's little brothers to five, but he buried them in similar fashion: 'five little stone lozenges, each about a foot and a half long, in a neat row beside their grave'.

Cooling Church has been redundant for many years, and the graveyard can be a gloomy and sinister place on a dark winter's evening. It is easy to picture that terrifying convict looming out of the mist over the marshes – 'a fearful man, all in coarse grey, with a great iron on his leg, a man with no hat, and with broken shoes, and with an old rag tied round his head, a man who had been soaked in water, and smothered in mud, and lamed by stones, and cut by flints, and stung by nettles, and torn by briars, who limped and shivered and glared and growled . . .'

Yes, Mr Dickens tells it far better than I ever could. I'll leave the graveyards to him.

MAPS

The maps on the following pages are intended for general reference only. They are not recommended as route maps. The use of your regular route planner is therefore advisable.

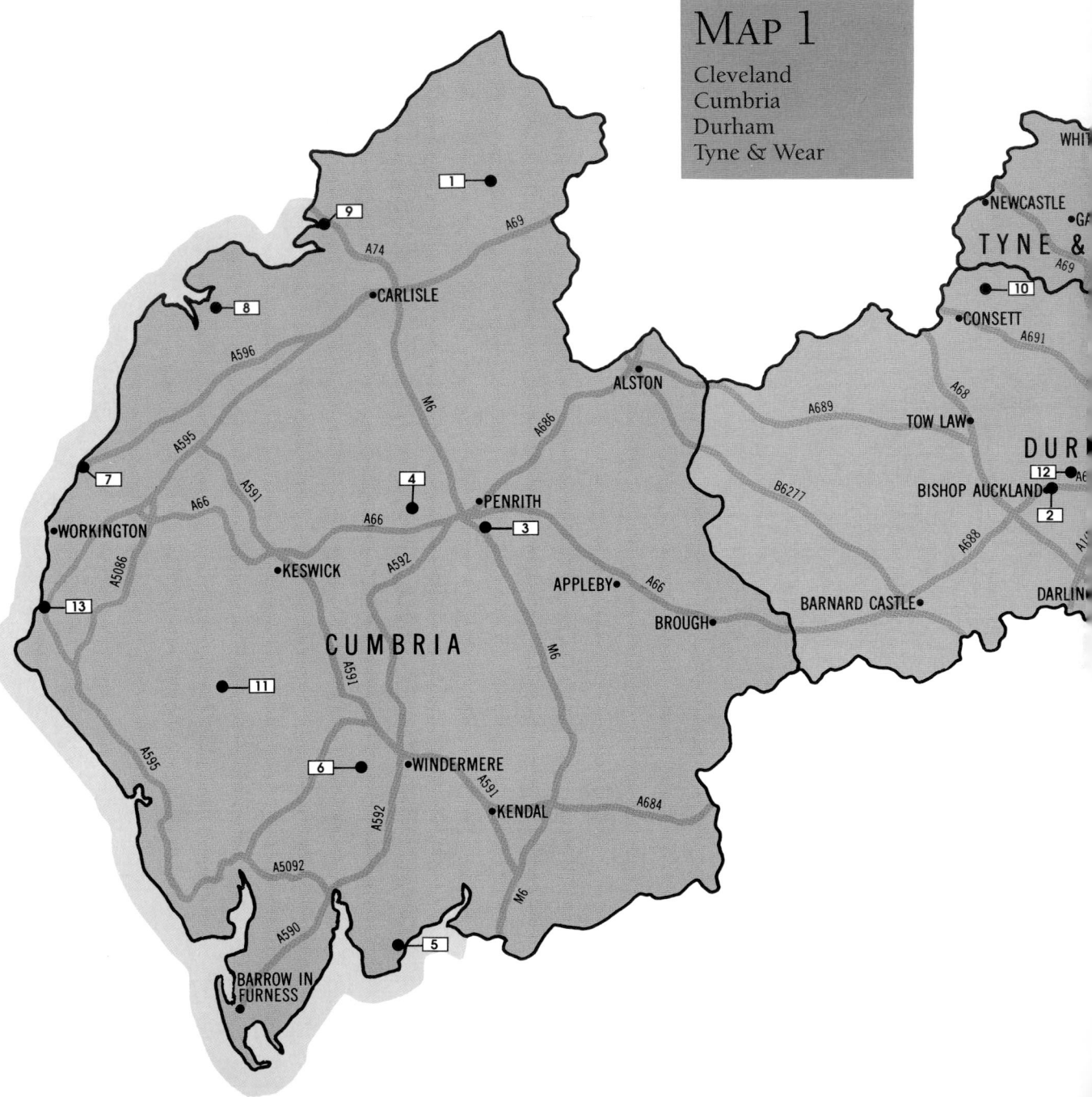

MAP 1

Cleveland
Cumbria
Durham
Tyne & Wear

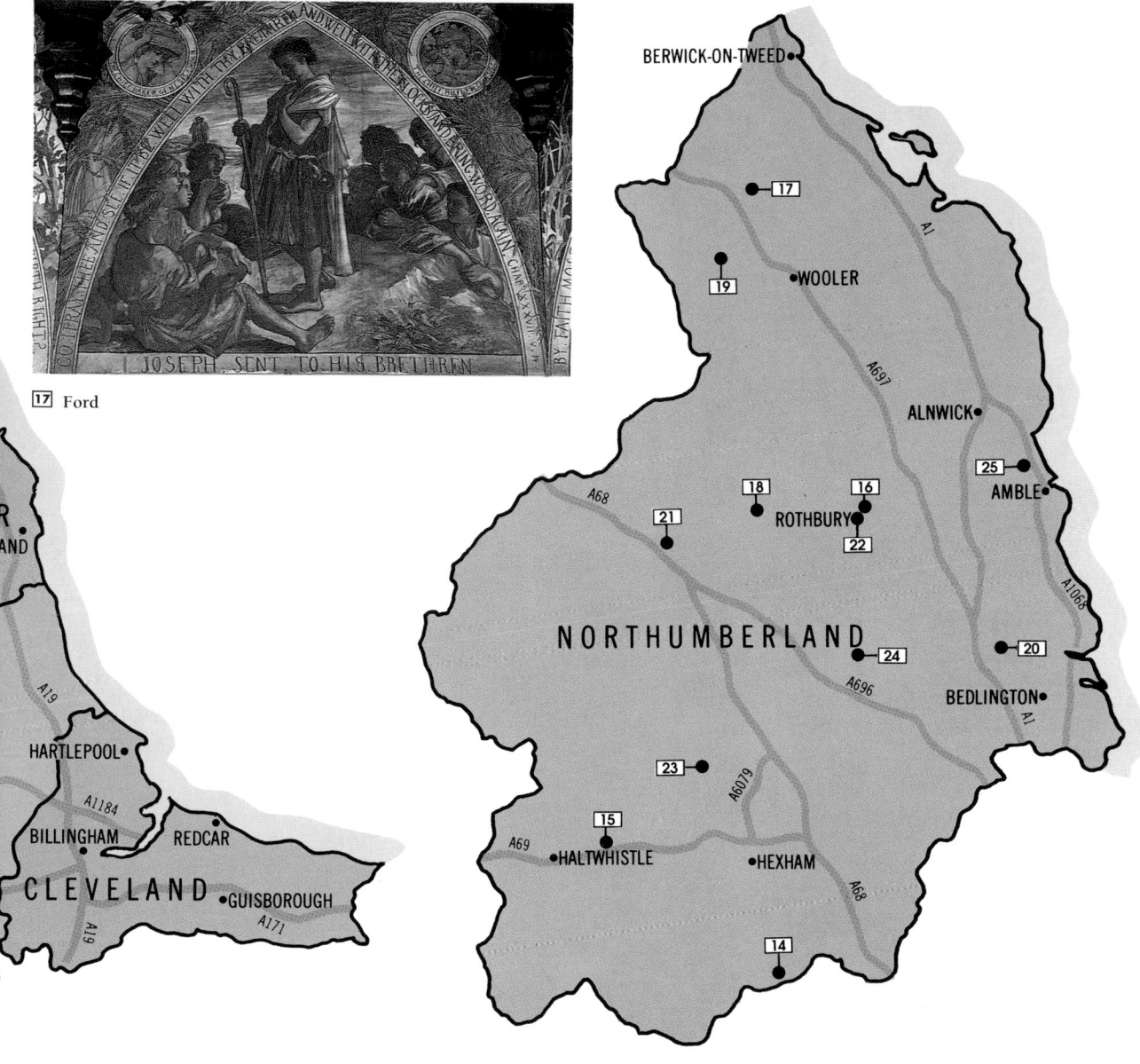

17 Ford

MAP 2

Northumberland

MAP 3

Humberside
North Yorkshire
South Yorkshire
West Yorkshire

41 Sledmere

STOKESLEY

RICHMOND

35 B6270

NORTHALLERTON

A1(M)

A167

A172

B1257

A6108

A1

HAWES

A684

A6108

THIRSK

A19

A170

A61

NORTH YORKSHIRE

29

A19

B6479

B6265

39

A61

A1

34

A65

33
SETTLE

36

A59

A64

A65

A59

HARROGATE

YORK

A19

ILKLEY

A65

30

A1

A61

A63

A6033

A650

A63

WEST YORKSHIRE

SELBY

BRADFORD

LEEDS

A63

A1041

37
A58

MORLEY

M1

A62

M62

WAKEFIELD

M1

A628

M62

HUDDERSFIELD

THORNE

A1

A18

BARNSLEY

A635

A628

44
DONCASTER

M18

A616

M1

43

ROTHERHAM

A631

SOUTH YORKSHIRE

SHEFFIELD

M18

29 Brandsby

MAP 4

Cheshire
Greater Manchester
Lancashire
Merseyside

MAP 5

Derbyshire
Lincolnshire
Nottinghamshire

MAP 6

Hereford &
   Worcester
Leicestershire
Shropshire
Staffordshire
Warwickshire
West Midlands

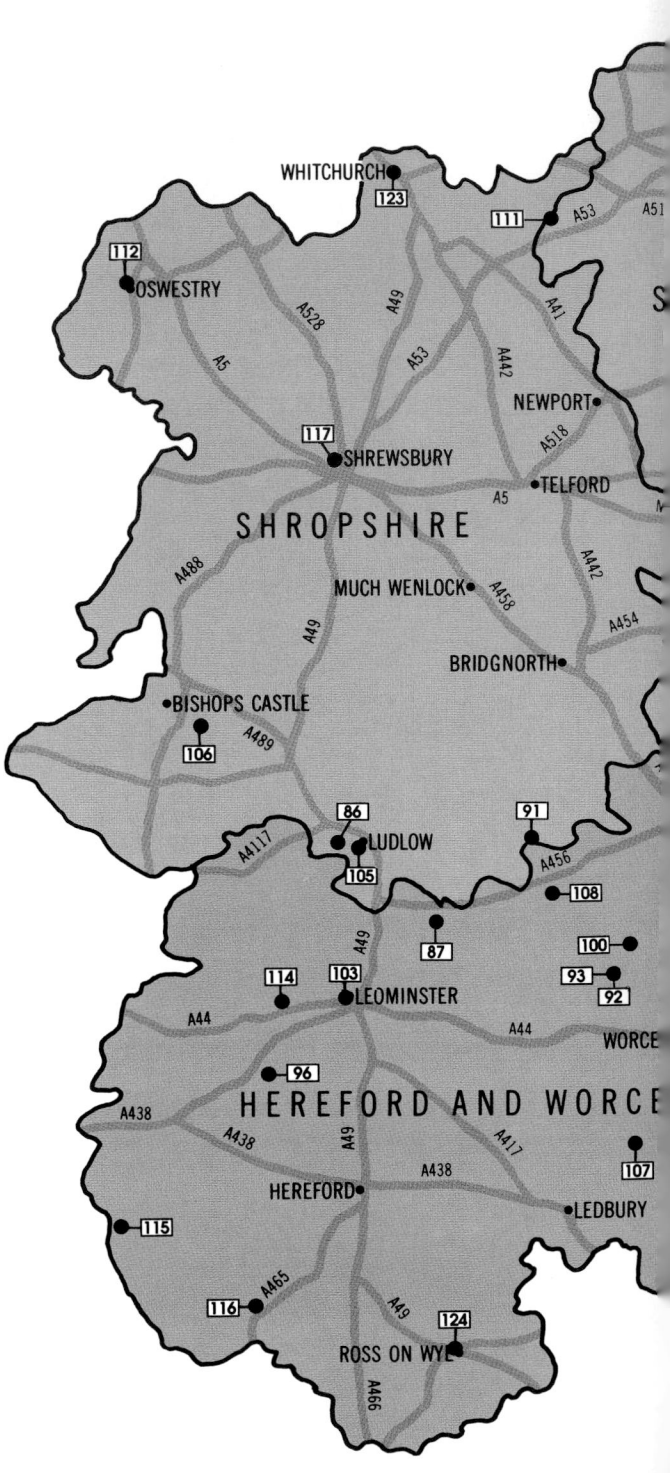

[90] Claverdon

[100] Great Witley

LEEK•

A53

A523

A520

TOKE ON TRENT

A50

A518

...FORDSHIRE

•STAFFORD

A449

[118]

[99]

BURTON UPON TRENT•

[101]

A515

A51

A38

CANNOCK•

A5

•LICHFIELD

A453

[89]

A453

SHEPSHED•

•LOUGHBOROUGH

A6

COALVILLE•

A50

L E I C E S T E R S H I R E

•LEICESTER

A47

[85]

A607

•MELTON MOWBRAY

A606

OAKHAM•

[125]

UPPINGHAM•

[120]

•WALSALL

[126]

M6

•SUTTON COLDFIELD

•HINKLEY

A6

M1

DUDLEY•

•WEST BROMWICH

[83]

•NUNEATON

[94]

M6

•BEDWORTH

A5

[95]

•MARKET HARBOROUGH

BIRMINGHAM•

[109]

[110]

W E S T M I D L A N D S

...MINSTER

A433

M42

•SOLIHULL

A45

[84]

•COVENTRY

A45

RUGBY•

M5

REDDITCH•

•KENILWORTH

[113]

A423

[104]

A34

A41

[90]

•WARWICK

A422

[82]

W A R W I C K S H I R E

A422

A45

[119]

A439

•STRATFORD UPON AVON

[121]

A422

A41

[88]

[98]

EVESHAM•

[102]

A34

MAP 7

Avon
Berkshire
Buckinghamshire
Gloucestershire
Hampshire
Oxfordshire
Wiltshire

163 Latimer

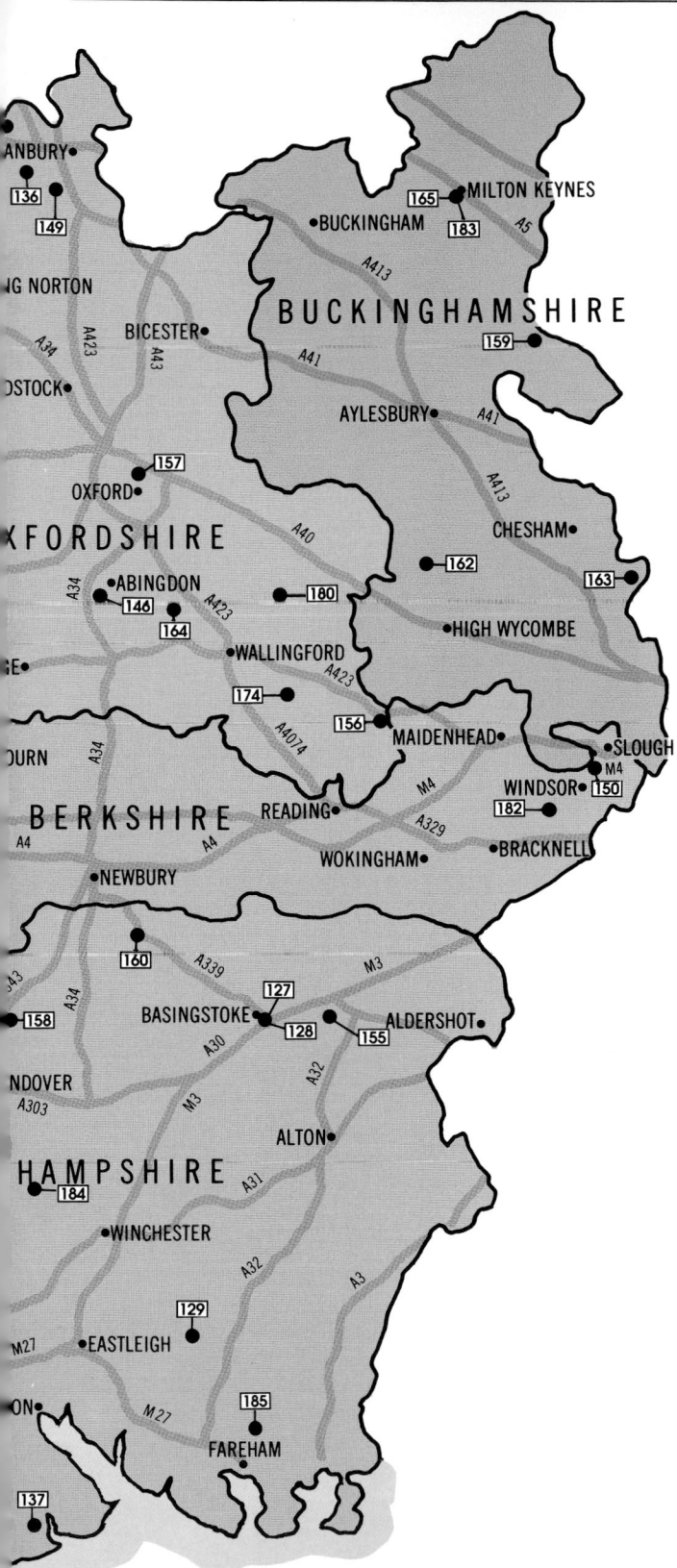

MAP 8

Bedfordshire
Cambridgeshire
Essex
Hertfordshire
Northamptonshire
Greater London

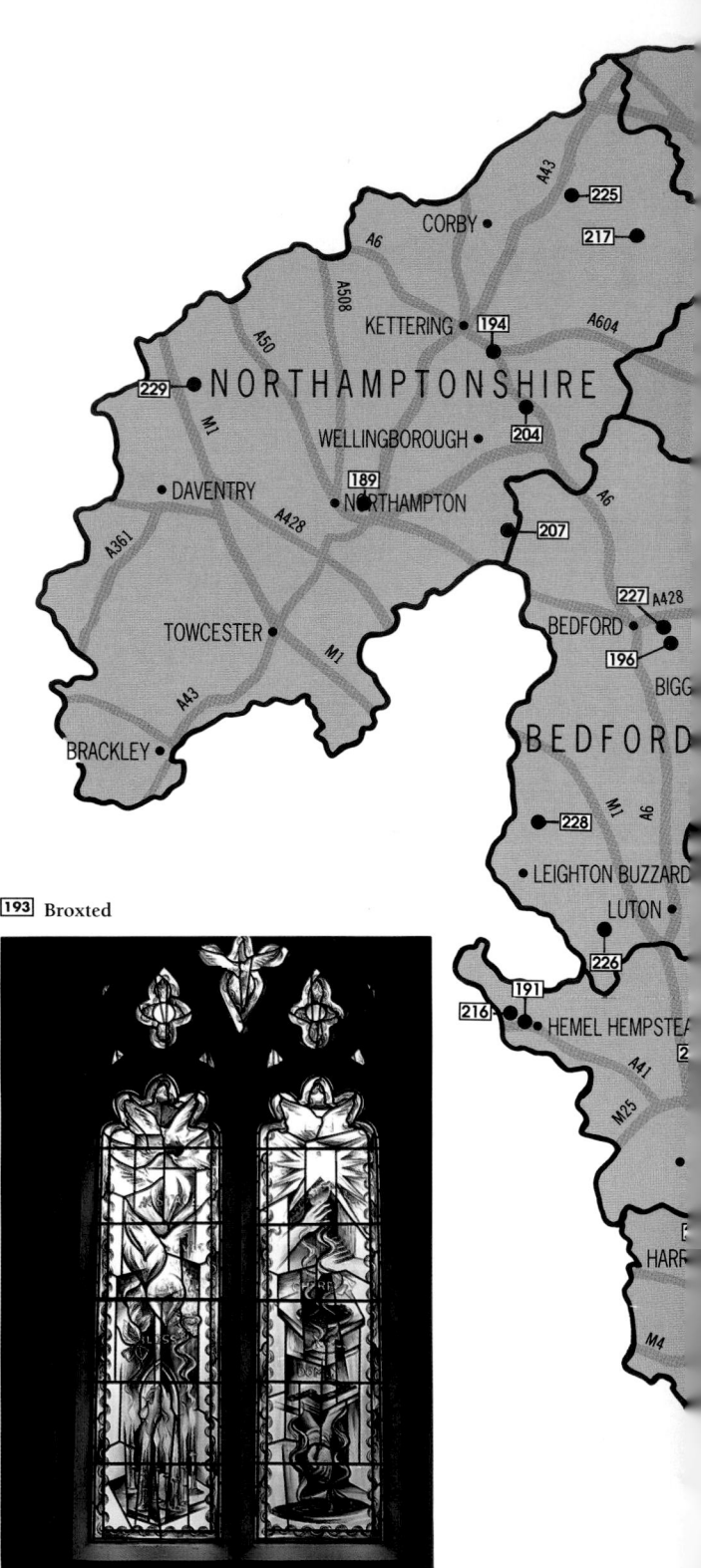

193 Broxted

WISBECH

A47

• PETERBOROUGH

• MARCH

A1

• RAMSEY

A141

A142

202
200

ELY •

A10

CAMBRIDGESHIRE

GDON •

210
218

• ST NEOTS

CAMBRIDGE •

A604

190

195

A14

197

A11

M11

ROYSTON
220
188

206

219

• SAFFRON WALDEN

221

BALDOCK

A131

• HALSTEAD

A12

A120

192

28

STEVENAGE

205

193

A120

A120

COLCHESTER •
214

CLACTON-ON-SEA

A133

197 Cockayne Hatley

ERTFORDSHIRE

224

ENDEN

209

A10

WARE

199

A1(M)

203

A131

A12

201

212

ESSEX

LBANS

M11

• POTTERS BAR

• EPPING

CHELMSFORD •

M25

A12

• ENFIELD

187

A130

08

A10

M1

• HAMPSTEAD

ROMFORD •

A127

• BASILDON •

DAGENHAM •

A13

SOUTHEND ON SEA •

A13

EATER LONDON

ENTFORD

222

A2

M20

SIDCUP

• WIMBLEDON

• CROYDON

M23

MAP 9

East Sussex
Kent
Surrey
West Sussex

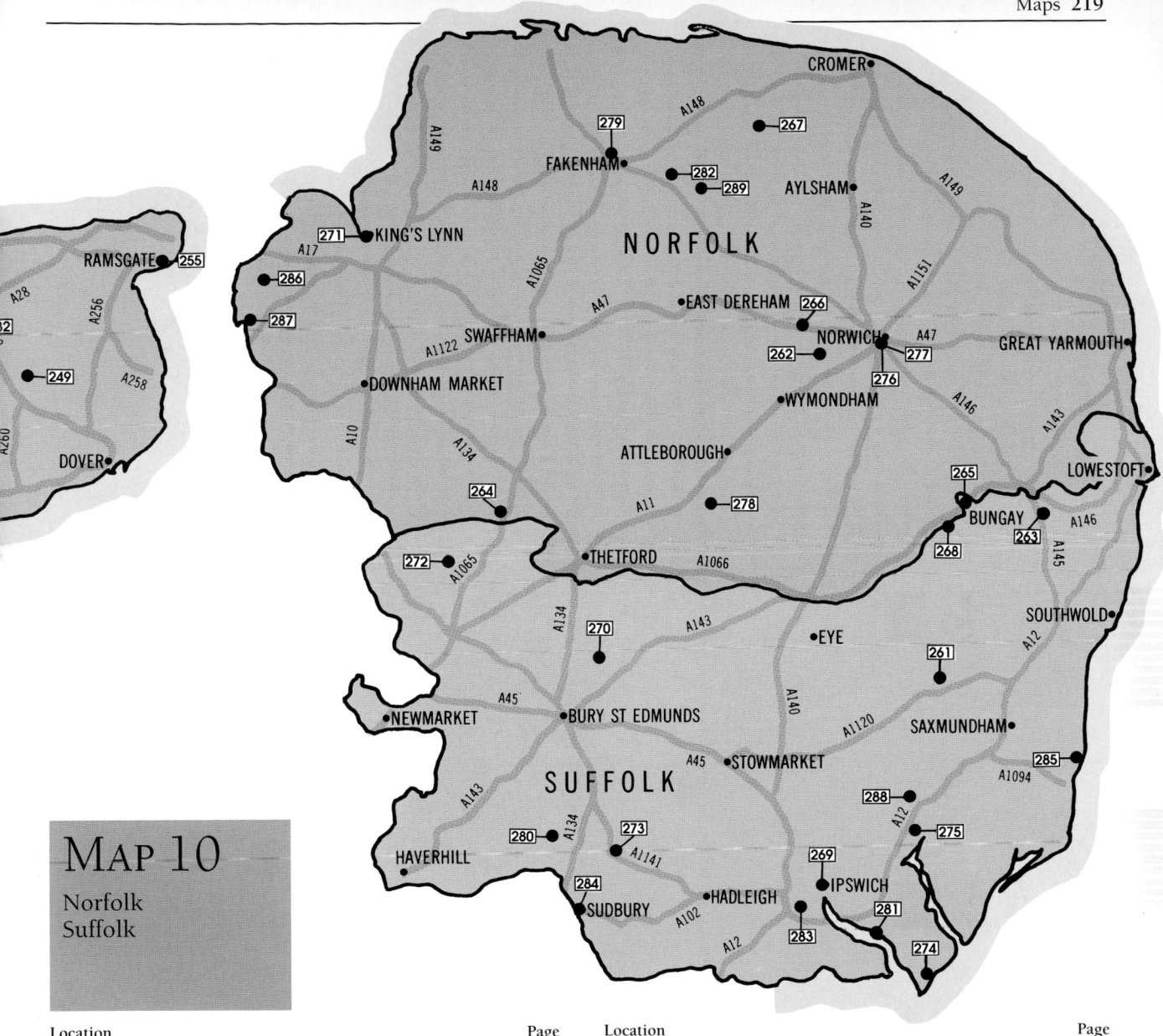

MAP 10

Norfolk
Suffolk

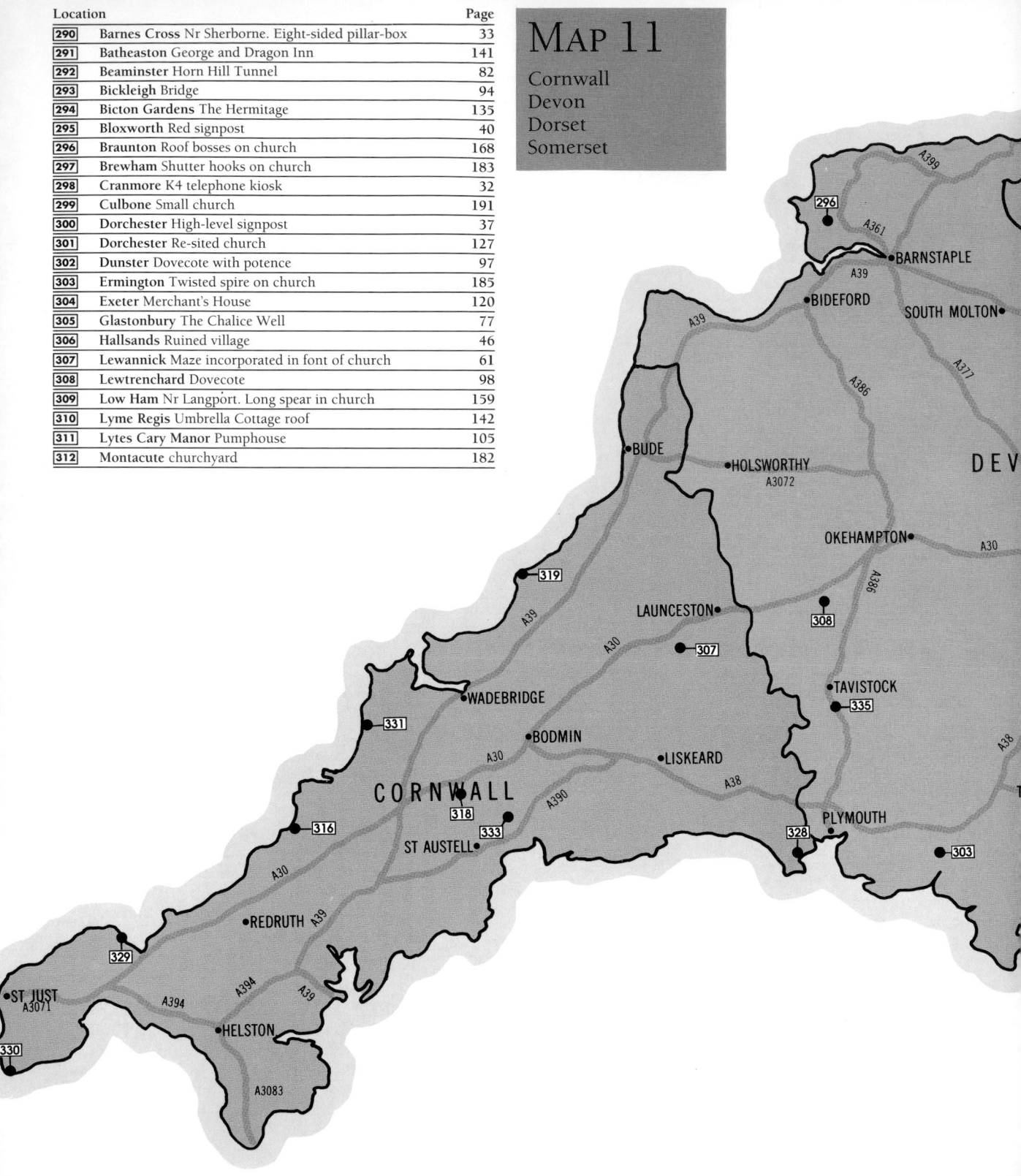

MAP 11

Cornwall
Devon
Dorset
Somerset

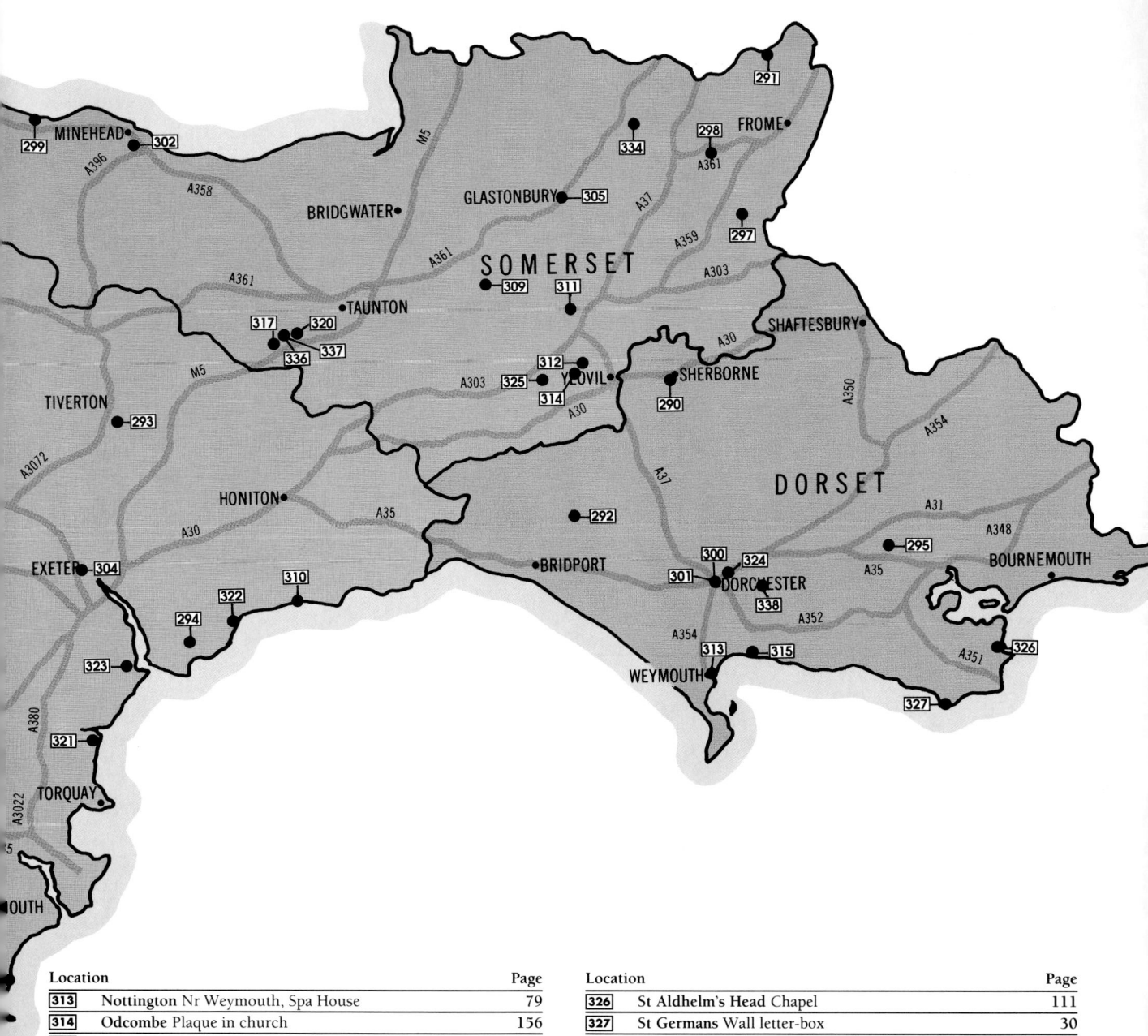

Index

Acknowledgements

The majority of the illustrations in this book
were specially commissioned; others supplied
to us, or requiring acknowledgement are
listed below.

37 *top right* By courtesy of Mr R. Miller. **47** *top left* By kind
permission of Royston Town Council. **52** By kind permission of
Horsham District Council and Sun Alliance Assurance. **57** *top right*
© National Trust 1991. **83** By kind permission of Shugborough
Estate. **84** BR Network Civil Engineers (John Goss). **97** By kind
permission of Mr D. MacDonald. **102** Dolittle Designs.
124 By courtesy of Mr P. Eely. **142** *bottom right* Michael J. Stead.
147 By kind permission of Dr and Mrs Cooper.
150 © National Trust 1991. **157** *top left* By kind permission of the
Trustees of the Thomas Hardy Memorial Collection, Dorset
County Museum, Dorchester.

The maps appearing on pages 205–221 are
based upon the Ordnance Survey map with
the permission of the Controller of HMSO,
Crown copyright reserved.

Every effort has been made to obtain the
appropriate rights or permission to publish
all copyright material. The publishers would
be pleased to acknowledge any omission in
future editions.

The publishers wish to express their gratitude
to the many individuals and organisations
whose specialised knowledge was invaluable
in the preparation of this book.

PRINTED IN BELGIUM BY
proost
INTERNATIONAL BOOK PRODUCTION

Printed and bound in Belgium